Loving Promises

The Master Class
for Creating Magnificent Relationship

By Richard Matzkin

Loving Promises, The Master Class for Creating Magnificent Relationship
Copyright ©2016 Richard Matzkin

ISBN 978-1506-902-44-9 PRINT
ISBN 978-1506-902-45-6 EBOOK

LCCN 2016945071

July 2016

Published and Distributed by
First Edition Design Publishing, Inc.
P.O. Box 20217, Sarasota, FL 34276-3217
www.firsteditiondesignpublishing.com

ALL RIGHTS RESERVED. No part of this book publication may be reproduced, stored in a retrieval system, or transmitted in any form or by any means — electronic, mechanical, photo-copy, recording, or any other — except brief quotation in reviews, without the prior permission of the author or publisher.

Grateful acknowledgement is made for the use of the following previously published material.
Ingrid Goff-Maidoff- www.ingridgoffmaidoff.com
Meher Baba- Avatar Meher Baba Trust- www.avatarmeherbabatrust.org
Cover photo, selfie by Richard and Alice Matzkin
Cover design by Pamela Grau

Library of Congress Cataloging-in-Publication Data
Matzkin, Richard, 1943-.
  Loving Promises: The Master Class For Creating Magnificent Relationship / Richard Matzkin
  p. cm.
  ISBN 978-1506-902-44-9 pbk, 978-1506-902-45-6 digital

        1. FAMILY & RELATIONSHIPS / Love & Romance. 2. / Marriage & Long Term Relationship. 3. / Friendship.

L9118

*To my parents, Ruth and Jack, whose love sustained me.
To the teachers and guides, whose love informed me.
To Swami Muktananda, whose love uplifted me.
To those who loved me and whose love I tried to return.*

And to Alice, whose love awakened my love and taught my heart to sing and my soul to dance.

Acknowledgements

Although her name doesn't appear on the cover, Alice is really the true author of this book. I have merely tried to put into words the beautiful person she is and the magnificent love and friendship that she gives.

The thoughts, insights and blessings of so many wise authors, guides, models and teachers have contributed to my understanding of love that it is impossible to name them all.

I would like to gratefully acknowledge the contribution of my editors, Cinnie Riddle and Pianta. Their work added clarity and correctness to the writing while allowing my voice to come through. I thank my brother-in-law, Robbie Long for his enthusiasm and patient, thoughtful reading, and our friends and relatives for their support and encouragement. Grateful appreciation is due cousin Pam Grau for her generous, loving advice and for creating the cover.

Lastly, I would like to acknowledge myself. I can honestly say that the process of thinking about love and writing this book has given me far greater understanding and made me a better lover. There have been very few projects in my life that I have brought to a satisfactory conclusion. This book is one of them, (although I know that as soon as it is in print I will want to make changes). I have poured my mind, heart and soul into its pages. Completing it has been my obsession for a long time, especially the last year. I feel good about it. With a bittersweet mixture of sadness because it's over and a sigh of relief, I finally lay down my pen.

Lovers—by Richard Matzkin. The sculpture is from our book, The Art of Aging: Celebrating the Authentic Aging Self. It is from the series, *Old Lovers*. The couple depicted is old, denoting an enduring relationship. They are naked, signifying openness and transparency. Their sensuous embrace indicates a continuing enjoyment of life and love.

AN EDITOR'S PREFACE

I was surprised and honored when Richard asked me if I would edit *Loving Promises*. My evenings and weekends were spent immersed in the precepts of a loving relationship as I meticulously parsed the manuscript, sentence by sentence. Eventually I got an early mockup of the original cover, which featured Richard's sculpture of a couple in a deep embrace. It spoke of trust, tenderness and caring. I focused on that photo while I searched my mind for the right arrangement of words.

My life was full. I lived alone in my beautiful home and was blessed with a wonderful circle of friends. I had everything I needed and was happy in my "singleness." Nonetheless, I felt the lack of a deeply committed partner.

As I completed more and more of the manuscript, I felt I was embodying the Loving Promises, creating an internal alchemy of Love. This book was not just a guide to being in relationship with another person – it was a guide to becoming a more loving person myself. I felt I was being transformed into someone who was kinder, more patient, less manipulative, more honest, less judgmental . . . This meditation on relationship was making me into a better person, emptying my persona of the selfish and uncooperative parts of myself that lay like landmines for the unsuspecting partner.

Several months into the editing process, I received an email from an old friend. For the last few years, Lincoln and I had hung out occasionally, meeting for dinner with friends or alone. Our connection had been open-hearted; he was kind and attractive, and it was easy to be together. We laughed and talked through each meal. But, no matter how much fun we had, he clearly wasn't interested in taking the connection beyond friendship. As we'd said goodbye last March, I invited him to come and visit some time. He seemed bemused, and I could tell that this Oregon guy had little interest in coming back to L.A., or in being any more than friends with me.

So I was surprised to get his email in October, proposing a visit in December. He said he was coming on a business trip and needed a place to crash while he was in town. I didn't think much about his visit, having heard from a mutual friend that he was still hung up on an old girlfriend. I stayed focused on my day-to-day life and *Loving Promises*.

When Lincoln finally arrived, I boldly asked him if he had come to be in relationship with me. Somewhat shyly, he answered that he had. We took it slowly, but soon it became clear that we both had come "Home." Our relationship was the one I had been waiting for, my entire life, and I was finally ready to receive it.

Love in the "third quarter" has its challenges (like love in any quarter, I'm sure.) How we work through those challenges remains to be seen. But no matter what happens, the truth is that I invited Love into my life, and Love showed up.

Loving Promises literally transformed my heart and helped me to become a more beautiful person, one who can give and receive love. My intimate journey with the book created an alchemical field of a higher kind of Love. As that Love grew inside me, I attracted a similar Love in a human form, a wonderful man with whom to share my heart and my life. I had deepened my intention to be with a loving partner; then I allowed myself to be transformed enough to pull him into my life. It was a transformation set in motion by *Loving Promises*.

Cynthia Riddle

Loving Promises

Someday, after mastering the winds, the waves, the tides and gravity, we shall harness for God the energies of love, and then, for a second time in the history of the world, man will have discovered fire.

Pierre Teilhard de Chardin

Table of Contents

PART ONE
Love 17

    Growing A Magnificent Relationship 19
    Full Pallette Love 33
    Our Love Is My Responsibility 47

PART TWO
The Promises 63

    Introducing The Loving Promises 65
    Understanding The Loving Promises 79

PART THREE
Fulfilling The Promises 223

    Encountering Conflict 225
    Ways To Work With The Loving Promises 255
    The Promise Of Loving 281

    Epilogue - Our Story By Alice 293
    Afterword - World Peace 309
    Appendix - Meditation 311

Introduction

Alice and I have a magnificent relationship. It is my crowning achievement, the accomplishment in my life of which I am most proud. There's nothing I have devoted so much attention to, nothing that is more important for me to perfect. And there is nothing that has provided me greater rewards than my relationship with Alice.

We are considered by the people who know us, to be models of a perfect couple. Even total strangers sense and comment on our obvious love for each other. Alice and I are best friends, each other's ardent admirers, cheerleaders, and helpmates. We invariably enjoy each other's company, settle our rare conflicts fairly and harmoniously, and wake up every morning happy to see that old face on the pillow next to us. We are as passionately in love with each other now as when we first met, fell in love, and married over three decades ago. For years our friends and acquaintances have been urging us to reveal the "secrets" of our loving, harmonious relationship. And so, with Alice's help and support, I have written this book.

The book you hold in your hands is many things. It is a thoughtful inquiry, a love story, a self-help book, a love poem to my cherished wife. Primarily, LOVING PROMISES is about our relationship. It is about the ways Alice and I are with each other. I have used our relationship as a laboratory to investigate love. The book contains no scientific studies, questionnaires, or clinical narratives. I wrote it through long hours of contemplation on the way Alice and I live together, play together and work together, trying to understand the elements that make our loving partnership so beautiful. I have attempted to communicate these elements as clearly and succinctly as I can, without distracting detail and analysis. I am not simply imparting information here or parroting what I have read in books. I am sharing our life experience. Alice and I are actually living what I have written here. This is what gives these words authenticity and power.

More than just a personal exploration of our relationship, the book is really about love. From the title, one would assume that the love referred to is restricted to the love between two individuals. This is not true. I have used this as a lure to attract interest; who would not want to better their relationship with their partner? Actually, the true subject of the book is much wider than the connection between two individuals. It is love itself, a love that encompasses friendship, family, erotic love, maternal love, love of humanity. I believe that all these forms of love combine to impact the quality of the love between intimate partners.

There is probably no concept in life more potent, more discussed, yet more misunderstood than this mysterious and confounding condition called love. The roots of love reach deep into every aspect of the human experience—work, family, health and more. Therefore, more than just about our relationship, or relationships in general, or love itself, the subject of the book is wider still. It is about living an openhearted life.

A proper understanding of life and love is important and that is the emphasis here. This, then, is not a "how to" book with lots of techniques, questionnaires and experiential exercises. It is more about gaining insight and inspiration. If the readers of the book are able to do no more than acquire a deeper, more comprehensive appreciation of what love is, how love can transform and what love requires in order to be magnificent, then they will have made real progress in their ability to love. I attempt here to tease out the laws of love, universal principles that I believe apply to all loving relationships. Those principles, being universal, are strongly reflected in the relationship I share with Alice.

It should be kept in mind that even though the laws of love as described here might be universal, it does not mean that they will be expressed the same way as with Alice and myself. Each person is "one-of-a-kind" and therefore, each relationship is unique. Everyone brings their own particular history, fears, passions, sensitivities, inhibitions and gifts into the mix. Never before has there ever been, and never after will there ever be, a relationship like the one you have. Because of that, there is never one perfect or ideal relationship. There are magnificent relationships – but each one is magnificent its own way.

The kind of love that is subject of this book is not the romantic, soap opera type, full with drama, trauma and heart pounding episodes of yearning, jealousy and scintillating high energy, (although this type of love is exciting and dramatic and certainly has its place). The love I explore here, though surely not devoid of passion and fire, also encompasses the comfortable old shoe, day-to-day companion and helpmate, "through sickness and health, richer and poorer, until death do us part" kind of love. It is a durable love that promises, through life's inevitable ups and downs, a safe harbor, a challenge to grow, and a fullness and sweetness that is infinitely more satisfying.

In the interest of honesty, I admit I am "a work in progress." I know more about love than I am able to put into practice. While I cannot say that I am a fully realized master of love, I can say that I am a willing student—a person intent on learning, practicing and perfecting my love. My relationship with Alice has been my schoolroom and has given me a quantum leap. It has provided me a glimpse of the magnificence that is possible when two hearts are one, and a grasp of what it takes to get there.

LOVING PROMISES

The understanding I garnered about love and relationships didn't come solely from my connection with Alice, and it didn't appear instantaneously. Though I didn't realize it at the time, every single person who has entered my life was there to teach me about love. That includes the angry ones, the greedy ones, and the hurtful ones – maybe especially those. The ones who loved me well taught me love by their example. Those who loved me badly also taught me by their example. Fortunately, I have had far more teachers of the former method then the latter.

The reality is that no one is ready for relationship. You get ready by doing. You get ready by being in relationship, by making foolish choices and learning from your stupid mistakes. I received practical nuts and bolts training in relationships primarily with the women in my three previous marriages. Through Jean, Tiana and Susan, I learned what it was that I did not want in relationship. I didn't want discord and conflict and unhappiness. But, that's what I had gotten. I got what I deserved. Those marriages were filled with large doses of neediness, hiding, deceit, jealousy, laziness, infidelity, selfishness, insensitivity, manipulation, immaturity and ignorance – mostly on my part. There were trips to hospital emergency rooms to repair the damage from my rage and frustration. Even now, I still feel pangs of remorse when I think of the pain I caused and the stupid, selfish, unconscious things I did.

I was immature, and instead of taking on the responsibility of becoming an adult, possibly living alone for a while in order to find myself, I inflicted my pain and immaturity on my partners. I addictively used the relationships as a drug. I used them to feel better about myself. I used them to fill my emptiness and allay my fears. I used them to satisfy my needs. I failed to honor these women and treat them as they deserved. Ignorance is no excuse. I owe endless apologies to those three women, and several others, among them Joan O, Katie E and Kevin S-B. I also owe them endless appreciation. I appreciate them for the sweetness and the good times and also for the bad times, for putting up with me, even when my selfish behavior caused them pain. Their forbearance allowed me to play out old destructive patterns so that I could leave my angst behind when I met and fell in love with Alice. The pain I experienced from those marriages and those relationships was not in vain. It tempered, ripened and matured me – made me ready for love. Almost immediately, Alice and I started out our love on a much more elevated level because of previous trials and tribulations. (Alice's prior marriage and subsequent relationships had also ripened her.) We were clean with each other and were able to circumvent pitfalls and avoid developing a backlog of hurts and unexpressed anger. When I look back at our history together, I find no remorse, no regret – just gratitude.

I didn't learn about love solely from my relationships. In great part, the foundation of my understanding arose from my lifelong study and practice of Eastern spiritual traditions. While I am not a particularly sophisticated thinker, I do have a nose for truth. I picked up the scent in the mid-seventies when I met the late meditation master, Swami Muktananda. The fragrance of his wisdom and my experience with him permeate this book. Years of study of Hindu and Buddhist literature, meditation practice, and time spent in a monastic environment and at the feet of elevated masters exposed me to a depth of wisdom that has been a guiding light in my life. And, it has proven invaluable in my day-to-day life with Alice.

Loving deeply and well requires, I believe, a level of emotional, intellectual and spiritual maturity. Maturity is grounded in autonomy. Mature people are not tied to their partners, nor overly dependent on them. They can feel and think for themselves, speak and stand up for themselves, act in their own and others' best interest. Without maturity, fused dependencies make it easy to become mired in conflict and discord.

Maturity, while related to the number of years lived, is not dependent on them. We all mature physically over time – boys grow to men, girls to women. We take on adult responsibilities; acquire the symbols of adulthood – degrees, careers, families, houses. But, while on the surface we appear as adults, most of us retain remnants of our infantile mind. That mind is immersed in self-centered demands – "I want, I want. What can I get? What can you give me?" The evolution from immaturity to maturity in relationship, however, is movement away from a self-centered, "What can I get?" to a generous, open-handed, "What can I give?" Giving is the key to a magnificent relationship and a magnificent life. It is through giving that we receive. And giving is the basis of the Loving Promises.

The ability to give freely is a hallmark of a mature person and a requirement for a mature relationship. While magnificent relationships require maturity, you don't have to first become a mature adult and only then be able to have a magnificent relationship. Relationship and maturity are ongoing growth processes. Open-handed generosity can develop through everyday living with your partner. In fact, relationship is the perfect place to learn. You receive instant feedback from your mate when you tread the loving path, and an even quicker response when you deviate.

I have read many relationship and self-help books. Most of them explain to the readers what they can do to find the right person, handle conflicts, get their emotional needs met, assert their rights, communicate more clearly, overcome relationship difficulties. They offer problem-solving strategies and procedures aimed at fixing any predicament couples can find themselves in. All this is valuable advice, but mostly from the perspective of "What can I get?" However, it is this "what can I get" perspective that creates many of the problems in the first place. This driving need to receive love and gratification from others keeps us out of balance. It prevents us from being focused on the very thing that will bring us a love that will satisfy us – which is the sending of our love out to others – serving them, uplifting them, making them happy.

This book is different. It intends to right that imbalance. It places the emphasis almost exclusively on "What can I give?" And it lays out specifically what that entails.

The heart of the book, and its central message, is the "Loving Promises." The Loving Promises are 39 statements of intention about love in relationship. The intentions are stated as behaviors because the most salient aspect of love is the way you behave toward your beloved. *They are promises you make to yourself, not to your partner.* This is because only you are in control of your behavior. The loving behaviors you bring to the relationship set the tone of the relationship and determine its trajectory and outcome. When you are able to bring more love, you are able to receive more love. It is as simple as that.

The Loving Promises constitute true love. They define love. Of course, any endeavor that seeks to define love with words will fall short. Love is a mystery, and when you attempt to pin down love, you will come face-to-face with the mystery. This doesn't mean that you should not attempt a definition. There is value in the endeavor. Most books about relationships provide a cursory definition of love. Not here. Defining love is essential to understanding love. Once you have a clear understanding of true love and a concept of the characteristics that go into making up a magnificent relationship, you then have a prototype, a model you can emulate. The Loving Promises comprise that model. They are an exhaustive list of attributes of love. Each Promise is a distinct facet of love. Nowhere else have I found love so clearly and comprehensively defined. That is one of the great values of this book and why I felt so moved to share what Alice and I have gained in our life and love together. The Loving Promises provide a clear vision of love and an intimate view into magnificent relationship. Understanding these Promises and putting them into practice in your life and in your relationship will bring love into your life – guaranteed – because, taken together, the Loving Promises are LOVE IN ACTION.

Since the Loving Promises *are* love, they are appropriate for nearly every type of relationship. I write from my personal experience as a heterosexual male, but these principles of loving are also applicable for the bond between family members, friends, gay and lesbian couples, and transgender individuals. With modifications, the Loving Promises can be adapted to apply to the important arena of parents' relationships with their children. What better way to start off life than for a child to be embraced by their parent's finest love? And what better education can you offer your children about life and love than to have your loving, giving relationship serve as a model for them? A whole book could easily be devoted to using the Loving Promises with families.

The Loving Promises are also applicable to adult children's relationships with their parents. For many adults, the backlog of hurts and resentments they hold toward their parents keeps them bound to the past. Applying the Promises can help loosen the bindings and liberate the love that both adult children and their parents may withhold from each other. Improving or repairing this primary relationship will have a beneficial effect on all other relationships.

The Promises are not exclusively concerned with humans. Our daughter's relationship with Bella, her lovable poodle mix dog, has opened her heart, taught her about caring for another living being, while transforming her relationships with the men in her life. When I re-read the Promises, I see that many of them apply to the way Angela and Bella are with each other. (It's no mistake that "dog" is God spelled backwards.) Love is love in all its many incarnations and permutations, and any variety of love can benefit from the Loving Promises.

Some words of caution: The Loving Promises and many of the ideas in this book are not for all couples. There are many different varieties of relationships and different levels of progress on the path of love. If you think of life as a school for learning how to love – and it is – some of our relationships are in grammar school, some are in middle school, some are in high school. Make no mistake; this is a textbook for a college level course – maybe even for a graduate or postgraduate course. Because of this, an aim of the book is not just to help people make their troubled relationships okay, or even their okay relationships good. Its goal is more ambitious and more unique. The book aspires to help couples whose relationship is already good, transform theirs into one that is magnificent.

Admittedly, this might reduce potential readership. Most couples are satisfied if their relationship is good, and couples in troubled relationships would be delighted if theirs were just okay. With such a refined audience for the ideas in this book, some couples will find very little of value here. Some might even find it harmful. If you are undergoing emotional crisis, mental instability or serious relationship issues like ongoing adultery, addiction, acute power struggles or domestic violence, this book is not for you. These issues are beyond the scope of the book and best dealt with by a competent professional. (In the case of domestic violence, it is a safety and legal issue before it is a psychological one.)

LOVING PROMISES

The ideas here are not meant to replace therapy or psychiatric treatment. There are many personal issues that individuals must tackle before they feel ready to focus on what they have as a couple. If you are dealing with personal issues like being a "people pleaser," looking for someone to rescue, having a persistent need for approval, not being able to say "no" or set clear boundaries, some of the ideas from the book may be at odds with what you may need right now. If you are in an out-of-balance relationship where you are already giving in far greater proportion than your partner, rather than asking, "What can I give?" which is the basis of the book, maybe you should be demanding "What can I get?" instead.

Not everyone who picks up this book is ready for a Ph.D level course in life and love. Such a lofty goal is not a requirement. Ideally, readers of the book will benefit if they engender three qualities – a desire for a deep, enduring connection with their partner, a willingness to do what it takes to work through the obstacles that stand in the way of that connection, and an openness to the idea that they themselves might be the main obstacle to a magnificent relationship, and thus, are entirely willing to do the essential work for their personal evolution. While working on personal hang-ups might not always be easy or comfortable, it is nowhere near as difficult and uncomfortable as surviving in a dry, unhappy relationship.

A magnificent partnership is not every couple's desire. Some couples might be perfectly satisfied with less intimate involvement and may even prefer a roommate type of relationship. Couples may have other goals and other interests. They may desire a magnificent career or want to pursue a magnificent project. They may consider couple relationships a diversion, a pleasant addition to their life, while work, friends or achievement takes first place. For them, the time and effort required for an intimate relationship is more than they are willing to devote. In spite of societal pressure to "couple up," the advantages of living without a partner – the freedom, privacy, simplicity and financial independence, attract many to the single life. This is a legitimate choice and perfectly all right, (as long as both partners are on the same page regarding their priorities). Everyone is different and must make decisions as to where they put their limited time and energies. There are many worthy ways to live out a lifetime, none of them "correct" or applicable to everyone. However, if, like me, your inclination is toward a deeply intimate, committed relationship, and you choose to spend your life in partnership, the energy you devote to perfecting that partnership will be amply rewarded, not just in your relationship, but in your entire life.

This book takes more of a spiritual approach to cultivating great relationships, as opposed to a psychological one. Psychotherapists seek to help the couple understand the sources of painful emotions and maladaptive behaviors that are causing strife. They look to improve clear communication and aid the couple to negotiate how to get each individual's needs met. All are important and useful objectives. I don't at all discount the value of psycho-dynamically oriented couple's therapy. The spiritual approach takes a different tack. It draws on perennial philosophy and the underpinnings of world religions and spiritual traditions. It is about cultivating, through understanding and ongoing practice, exalted human values such as kindness, patience, generosity, honesty and compassion. These are values that are characteristic of magnificent love. As these values evolve in an individual, that person's ability to love evolves. Developing these values is healing and will bring peace and harmony to the individual, the couple and to everyone they encounter. This approach I have found most fruitful in my life and is the foundation of Alice's and my magnificent relationship.

The spiritual approach is not about making the relationship comfortable or becoming "nice" with each other. It is about using the relationship and everything that occurs within it as grist for the mill for profound inner growth and change. It is about plumbing the depths and scaling the heights of love, of life and of spirit. This is not an easy way, nor is it quick. There are no magic formulas. But, it is all I have to offer. It is our truth and our path. And the journey and destination is magnificent.

There is a belief in many schools of psychotherapy that inadequate parenting and childhood trauma in the past determine relationship dysfunction in the present. This can be true and focus on the past can be an effective therapeutic approach. However, I believe the past can only influence the present, but it cannot determine it. It is not my intention or role to examine or revisit the traumas in an individual's history. None of us were perfectly loved exactly the way we wanted by our imperfect parents. None of us have escaped heartache from previous relationships. Here the attention is not focused on healing past pain and trauma in order that you can move on. Rather, the focus is about moving on, and in the process, past pain and trauma may be healed.

While I'm very respectful of people's life stories and narratives, I realize it's too easy for a person to get caught up in those long-standing stories, so much so that they are reluctant to let them go. Their stories become their identity, their belief about who they are. We have a friend who visits his analyst every week, spilling the contents of his mind – and he has done so for over 20 years. While he has great insight about his history and childhood and the causes and effects of his psychological issues, he still has most of those same issues he had 20 years ago.

If we put our energy into moving on with our life – working at becoming stronger, wiser, more generous, more loving, we will be calling forth the highest and best in ourselves – our strength, intelligence and autonomy. In the process, the emotional impact of our past pain will fade and traumatic memories will recede. As we embody the highest and best in ourselves, we will call forth the highest and best in our partner. Then we both will be able to spend more of our time enjoying the fruits of love, rather than chewing on the pits.

Try to resist the temptation to read page after page and finish the book cover to cover in a few sittings. This is not an easy book. The subject is vast and the writing is dense. I try to simplify, but the ideas are complex and the reader needs to take time to contemplate and process. There are jewels to be mined here, but they need to be discovered and given respectful consideration. Read for more than to simply receive information, although just by understanding the concepts you will receive value. If you relate the ideas to your life and your experience, you will receive more value. But if you put the ideas into practice, you will receive the greatest benefit.

Keep in mind that everybody is different and no two people and no two couples love in the same way. Don't take the words of this book as gospel truth. Use them as a guide. Accept what fits for you; reject what doesn't. It is not the purpose of the book to tell you what is right or wrong for your relationship and for your life or promote a model that will work for everyone. What I am trying to do here is provide you information that can help you explore and discover for yourself. You are the expert of your relationship and the director of your life. Contemplate the ideas. Sense what feels right for you. Let your own intuition be your ultimate guide. Experiment. Stay awake. As your heart opens, it will speak to you and you will *know* from your inside.

Think of the book as a map. A map will not take you to your destination, but it will show you a route you can take to get there. You must set out and travel in order to arrive. But without a map and without knowing the path to your destination, it is easy to go astray.

The book is in three parts. **Part One** is about love and what it takes for love to survive and thrive. I describe the many varieties of love and introduce a series of ideas about the power each individual has to create the magnificent relationship they desire. **Part Two** is about the Loving Promises themselves. I provide a rationale for the Promises and go into detail about what they are and how they work. **Part Three** is about employing the Promises in your relationship. I explain ways to deal with conflict and offer suggestions on ways to implement the Promises in everyday life. In the last chapter I introduce the final Loving Promise. It is about the power and transformative potential of expansive love. In the Epilogue, Alice tells the story of our loving relationship. It is such a beautiful story that I wanted to share it. Reading the tale of our shared journey from her perspective adds another dimension. If you would like to get to know us better right off the bat, you might want to read that chapter first. This is followed by a short contemplation on love and creating peace in the world, and the book concludes with a brief summary of meditation techniques.

A note about the writing style – In the process of writing this book, I noticed that the Loving Promises and most of the chapters took on the form of short, concise statements, followed by explanatory commentary. This occurred automatically, without my conscious intention. I realized that this resembles a *sutra*, which is a literary form used for millennia in religious and philosophical texts in the Far East. Sutras are short aphorisms, highly condensed statements of ideas. They originated from ancient oral traditions, as a memory device. Later, written commentaries (and commentaries on commentaries) supplemented the sutras to explain and clarify them. Although somewhat formal and a bit unusual, this style is an excellent way of organizing and communicating ideas.

I am in my seventies now, an age when a person has gained some wider perspective. It is from this perspective that I write. Many gifts have been given me in my life, and I have been feeling the strong urge and inner calling to give something back. I am in a stage of life where I don't need a career, I don't need fame, I don't need more money. This book is my gift. I offer it from the depth of my heart. I am honored to take on the privilege and responsibility of being a teacher, especially of a subject of such vital importance to everyone. Writing has not been easy. Words do not flow smoothly from my pen. The process has taken many years. I persevered with a growing sense of mission that has been driving me to finish the manuscript. The urgency that motivates that mission is the recognition of the pain and confusion that I see all around me – people making the same mistakes I made, and reaping the same suffering. This doesn't have to be.

It is possible for you to attain a magnificent relationship. It is possible, if your relationship is good, for it to be great. It is even possible, if your relationship is bad or just limping along, for it to become magnificent. We know many couples who have attained magnificent love.

The fact that you have read so far attests to your desire to welcome more love into your life. If you were not attuned to love, you would not have even picked up this book and opened it. Your desire, conscious or unconscious, invited this book into your life. Now I propose you invite the book into your heart. Before entering into the first chapter, I'm going to suggest to you a little ceremony that can work with your intention. You might like it, or you may think it is silly or crazy. Try it anyway.

Take the book in your hands and press it to your heart. Intend that all the love you desire for yourself and your loved ones, all the love that went into the writing of this book, all the love that emanates from Alice and my relationship, is absorbed from the book into your heart and fills it with loving kindness toward all, including yourself. Call in your God, your protective angels, your beloveds, to be present and stand by you as helpers and guides. Ask for gifts that will assist you in manifesting the love that fills your heart. Ask for gifts which clear away blocks that prevent you from giving and receiving magnificent love. Feel love as a continuous warm presence in your chest.

After you have finished this process, and throughout your reading, hold in your mind the awareness of this book as a powerful love talisman, an object that contains the energy of love that will clear, protect and bless your relationship.

This may seem like magical thinking to you, but intentions are powerful. Sometimes intentions can work magic. It is my fervent wish that you, the reader, are touched with the same spirit of love with which this book was written. May you be inspired by Alice and my journey of love to realize that a magnificent relationship awaits you. It is within your grasp. May you reach out for it.

Because living an openhearted life is so essential for happiness, one would think that information about love would be available to every child. It would be expected that every school would have classes on love along with English and math, and there would be a required love course in every college and university. But no. Instead, children grow to adulthood learning about love by painful trial and error. Examples of mature, abiding love that we can emulate are few and far between. Our most pervasive models of love we experience through the popular media--television soap operas and "reality" shows, popular songs, romantic novels--models that extol emotional upheaval, obsessive attachment, lying, manipulation and deceit. This book is an attempt to fill the gap and provide a model of a deep, enduring, mature love. Think of it as a master class for creating magnificent love. Contained herein is the course curriculum.

Part One

Love

Chapter 1

GROWING A MAGNIFICENT RELATIONSHIP

The Longing for Love

Let's start out with a question. This is probably one of the most essential questions that can be asked of you. What is your life's purpose? Why were you born? Were you born simply to survive by satisfying biological needs for air, water, food, elimination? Were you born to reproduce in order to insure the continuation of the species? Were you born to work, to provide food, shelter and protection for yourself and your loved ones? Were you born to enjoy sense pleasures, to savor delicious food, possess beautiful objects and engage in sensual delights, to be entertained by your favorite TV. program? Survival, procreation, security, enjoyment – all are good answers, and all important aspects of a well-rounded life, but incomplete.

I believe we each have a yearning to fully express our unique selves. Every one of us comes into the world with innate talents and abilities, which we can cultivate or allow to lie fallow. We also have deficiencies that hold us back and with which we can live or strive to overcome. To fulfill our promise and grow into the person we are meant to be, to maximize our gifts and overcome our deficits, and to take our rightful place in the world–those are what gives us a sense of satisfaction and fulfillment. But, that is not all; that is not enough. For most of us, life can never be complete; we can never be fulfilled without an additional ingredient. The quintessential ingredient that alone makes life delicious, is love.

Love cannot be seen or heard or touched or tasted. It cannot be perceived or understood through the mind. Like everything in life that is essential, love can only be known through the heart. The heart I am referring to is not the physical organ located in the chest. Rather, the heart is a reservoir of energy, an energy that both receives and broadcasts our deepest feelings. It is all feeling, no mind. It intuits and knows without conscious thought. Our heart tells us when we love someone and when someone loves us. It provides us the sense of connection with those we love. It guides us as to when and how we express our love. Our heart is *home*.

With the exception of the rare hermit or the person with severe mental and emotional disabilities, every human being's physical, psychological and spiritual well-being is dependent on the presence of love in their lives. Without giving and receiving love, life can be barren, empty. We can have riches, fame and the admiration of multitudes, but what is it worth if at the end of the day we come home to a cold and loveless house? Could it be that our frantic pursuits, our mad addiction to prestige, success, power, money and sex, are but shallow substitutes for love that is lacking? Healthy, heartfelt love is a balm for loneliness. A deep intimate connection with another makes it possible for us to break out of our separate universe and touch (however briefly and tentatively) the separate universe of another being. That loving touch marks the end of loneliness and the possibility of the beginning of a sense of kinship with all beings.

Our heart opens through love. We feel so good when we love and are loved. Love cradles us in its beckoning embrace. Around our beloved we feel warm, full, engaged, connected, at ease, safe, open, happy. We feel good about ourselves, valued and valuable. We can be relaxed, at home with who we are, not having to play act at presenting a phony image. We are able to feel more alive because love awakens us and brings us into the present. Loving and being loved brings us joy.

As sweet as love can be, we can never know the full extent of its sweetness and preciousness until we lack it or until it has abandoned us. The emptiness, the loneliness we experience from love lost proves how central love is to our wellbeing. Nothing shows us the importance of love in our life more than its absence.

Even though living immersed in love is so delicious and so nourishing, and living without love leaves us so hungry, true love usually doesn't come easily to most people. Few of us are able to escape our past without experiencing deep scars from a difficult childhood, a tortured love affair, or a betrayal of trust ... scars that can leave us sour, cautious, unwilling to risk giving our heart to another. Giving of our vulnerable heart, however, is the very thing that heals us. Yet giving our heart and opening ourselves to yearning for another is the very thing that is most difficult for us to do. It exposes us to the potential danger of being hurt. It brings up our deepest fears and clenching, resistant defenses. These can be primal issues.

LOVING PROMISES

Those fortunate among us who were welcomed at birth into a safe, supportive environment may find it easier to make trusting connections with others. (I remember graham crackers and milk waiting for me when I returned home, and being carried to bed, half asleep in my father's strong arms.) These lucky ones like myself tend to encounter fewer obstacles on the path to love. Others entered life in an environment of neglect and abuse. (My friend remembers fists, screaming arguments and the sound of breaking glass.) These unfortunate ones like my friend tend to develop an orientation of fear, and face greater obstacles. The distance they must travel on the path to a magnificent relationship is greater and the way can be more challenging. However, the challenges are not impossible to overcome.

Whether our past has left us with superficial scars or deep, unhealed ones, it should be remembered—we are all wounded in some way. No matter how well put together we may seem on the surface, every one of us has a sad, scared little child somewhere inside us, a child in need of love and comfort. Though we are usually tuned in to our own wounds and imperfections, remembering that our partner also carries their own wounds and imperfections will help us look upon our lover with more patience and forbearance. As we maintain the awareness of our partner's vulnerable inner child, we are more apt to offer empathy, kindness, forgiveness, praise and support, all elements which bring about their healing. Through the process of offering our healing energy, we also bring about our own healing.

There are many arenas where anyone can offer their heart and take up the challenges of learning how to love more deeply. People can give of themselves through raising a child, ministering to aging or ailing parents or providing ongoing care and support for friends or strangers in need. Giving oneself in love and service to family and strangers is noble training for love. However, the most comprehensive, difficult and confounding arena for learning to love is intimate couple relationships. There is no more difficult practice for the learning of love than the day-in and day-out demands of two adults, usually of different gender, different upbringing, different education, different values, different beliefs, different habits and different likes and dislikes, who are living together in close proximity, trying to slog through conflicting needs and desires. Their task is to work through their differences, live and work together peacefully, share graciously, communicate clearly and appreciate and support one another. Not an easy thing to do.

Intimate relationship is a hard taskmaster. It is very demanding. It demands that we be vulnerable, that we expose our fears and weaknesses and our undefended hearts and put our fragile egos on the line. In intimacy, we give our partners the power to reject us and hurt us. We hold the same power over them, yet we both must refuse to abuse that power. Intimacy demands, even if we feel threatened and uncomfortable, that we accept our partner just as they are, without trying to change them into our image of who they should be. Intimacy demands we break out of our selfishness and share of ourselves, even at times when we feel like hoarding – *especially* the times we feel like hoarding. Intimacy demands we compromise, remain flexible and accommodate our time, habits and preferences to the needs and desires of our partner. These are not things that normally inhabit our comfort zone. It can sometimes necessitate grueling effort over an extended period to become comfortable with the requirements demanded by a close, loving relationship.

If we take up the challenges that intimate relationships demand of us, it can transform us. Love's power is explosive. The force of love and the strength of attachment is so powerful that it can rattle our world. The love we have for a partner can touch us so deeply and envelop us so completely that it becomes an earthquake that shakes what we thought were the solid foundations of our life. The tremors can transport us to heaven and the next moment send us crashing down to a hell of pain, jealousy and frustration. Love's seismic shockwave can destroy, but the destruction can be beneficial. It can take down outmoded, detrimental ego structures and begin to erect robust and healthy ones.

Because of the difficult terrain, the path of close partnership can be daunting. It is no wonder that many of us, either through ignorance or fear, do as I did for many years and take the easy way out. We tune out, hide our true feelings, acquiesce to avoid conflict, and attempt to manipulate or control the other. Or, we give up the challenge and separate or divorce. By not working through our obstacles to feeling and expressing our loving heart, we sentence ourselves and our partners to half-loved lives. We play-act at love, never tasting the real sweetness of an open-hearted and loving partnership. What a loss.

Though the challenges of intimate partnership can be demanding, many couples are willing to undertake those challenges. We ask ourselves "Why have we chosen to be together? What is the purpose of our relationship? What are its rewards?" I think Alice's and my answers echo every loving couple.

We enjoy each other. We got together in the first place because it feels good to be in each other's company. We laugh and have fun doing exciting things and making love; in general, we delight in being together.

We share life's burdens. Our life is easy and more manageable when we have a helpmate who nurtures us, helps carry our load and comforts us when we are down. Even the simple act of making our bed is so much easier with two than with one.

We grow together. Living with this other being who has divergent tastes, habits and perspectives, expands our universe. We illuminate each other through our diversity. In the process, we discover how to be ourselves.

We learn to love. By enjoying each other, sharing life's burdens and growing together, we learn how to love. That education is the most important thing life has to teach us. We bring that love out into our world and share it with everyone we meet.

Necessary Conditions for Love to Survive

Each couple's relationship is unique. Both partners bring their individual upbringing, genetic makeup and life experiences into the soup and the combination of the two unique flavors gives the relationship its inimitable taste. I believe that even though magnificent relationships all share certain qualities, some of those qualities are essential – love cannot endure without them. I have termed these, Necessary Conditions—qualities without which love will wither and die.

Maintaining and cultivating the love between two people is like caring for a tender young plant. A seedling needs basic, necessary conditions in order to survive. Without those conditions – proper moisture, abundant sunlight and essential nutrients in the soil, the plant will wither. And so it is with love. Love will wilt without proper ingredients and proper care. As I see it, the main Necessary Conditions that an individual must have in order for love to survive, are the need to feel *safe*, the need to feel *appreciated*, and the need to feel *connected*. If even one of these conditions is absent, love cannot persevere. The relationship may continue to exist, but it is unlikely be a deeply loving one.

THE NEED TO BE SAFE

Love will wither in an atmosphere of fear and distrust. We all have a vulnerable center . . . a soft, tender place where we can be wounded. Maybe in the past we have been betrayed by someone we trusted, severely judged or harshly put down, ignored, or abandoned by someone who left us or passed away. Or, we might even have been physically harmed or threatened. We may cover up our hurt and our fear, but we are still supersensitive to potential threat. Like a turtle, we pull in our vulnerable parts behind a protective shell if we sense we are in the presence of someone who might hurt us. However, if we are in the presence of an individual who we know is safe and trustworthy, who has tender caring for our well-being, and who will tread carefully around our raw spots, we can allow our protective walls to dissolve. With the relationship as a safe sanctuary, and without the need to be on the alert to protect ourselves, love is able to flow unimpeded.

THE NEED TO BE APPRECIATED

We all need to be appreciated, to be valued for who we are, just as we are, not as others want us to be or expect us to be. We need to be trusted as independent, autonomous adults who are able to care for ourselves and make judicious choices. Every person's sense of self-worth is an inside job. Each of us alone is the one who can appraise our own value. Yet, it is very difficult for us to appreciate ourselves if those who are important to us fail to see and value us, and fail to express their appreciation in words and action. It is even more difficult if they judge us harshly, belittle us and withhold genuine affection from us. To be appreciated requires that our beloved is sincerely interested in us. They personally attend to us, listen to us, watch us, and try to understand us. Only when we are known can we be truly appreciated. Being known and appreciated allows us to blossom.

THE NEED TO BE CONNECTED

To be connected to another person is to feel a union with them. You are attuned, open and responsive to each other. When you are connected with your partner, you are interested in each other, inspired by the other. You communicate; you care for and about each other's safety and happiness. Too many relationships survive for years without connection. Couples suffocate in stagnant partnerships and live out their separate lives deadened to each other. One or both are too afraid, too confused, or too complacent to make the move to either separate or to initiate changes that will revive the closeness that was originally there. In failing to do so, they write off a chunk of their lives. Yet, isn't the potential for shared passion, communication, romance, sexuality, affection, comfort, humor, joy and the opportunity for new challenging and exciting shared experiences the reason why we get together in the first place? It is the presence of these things that make a relationship so gratifying, and their absence, so dull and lifeless. Connection is the glue that holds the relationship together.

Safety – to know we will not be purposely hurt. *Appreciation* – to know we are seen and valued. *Connection* – to experience bonding and intimacy together – these are the minimal necessary and sufficient conditions that need to exist in order for a relationship to survive. But, mere survival is not enough. There are other qualities that foster love and allow it to thrive. I call these, Optimal Conditions.

Optimal Conditions for Love to Thrive

We all want more than to have our relationship merely survive. We want to have our relationship flourish. What then are the conditions that need to be present in order for love to do more than just survive? What is necessary in order for love to thrive? What does it take for a partnership to be magnificent? I have looked at my life with Alice, searching for those conditions that we both needed in order to be fulfilled with each other. These are listed below. Know that this is our list, and though to me it seems to be universally applicable, others might add some to the list or take some away. Note that for each condition that I wish for Alice to fulfill for me, I must also fulfill for her. Note, also, that all conditions fall within the categories of safety, appreciation and connection.

I want **integrity** in our relationship. I want Alice to be principled and truthful with me. I intend to be principled and truthful with her. Integrity is a bottom line in our relationship. I need to trust Alice. If I saw that she would be unprincipled and would lie, cheat, hurt and steal in her dealings with others, I could never feel safe with her. If she would do that with others, why would she not do that with me? She, too, deserves to be treated with integrity by me.

I want **authenticity** in our relationship. I want Alice to be able to reveal her genuine self to me and I intend to be authentic with her. If Alice and I censored what we revealed to each other about ourselves, holding back parts that we are ashamed of, that make us look bad, while displaying parts that makes us look good, this would make true love impossible. Our connection would be fraudulent. We would be like actors relating onstage as scripted characters.

I want **stability** in our relationship. I want to know that Alice is committed to be with me for our lifetime, and I intend to be with her as long as we live. I came of age in the 60's when, for many in the younger generation, the idea of a lifetime, committed relationship was considered passé. When the going got tough, you got going. This never worked for me. I thrive knowing that Alice will be here for me the rest of our lives through good times and bad. The strong roots of our relationship, forged by an enduring commitment to each other, have allowed us to plumb the deepest levels of love.

I want **kindness** in our relationship. I want Alice to feel empathy toward me and for her to treat me with compassion and respect my dignity. And I intend to be empathetic and treat her compassionately and respectfully. Every human being is deserving of being treated with kindness and respect. If you don't do so, you diminish yourself, as well as them. This is especially true with those who are close to us. Alice and I learned that if we were to let our guard down and treat the other with less than perfect kindness, we would both feel it acutely. This keeps us keenly attentive in all our interactions.

I want **generosity** in our relationship. I want Alice to freely and joyfully give to me and take care of me without demand for equal reciprocation. I intend to attempt to freely give to her without expectation. The thing about generosity is that it is contagious. When someone is generous with me, it makes me want to return the same. This is exactly what happened when I met Alice. I tend to be stingy, while Alice is the picture of open-handed giving. Alice's generosity with me and others inspired feelings of generosity in me I had never before experienced. This helped me to loosen my grasping tendencies.

I want **independence** in our relationship. I want Alice to feel comfortably able to view herself and me as independent individuals with separate likes, opinions and choices. I intend to see her and myself as free and autonomous individuals. One of the dangers of being a close couple is that you can lose yourself in the other and end up not living your own life. Alice and I spend a lot of time together and do a lot of compromising, but we maintain clear boundaries and respect each other's freedom to think, say and do as we each think best.

I want **maturity** in our relationship. I want Alice to bring her wisdom, perspective and careful judgment into our relationship, and I intend to bring mine. A magnificent relationship requires maturity. The relationship of two people with childish psyches clothed in adult bodies will consist of constant clash of needy egos. Alice and I met later in life and had both matured by living through a wide variety of life experiences. Our relationship quickly blossomed with mature love.

LOVING PROMISES

I want **acceptance** in our relationship. I want Alice to appreciate and value me for who I am, as I am. I intend to appreciate and value her as she is. In previous relationships I was often judged and criticized. Naturally, I became cautious and self-judgmental, editing what I would say and do. Not so with Alice. There are a few things about each other we would prefer to be different, very few. Alice and I love and accept the whole package as we are. It is a relief to be appreciated and not pressured to change.

I want **presence** in our relationship. I want Alice to receive who I am. I want her to profoundly see, hear and know me, and I intend to use my mind, senses and intuition to know her. When Alice and I are interacting, I usually feel that we have genuine interest, attention and sensitivity to each other. Being awake and attentive to each other in these ways awakens and enlivens each of us.

I want **joy** in our relationship. I want Alice to feel free to play and laugh, and celebrate life with me, and I intend to enjoy and celebrate with her. To enjoy each other's presence and enrich their lives is the reason couples come together. In Alice, I have found a playmate and helpmate. Even in our seventies, we play together with childlike glee.

I want **sensuality** in our relationship. I want Alice to be free to enjoy my body sexually and sensually, how and when appropriate, and I intend to feel free to enjoy her body in mutually appropriate ways and times. We have always taken great joy in touching each other, from holding hands, to a sexual embrace. A loving touch is the physical demonstration of our caring and generous feelings for each other.

I want **stimulation** in our relationship. I want Alice to explore, grow and challenge herself and me, and I intend to explore, grow and challenge myself and her. Alice and I are not content to allow ourselves and our relationship to stagnate. We purposely engage in pursuits that will keep us evolving as individuals and as a couple.

I want **ease** in our relationship. I want Alice to feel comfortable, relaxed, effortless and problem free in my presence, and I want to feel the same in her presence. When most or all of the Optimal Conditions are present in a relationship, the result is an easy, uncomplicated partnership. This quality of ease is a hallmark of a magnificent relationship.

The foregoing conditions are what Alice and I have asked of each other and of ourselves. They are what we want for our relationship and what we are willing to give. We have tried to abide by them and for the most part, we have. To the extent that we have been successful, our love has flourished. Aside from being qualities that are essential for a magnificent relationship, there are deep truths about love and relationships contained in this list. The Optimal Conditions stress how important it is for both parties to embody those qualities. I cannot ask Alice to be honest or generous or kind to me if I am myself unable or unwilling to be honest, generous and kind. Like attracts like. You will likely attract the kind of person you are. You will also recreate in your partner the person that you are. What this means is that you must be the lover that you want in a partner.

Integrity, authenticity, stability, kindness, generosity, independence, maturity, acceptance, presence, joy, sensuality, stimulation, ease – when these are present in our life and in our relationship, our love grows sweeter and our partnership is characterized by peace and harmony.

Cultivating a Magnificent Relationship

The Optimal Conditions That Allow Love to Thrive form the backbone of the Loving Promises. The Promises themselves are a more detailed and comprehensive version of these Optimal Conditions. A magnificent relationship is built on the foundation of the Loving Promises.

What is a magnificent relationship? What does one look like? I think it is inaccurate to generalize and assume that one magnificent relationship is the same as all others. As I had written before, each couple's partnership will be unique because each partner is unique. Great relationships can never be flawless and complete. They are not a project to work at, perfect, and once attained, retain their perfection forever. Relationships are an evolving process and an ongoing practice. They are something you continuously work with throughout the course of your lifetime together. The events and challenges that inevitably come up through day-to-day living are grist for the mill and provide the raw materials that allow you to perfect your practice and deepen your love.

Like all interpersonal relationships, a magnificent partnership is not stress-free or devoid of problems. But the strength and durability of the bond and the power of love between the partners make the stress manageable and the problems less frequent, less intense and more workable. An extraordinary relationship is not necessarily an entirely compatible one. In fact, it is the differences – the parts that chafe against each other, that provide the impetus to stretch and grow and heal in love. Because the difficulties a healthy couple encounters are dealt with loving care, they deepen and strengthen the bond rather than weaken it.

Magnificent relationships engender an ideal, a goal to strive for. Couples in such a partnership don't just live from day to day. They have an ideal vision for the way they wish to be with each other. They work to live up to that ideal. The ideals they hold furnish the couple with ongoing guidance and inspiration. They provide direction. Lost in the forest, Alice in Wonderland comes to a fork in the road and stops to ask the Cheshire Cat for directions. "That depends a great deal where you want to go," said the Cat. "I don't much care," said Alice. "Then it doesn't matter which way you go," said the Cat. The Cat was right. You have to know where you are headed.

The Loving Promises provide explicit directions to take your relationship to a place of magnificence.

Some people may denigrate the power of the Loving Promises in our relationship, saying, "It's easy for you and Alice to have a great partnership. You two are in alignment. The roles you play in each other's lives are a perfect fit. Most couples are not so compatible." It's true; we are compatible. The fact that we are in agreement in so many ways has helped make the road easier for us, but it doesn't determine that our relationship will be magnificent. It is magnificent because we make it so – every day. Every day we maintain the intention to be happy with each other. Every day we do what it takes to make that intention real—we honor each other, we are kind, we are truthful, we are generous with each other.

If we didn't continuously work at applying principles such as Loving Promises with each other, our relationship could easily go downhill and we could lose the happiness we have worked so hard to garner. We know couples who started out with a "perfect fit" but didn't follow up with kindness and generosity, and ended apart. It's not so much who you start out with. Magnificent partnership is more about how you view and what you do with who you've got.

One thing that sets a magnificent relationship apart from a good one or just a so-so one is that normally, couples view the problems they have with each other as obstacles to avoid or impediments to be gotten rid of. However, couples in magnificent partnerships tend to view their difficulties and crises as opportunities to grow. Problems are painful, but useful. The pain grabs their attention and shows them right where love is needed. Relationships expose a couple's dark places, their fearful places. How else will these parts be healed except by bringing them to the light? Instead of hiding from problems, these couples bring them out into the open, examine them, claim responsibility, dialog.

GROWING A MAGNIFICENT RELATIONSHIP

Our problems and personal issues are like compost for the garden. Compost is made up of things we don't want or need—grass clippings, leaves, old flowers and rotted veggies. This concoction may look disgusting and stink, but when dug into the soil, it enriches it and produces beautiful flowers and delicious vegetables.

Continuing with the analogy, growing a magnificent relationship is an organic process, much like cultivating a garden. Of course, you first must have the basic necessities – proper soil, sunlight, moisture and suitable climate. This would correlate with The Necessary Conditions for Love to Survive – safety, appreciation and connectedness. But in order for your garden to flourish, it takes ongoing care that will keep the plants healthy and protect them – continuous attention to weeding, watering, fertilizing, eliminating insects and diseases. This would correspond to the Optimal Conditions for Love to Thrive – the daily maintenance of integrity, authenticity, generosity, kindness and the rest.

Think of these qualities as actions needed to care for seeds. Each of us has many kinds of seeds buried deep within our consciousness. Some are negative – lying, selfishness, impatience, etc., and some are positive – honesty, generosity, patience, etc.. By continuously attending to the positive seeds, we encourage their growth. By neglecting the negative seeds, we prevent them from germinating. The Loving Promises are an ongoing practice for eliminating those negative seeds that weaken relationships, while cultivating the opposite, the seeds of honesty, generosity and patience. As these qualities mature and ripen, the seeds will then produce beautiful flowers. The monk Thich Nhat Hanh has said that we all have flowers as well as garbage inside us. We should water the flowers and remove the garbage, or at least don't bring any more in. You are the gardener and you are the garbage collector.

The Loving Promises are merely a bunch of good ideas unless animated by action. They need to be imbibed, ingested, and practiced. They are also ideals, goals to work toward and an ongoing learning process. As you work with the Loving Promises day by day, love becomes integrated into the fabric of your being. You become so filled with love that everything you experience is infused with love. The whole world seems made of love because you are viewing with love-tinted glasses. Love becomes the way you operate in the world. Then the way you love becomes the way you live, and the whole of your life becomes an expression of the love that resides inside you.

When that happens, your entire being expands. Your small pond becomes the ocean. Rather than feeling that you are a separate island, you will open to feel a deeper love and greater connection with everyone and everything. Your beloved family will expand beyond your immediate loved ones to encompass the whole world – all living beings, all things animate and inanimate – the trees, the wind, the stars. This is the goal, the ultimate flowering of the Loving Promises.

Chapter 2

FULL PALLETTE LOVE

The word "love" can have many meanings. It could refer to anything from a teenaged crush on a pop idol, to the profound melding of a couple in a fifty-year marriage, from a mother's boundless bond with her newborn, to the deep, mutual feeling of lifelong friends, from the forbidden sensual thrill of an adulterous affair, to a religious person's transcendental relationship with God. Love, as used here, will primarily refer to the intimate connection between two adults. That love can take on many forms, many colors.

Love's Many Colors

In my earlier relationships, I had a narrow concept of what my role as a partner should be. My constricted beliefs about the ways I was supposed to think and act limited the full range of color that was available in the relationship. My idea of what was required for me to be an ideal husband was formed by how I saw my parents interact and by the depiction of familial roles in television and movies of the time. Robert Young on *Father Knows Best* and Hugh Beaumont on *Leave It to Beaver* were my models. In my family, my father took on the traditional paternalistic function that was prevalent in those days – breadwinner, pillar of strength, emotions held in check, the one who is knowledgeable and makes all the important decisions and who is served by the "little lady." When a man takes on the paternal role like this in a relationship, his partner, if she sticks around, is forced to assume a pliant, daughter persona or else be a rebellious woman/child. Things worked out well with my parents because my mother had been the youngest in her family of origin and was comfortable playing the role of a daughter in their marriage. Thankfully, none of my wives were content being placed in a subservient position. My effort to "father" them was a source of friction and ultimately, because they stood up for themselves as independent women, was a source of growth for each of us.

The fact is, if we are rigidly locked into a role in our relationship, any role, we limit ourselves and cannot give expression to our full being. If I allow myself to be only "husband" to my wife, how can I also be "friend" or "playmate," and how will I be able to learn from her if I am unable to accept her as "mentor" to me. Also, by confining ourselves to one or two roles, we limit our partners' expression of their full selves because they are forced into a complementary role. For example, if I am locked into a dependent child role in relationship to my partner, I am unable to experience the potency and autonomy of being an adult. And by my taking on this dependent role, my partner is forced into assuming a parental function in order to counteract my lack of assertion, thus limiting her own expression. Because I am not available to her as an adult, she cannot allow herself to let go and be a child at the times she needs the support of a strong partner. Nor is she able to give full expression to her feminine power that a strong male would evoke. Instead, she must "mother" me.

There are a wide range of roles we can adopt in our relationships, each role adding a different color and texture. If we are free to embrace most or all of them, we can add immeasurable breadth and depth to our partnership and to our life. A description of some of these roles follows.

I want to love you . . . and I invite you to love me,
as friends and siblings love each other.

Alice is my best friend, my trusted companion. With years of shared history, we have become family in the truest sense, closer than a best friend – a sister, a brother to each other. We get to share stories, gossip, recount our history, and discuss our concerns. We give and receive support. Sometimes Alice can be the older mature sister, or the younger naïve sister, sometimes I'm the older or younger brother. But the underlying understanding we both hold is that neither of us is greater or lesser than the other. We are equals and we respect each other and stand up for each other.

I want to love you . . . and I invite you to love me,
as a romantic partner.

Romance is flowers, gifts, surprises, special meals together, candlelight, picturesque getaways, holding hands while gazing at the full moon. Romance says, "I care about you. I find you enchanting. I think you are special, I love being with you. Romance is whispering in Alice's ear, "I love you," meaning it, and making sure she knows it.

I want to love you . . . and I invite you to love me,
as my erotic lover.
How great it is to be able to cuddle, nuzzle, caress, and pleasure and be pleasured by the most important, intimate person in my life. Physical union is the fusion of two bodies, two senses. I am embraced by Alice, and physically become part of her. Our senses meld. We generously give and receive and we lose ourselves in lust for each other. What a unique and beautiful dance. Sexual congress is the physical affirmation of our love.

I want to love you . . . and I invite you to love me,
as a mother loves her child.
A mother's love for her child is the closest to unconditional love. Sometimes I watch Alice sleeping, awed by her innocence and vulnerability. At these times, the predominant feeling I have towards her is one of motherly love. I want to nurture her; I want her to feel secure. I am overcome by soft, gentle feelings. Discovering this motherly aspect in myself has surprised me. Mother love is not something I would normally ascribe to myself. But this tender, protective feeling evoked by my love for Alice has helped bring out my tender, protective feelings toward all living beings.

I want to love you . . . and I invite you to love me,
as a father loves his child.
Our mothers are our original models of love. The archetype of mother love is more concerned with nurturance and the inner world of feeling. The father's influence typically comes later in the child's development. It is more concerned with the outer world. The father archetype is protector from dangers of the world. The father champions independence and responsibility, calls us to adventure and challenges us to stretch the boundaries of our body and mind. Father love can be conditional, has expectations of us, lays down limits, provides guidance and is willing to discipline when necessary. Father love is not invariably tied to the male gender. Alice has the ability to love me with fierce father love if necessary.

I want to love you . . . and I invite you to love me,
as a child loves its parent.
This role makes me uncomfortable. It pushes my buttons to be considered a child, lacking power, requiring protection, not manly – Alice's child. But coming

under the nurturing and protective wing of Alice's parental love stretches me. Though I shy away from her motherly love, I also crave it. It fills me. I am at peace. Often when I am enfolded in Alice's loving arms, my mind is completely at rest. My breathing slows. My body relaxes. I luxuriate in Alice's protective love. These feelings, when being embraced by Alice's mother energy, come from a place so deep, so primal within me, I cannot begin to understand with my mind.

I want to love you . . . and I invite you to love me,
as a child loves its playmate.
Our age notwithstanding, Alice and I are a couple of kids. We love to play with each other. Our life together and our home and studio is our sandbox. We can be adults when the situation demands, but it is so much more fun being playmates. We take every opportunity we can to laugh and joke, celebrate and play with the innocence of children.

I want to love you . . . and I invite you to love me,
as your mentor.
A value we both hold is to grow and learn from each other. I have much to teach Alice. I don't take lightly my job of mentoring her. I am not her instructor, no formal classes and lectures. I teach by the way I live my life and the way I interact with her and others. Because I understand I am her mentor, I must be an honorable model for her. I must live my life with integrity and high ideals, therefore being her mentor has helped me grow. It is said that the best way to learn is to teach. I believe the best way to teach is by example.

I want to love you . . . and I invite you to love me,
as my mentor.
Being with Alice, loving her and being loved by her and watching how she loves others, has taught me so much. Her easy, open-handed generosity, her free-flowing emotions, her graciousness in social situations, her demand for scrupulous honesty, the way she is always herself – no artifice, no falsity – her respect for all living beings; these things and so much more make me admire her and want to emulate her. She is my teacher, my mentor, and I am grateful to be able to be her pupil.

I want to love you . . . and I invite you to love me,
as an elder to an elder.

LOVING PROMISES

I observe as Alice and I grow old. Our love becomes sweeter with the passing years. We know our time together is limited and this adds to the sweetness and the poignancy. Aged love has its special quality, its simplicity. That quality is unavailable to the young. Things that were important in our earlier years – ambition, physical beauty, recognition, running, doing, having – these fall by the wayside. Life's battles fought, old hurts forgotten, not driven by needs, we are as we are and can simply be present together – familiar, comfortable. We smile and wink at each other. We understand.

I want to love you . . . and I invite you to love me,
as I love myself.
Self-love is the primary love and is the basis for our love of another. I love myself and desire happiness, peace and freedom from suffering in my life. After years of living and loving, Alice and I almost have a shared nervous system. What harms her, harms me, what benefits her, benefits me. Our destinies are tied together and so my love of self encompasses her.

I want to love you . . . and I invite you to love me,
as I worship a deity.
Alice is more than flesh and bone, more than her mind and her personality and her history. She is spirit. Her body is the vehicle for the Divine spirit that resides within her. When I honor her as spirit, as the best and highest manifestation of who she is, I elevate myself as well as her. I get in touch with that which is holy in both of us. In the Hindu tradition there is a ritual called *puja*, where worshipers, with an attitude of gratefulness and devotion, wave candles and incense in front of their chosen deity to honor the holiness of that deity. Alice and I do puja to each other.

I want to love you . . . and I invite you to love me,
as a god would love us.
How would a god love? Let me conjecture about how an infinite being would love his creation. It is useful to do this because if we can imagine heavenly love, it can provide us a touchstone against which to measure the best of earthly love. (This is all pure speculation and for purposes of clarifying ideas. It is not meant to contradict traditional religious teachings, as evidenced by lower case "g," Based on convention, I use the masculine "he," again lower case).

Unconditional acceptance – Needing nothing in return, a god would cherish us without placing any preconditions on how we should think, act and feel. A god's love would embrace us, whoever we are and whatever we do – good or bad. That love wouldn't require reciprocity. It wouldn't depend on whether we loved him in return. We wouldn't have to worship him, wouldn't have to obey him, wouldn't have to give back, and wouldn't even have to be grateful.

Infinite goodwill – A god would want the best for us. He would want us to thrive, to be happy and healthy, and to live up to our highest potential. A god would never want to hurt us or wreak revenge if we were bad.

Inexhaustible giving – A god's giving is an expression of his infinite goodwill. He would make available to us whatever we needed in order thrive. Such a god would have created a world of abundance for us, where, if we have the desire and the will and the energy, we can obtain whatever we want.

Boundless vision – A god is all seeing and all knowing. He is aware of exactly what is needed to make us happy and help us to grow into our highest and best selves. He knows what we should avoid and he points us in the right direction. However, if we needed to learn painful lessons, a god, in his infinite wisdom, would not prevent us from experiencing the pain that is the consequence of our greedy, unkind or unscrupulous behavior.

Consistent caring – A god's love would be continuous. There would be no breaks or gaps in his love or times where he stops loving us for even a moment. Another meaning of consistency is that it is steady – the love would never decrease. It would never increase either, because godly love is 100% full and overflowing.

All-inclusive – A god's love leaves no one out. Saints or sinners, angels or devils – all would be loved consistently with unconditional acceptance, infinite goodwill and inexhaustible giving.

This is my conjecture about what the purest of pure love is like. Pure love is in the domain of a god, but is it possible for humans to love this way? The simple answer is a resounding NO! Pure love of this magnitude is impossible for us humans (save for a Buddha or a Christ) because of limitations in our physiological and psychological makeup. Even though we cannot love as a god loves, we can, using godly love as a model, attempt to mirror this purest of pure love in our relationships.

LOVING PROMISES

The Human Face of Godly Love

The aspects of what I have called "godly love" can correspond to human love. If I were to give the human form of godly love a voice, it might sound something like this, if a lover were speaking to their beloved. (And this is the way I would speak to Alice from the place of my highest intention for our love).

Non-judgmental acceptance – *I accept you as you are and refrain from judging you.* I view you as full and complete as you are. I don't require you to do anything or change anything to please me, or be anyone other than the person you are in order for me to love you. Essentially, I place no conditions that you must first fulfill in order to earn my love. If you are at present not living up to your potential, this does not negate my fully accepting you as you are. I recognize that you, as well as I and everyone else, are a "work in progress," a person on a journey to discover your true self. Accepting you non-judgmentally does not mean that I have no judgments about the way you are and what you do. I may have mountains of judgments, both positive and negative, and they may be accurate. Refraining from judging you means that whatever judgments I make about you have no power to shake my deepest feelings about you. When I don't take my judgments seriously, I realize they are my preferences, a product of my mind rather than my heart. Whatever judgments I may have (especially my negative ones) are my business. I don't necessarily have to share them with you.

Supportive Goodwill – *I want the best for you.* I want all the things for you that I want for myself – health, joy, prosperity, laughter, good fortune – without reserve, without jealousy, without competition. I also want to see you evolve into the very best you can be, in the direction and at the speed that your inner guide dictates. I want to see you cultivate your special gifts and overcome your disabilities. Wanting the best for you, I am **for** you, available to you, in your corner – one hundred percent.

Generous giving – *I am willing to give of myself to you – without demand for equal payback in return.* I am eager to help you have the best and be your best by giving my best. If needed, I will offer my attention, time, energy and resources. More than this, I will give of myself to you that which makes me alive – my joy, sadness, fear, and understanding. Since I love you and want the best for you, my giving will be easy. It will come as a natural expression of the love I have for you. I will not feel it is depleting me – as a giving away or a sacrifice I make, or as something I feel I should do. My giving to you is an expression of the abundance I feel. Part of that abundance is that my heart is overflowing with love for you. Generous giving asks more of me than simply giving. It asks me to give without demand or expectation for you to give equally in return. My gifts are given even if I receive no "thank you," congratulations on my generosity, or gifts in return. My reward for giving to you is that it affords me an opportunity to love. I give to you because it fulfills my desire for your happiness. I give to you because when you are happy, that makes me happy. This doesn't mean that I am indifferent to receiving from you. Of course, I want my love to be reciprocated. Of course, I would prefer to get goodies from you, even if just to allow you the opportunity to experience the joy of giving. But my love is not based on what I hope to get back.

Informed service – *I will pay attention to you and know you so I can best serve you.* I need to observe you, listen to you, intuit you and think about you so that when you need me, I can be there for you in a way that will serve your best interests. I will not be overly protective of you, so you will have the freedom to make your own mistakes and experience the consequences of those mistakes.

Consistency – *My love for you will not be interrupted or diminished.* We may have disagreements, maybe even fights. In the heat of the moment I may judge you and even feel like I can't stand your guts. Though I may withdraw momentarily, I will never withdraw my love. At bottom, my love for you will remain steady. This constant love is the bedrock of my relationship with you.

Inclusivity – *My love is to be shared; it is not reserved exclusively for you alone.* Because my love is so much of who I am, it radiates from me to everyone. I cannot be a loving partner to you without also being a loving child to my parents, a loving parent to my children, a loving friend to my friends and even a loving adversary to my enemies. I recognize that I am related to all beings. To all those who enter my life, I strive, whenever possible, to accept them. I wish for their well-being and am willing to serve their well-being through my actions. The love I share with others enhances the love I share with you.

These conditions – non-judgmental acceptance, supportive goodwill, generous giving, informed service, consistency and inclusivity – are all part of the human face of godly love. If even one of these conditions is lacking, the purity of your love will be degraded. How would it be possible to love a person and, at the same time, reject significant parts of them? How can we truly love them and not wish wholeheartedly for their happiness and evolution? How can we truly love them and be unwilling to give of ourselves for their happiness? How can we truly love them, yet not really make the effort to know them? How can we truly love them if our love is turned on and off like a faucet? And how can we cherish only them, yet be indifferent to the rest of the world?

When we model our love for our partner on the idea of the way a god might love, we bring in divine light, lift each other up and raise our life and our relationship to a sacred level. Here we can interact with each other from the dictates of our heart and soul rather than our mind and ego.

Men and Love

Few things have greater influence on the colors of our love palette than our gender. The genetic accident of being born male or female sets the trajectory of our life and puts restrictions on the path of our love. Our hormonal makeup, parental injunctions and societal mores confine and define how we are expected to be in relationship.

There are two fundamental principles that exist in the universe—active and passive. Active is movement, doing, effort. Passive is receptive, patient, letting be. Emphasis on the active principle is most often ascribed to the male, while the passive principle is most often ascribed to the female. These principles, working together in harmony, are at the root of any successful relationship. When a man can incorporate his passive feminine energy, and a woman her active masculine energy, they bring healthy balance to themselves and enrich their relationship. If they cannot incorporate both those energies, they become caricatures; the man a hard, unfeeling, dominating brute, and the woman a fear filled, dependent, nonentity.

Masculinity (active) and femininity (passive) are not inevitably tied to gender. Whether we are male or female, every human being has a mixture of masculine and feminine qualities. Alice and I are flexible in this respect. While I am usually the "guy," Alice can at times be free to play a dominant role in our relationship, as I can feel free to play a passive role. Assertive or receptive, we play as the inspiration moves us. This freedom allows us to more completely express the full spectrum of who we are, moment to moment.

Men and women generally are dissimilar in their approach to love and tend to exhibit differences in the way they perceive love, value love, express love and view the Loving Promises. I feel it is important to address these differences, especially in regards to men. For most men, love and relationships are a wonderful addition to their life. They consider love to be the frosting on the cake. The cake itself is their work, their career, their mission in life. This is where they find their greatest "juice." Until they lose it, they don't understand how vital the importance of love and relationship is in their life.

For most women, love, relationship, emotional engagement are the important things in life. This is where they get their "juice." They, by nature, tend to take on the nurturing, care-taking functions that are an essential part of love. Women will tend to be more receptive to the ideas in this book than men and find it easier to engage in Loving Promises. The times are changing, and more and more women are valuing career over relationships. While men are becoming more open to their softer side nowadays, there are still plenty who are allergic to the word "love" and who consider matters of the heart the exclusive domain of the "weaker sex."

Peer pressure from an early age, primarily enforced by other boys and men through public shaming, berating and exclusion, has kept the focus of "real" men's attention on sports, work, cars, politics, money and sexuality. Growing up, boys are shown the ideals of being a man – athletic prowess (size, skill and physical power), economic success (career, influence, money and possessions) and sexual conquest (bedding the greatest number and most desirable). Women are trophies, playthings. Feelings are off limits and "shameful" qualities like fragility, dependency, fearfulness and indecisiveness are to be hidden from others and from themselves. Discussions concerning relationships and emotions are left to the women. There is, for many men, the captivation with a "wild side" – a part of themselves that resists being "domesticated" by women. This is a personality characteristic they often aspire to and admire when they see it in other men.

For millennia, across time and cultures, men have subjugated and disempowered their women. There is reason they have done this. The power of love and the power of the feminine are awesome. If a man is not strong within himself, he might easily feel threatened by that power. It is an essential part of true love that a man be able to honor and appreciate the power of his woman. It is crucial for his own empowerment that he respect and treat her as an equal partner. By attempting to quash her strength, he can never feel his own power, nor will he be able to meet with her in true love.

Both men and women desire intimate connection. But women tend to be more comfortable with emotional closeness than men. The letting go of control and dropping of defenses that intimacy requires seems more threatening to a man than to a woman. Both genders have their favorite methods of avoiding intimacy and making sure that their connection doesn't go too deep. Some preferred escapes from intimacy for men include being so engrossed in work and career that there is little time for home and hearth, engaging in hobbies and activities that exclude their partner, such as viewing or participating in sports, going out drinking with buddies, withdrawing to the privacy of their man-cave. While these kinds of activities, in moderation, can be natural and nourishing for the man, when used as an escape from intimacy, they can be harmful and an indication of deeper problems.

Though some men may deny and resist it, tenderness and vulnerability are essential parts of every man's makeup. If suppressed, these fundamental aspects of the human experience are pushed underground, never to be felt or tasted. The man is out of balance, forced to demonstrate only "manly qualities," leaving it up to his partner to be the sole agent of expression for the softer qualities he rejects in himself. Finding balance – having full access to both feminine and masculine energies – allows a man to experience a more extensive range that encompasses who he is and who he can be.

For a man to engender the soft, feminine qualities, especially in the face of peer resistance, takes tremendous courage. "En-couragement" in this area is what many men will need in order to take on the Loving Promises. Many of the Promises will perhaps sound "submissive" and will seem deferential to their partner, and this is hard for a "real man" to swallow. True love requires that a lover surrender to and honor their mate, express feelings and be sensitive and nurturing at times. These are admirable qualities of a superior human being, not just restricted to a female or a male. If a man can clearly understand that the path of magnificent relationship is not for sissies, but a heroic journey, and that even the softer, "feminine" aspects of the Loving Promises require great strength, guts and fortitude, he will be more likely to take to the path with vigor and conviction.

When men bring their tenderness and vulnerability to the relationship, it makes them more of a real man. But women want more than just tenderness and vulnerability from their man. An emotionally mature woman will invariably be allergic to chronic neediness in her partner. A man who is insecure and overly dependent on his partner, who is threatened by her strength, who is afraid of making decisions alone, who has no separate passions, is a turnoff to his mate, sexually and psychically. Several of the Promises stress the importance of self-reliance. Self-reliance and self-assuredness are qualities most women especially value in their men (and men value in themselves.). But those qualities must be genuine. A woman will want more than a counterfeit man, a man who just has the toys, swagger and outward appearance of masculinity.

At the risk of oversimplifying and sounding like a throwback to caveman times, I assert that most women have a side of themselves in which they yearn to surrender to their man, to be "owned" by him. They crave a man who will show up, commit to care for her, pursue her, connect with her with love and presence so strong that she is helpless to resist. If she fails to receive this potent love from her partner, she may test in order to try to bring it out in him. She probes for his weak spots in order to discover his strength. She tests by complaining, challenging him, pulling away, withholding sex, threatening or expressing anger or judgment; becoming a "ball buster." All the while, she really craves for him to stand up and pursue her, meet her with his full presence of being, with soul and guts and balls. She won't stand for anything less. If her man "wimps out" and doesn't step up to her challenge and withdraws into his mind, holds on to his hurt feelings, or retreats to the computer in his man-cave, she might ratchet up the intensity of the test. Or she might give up and leave, literally or figuratively.

Couples can remain in this dry standoff forever unless someone makes the first move. One or the other must say, "We cannot go on like this. We have to communicate. We have to tell the truth. We must make changes. Our relationship is too important not to do so."

I think in most cases the first move is more appropriate if it is taken by the man. That courageous reaching out is a clear demonstration of love and strength of commitment, and it is a powerful response to her challenge. If motivated by desire rather than fear, the man breaking the standoff displays true masculine power. Such power has the ability to crack her heart open. And the strength and authenticity of his response confirms the wisdom of her willingness to place her trust in him. This can give him a shot of potency and vigor that can reaffirm his sense of maleness.

Sometimes a woman will get into a relationship with man with the idea that she will change him, teach him, make him grow up. A woman who does this is taking on the position of his mother. A grown up man doesn't like being corrected by his mother. In fact, he will be turned off by such a woman, unless he has a boyish and immature personality. In that case, he will look forward to being controlled and mothered. He will seek her validation and will be satisfied with an occasional pat on the head and being told what a good boy he is. If she enjoys being in relationship with a boy, they will be a good fit for each other, but they certainly won't have an adult relationship. A woman trying to change her man is very different from a woman who will not accept selfish, dependent and immature behavior from him. Such a woman is not trying to make him over, but simply demanding he act like an adult and asking he treat her with the respect she knows she deserves. A strong man admires a strong woman like that. He will want to be with her and is willing to learn from her.

Strength, maturity, authenticity, confidence and integrity are qualities a woman admires in her man. If he has these qualities, she can forgive him for other failings and inadequacies he might have. She can be smarter than he, make more money, be in a position of power and influence, while he stays at home taking care of the kids and doing the laundry. It won't matter. What matters most to her about her man is that he live his life as a strong, mature, authentic, confident person with unfailing integrity.

Much has been written and spoken about the occasional emotional moodiness that is typical of women. This can be accounted for by hormones or brain structure or enculturation or whatever. The fact is that a man and woman tend to feel and think in different ways. If she is in an emotional mood, a man should treat her differently than he would a male friend. Often, it is fruitless to try to reason with her. She can't be talked out of a mood by analyzing and strategizing, though if there is a problem that needs solving, a meaningful conversation can help. Rather than his words, her man's intervention with his focused presence and the strength of his positive masculine energy, love and humor, can help pop her into her normal, sweet disposition. Men, don't be pulled from your center and follow her down the path of her emotion. Be steadfast in your loving and solid in strength. Your warm hug and kiss, words of love or a goofy dance in your underwear can work wonders. Just her knowing you love her can help. And don't be overly alarmed. Her moodiness may be like the weather, a storm that will pass on by itself.

Because women tend to be the experts at nurturing and care-taking, it can become easy for her to fall into the habit of doing all the supporting while he does the "important" work. It is necessary that he realize, *it's <u>all</u> important work.* Some women wake up in the morning, prepare their family for the day, go to work, work all day, come home, cook, clean and fall in bed exhausted, while their mate, after a grueling evening of television watching, comes to bed feeling randy. Relationship is partnership. Don't be lazy. Nothing is more important than being a full partner and generous support for this person who shares your life.

In love and relationships, typically, what does a man want? A man wants all the things that a woman wants, but he especially wants his talents recognized by his woman, his body appreciated, his words and thoughts respected, his accomplishments admired and his comfort looked after. And what does a woman want in love and relationships? A woman wants all the things that a man wants, but she especially wants to feel loved by her man, her emotions listened to, felt and appreciated by him, her body accepted and cherished, her house comfortable and the safety and security of her home and family guarded. If a man would honor his partner's feminine needs and give his woman what she desires, and a woman would honor her partner's masculine needs and give her man what he desires, what a beautiful relationship would blossom.

I have one parting piece of advice for men on how to have a magnificent relationship. **Make your beloved happy.** Cherish her feelings and desires. Find out the things that make her glow with contentment and do them day after day. In their role as mothers, lovers and caretakers, women tend to be more experienced at this than men. Men need to learn.

Full-palette loving refers to many roles we play in each other's life. While it is healthy for individuals to be able to expand the roles they play in their partner's life, it is not healthy for their partners to expect and demand that their beloved should exclusively fulfill those roles in the relationship – to be their "everything." And it is not healthy for you to expect that it is up to you to fulfill all those roles for your partner. What an impossible burden that would be. How confining to the relationship and how confining for you! In order to have a satisfying life, in addition to an intimate partner, we need a full complement of friends, family, mentors, etc., to be a part of our entourage. Both partners need to be able to exercise the freedom to bring persons into their lives that will allow them to fulfill their intellectual, social, emotional and spiritual needs, and to be able to do so without fear of arousing their partner's jealousy or blame.

The purpose of this chapter is not about inciting "shoulds," like you should be a great lover, mentor and best buddy to your partner. It is about opening to possibilities. Loving with a full palette – using all your colors through all your roles, from loving as a child, loving as a parent, loving as an elder, all the way to loving as a god loves, expands your ability to utilize and experience all parts of yourself. Every pigment from your palette is available to you in potential form. Discovering those colors will involve opening to new ways of being with your partner and exploring and experimenting with aspects of yourself that may previously have been ignored or buried. Uncovering those aspects is an adventure. It is a shared adventure that makes you whole and allows you to enjoy more of yourself and offer more of yourself to your partner. All who enter into your orbit become beneficiaries of your expansive love palette and are able to enjoy, in full Technicolor, the beauty of who you are.

Chapter 3

OUR LOVE IS MY RESPONSIBILITY

Before moving on to the Promises, I want to examine a very important issue. The practice of the Loving Promises may entail a lot of difficult work, work that might require radical shifts in beliefs – major behavioral changes – even real sacrifice. People will undergo so much hard work and sacrifice only if they clearly know that their efforts have the capacity to bring about the desired results and they will personally benefit in the end. The effort we expend *will* produce the results we want, but not by luck; by our effort alone. This chapter will examine the fundamental issue of personal responsibility and explore an essential concept behind the Loving Promises – the tremendous power each of us has to create the relationship we desire.

FAIRY TALES

Here's a question to ponder. Research indicates that happy people tend to have happy relationships. Is that because their happy relationship is what makes them happy people, or is it because being a happy, well-adjusted person helps make the relationship happy? Your answer to this question will have a lot to do with how you approach being in a relationship. If you believe that the basis of a good relationship is the result of two healthy, happy, mature people coming together, you will put your efforts into becoming a healthy, happy, mature person. If you believe that it is the partner you have chosen for the relationship that makes you happy, you will put your effort into searching for and finding the right mate for you.

The search for the right mate is the preoccupation of many single people. At some point, we have all had the belief and the hope that the perfect person will show up and make our life complete. Once upon a time, a handsome knight in shining armor will sweep us up into his strong arms, carry us off to his castle and life will be good forever after. A beautiful princess will enter our life and shower us with love and admiration, nurture us and heal our wounds, and life will be good forever after. Sleeping Beauty awaits the kiss of the prince in order to awaken. The lowly frog awaits transformation by the princess' kiss. This fairytale, that the right man or woman will come along and fill our emptiness, take away our pain, and make our life complete, is the source of much suffering and disappointment.

The simple truth is that knights and princesses live only in fairytales. When you begin to become complete within yourself, not starving for love and hungry for relationship, the right individuals are more likely to arrive at your doorstep. Until then, the potential mates that knock on your door are often themselves incomplete, needy people, seeking security and wanting to complete themselves through you. They want *you* to be the knight to their damsel in distress or the princess to their hapless knave. When both partners are hungry and needing to be fed by the other, it doesn't bode well for the relationship. Each will be grasping for scraps for themselves rather than trying to provide nurturance for the other. Each will gobble up every word of praise, every smile, every approving pat on the head. The relationship will be driven by mutual hunger. There will be competition rather than cooperation.

The reality is that in order to attract the right partner, you must BE the right partner. To sustain a relationship that is fulfilling requires that you maintain a life that fulfills you. It all starts with you. Love originates within you and the power to create a magnificent relationship lies in your hands.

There is such a thing as a "soulmate," but soulmates are created; not found. You create your soulmate by loving with an open heart. Everyone has thousands of potential mates in the world they could be blissfully happy with. Each pairing would bring deep satisfaction, and each would be totally different. The joy you experience in any relationship is a result of the love you bring.

Here's another common fairytale. Once we are in relationship, we long for the touch of the magic wand of the fairy godmother, the wish granted by the genie or some magic potion that will transform our ordinary partner into the prince or princess we want them to be. We have all at one time or another had the firm belief that if only our mates acted differently, spoke differently, thought differently, even looked differently, our relationship would be so much better. It is *they* who are holding us back, *they* who are doing it to us, *they* who are the source of our problems. *They* cause our unhappiness because of what they don't understand, what they need to learn, what behavior they need to change. If only *they* could just see that, and make the changes that seem so obvious to us, we would all be happy ever after. This assumption, that the fault of our partner is the cause of our own unhappiness, is as much of a fairytale as is the belief in waiting for a kiss from a prince or a princess to make us happy.

Criticizing and assigning blame to our partner for our problems and pain is easy; taking responsibility is hard. Blaming others closes our mind and cuts off the possibility of our learning. It makes it unlikely that we will see our part...and we invariably do play a part in causing problems in our relationship. Blaming gives away our power by making the other person responsible for our happiness or unhappiness. In our mind we become the hapless victim. It's no fun being a victim. The truth is that we alone hold responsibility for our own happiness and unhappiness, and if we assume that responsibility by looking inward for causes and solutions, we can attain the satisfaction we seek and have greater control of the destiny of our relationship.

The misguided fairy tales that promote the false belief that another person is the source of our happiness and the belief that another person is the source of our problems and unhappiness are ways we abdicate responsibility and toss away our power to find fulfillment with our partner. Realizing the falsity of these fairy tales and assuming responsibility for the state of our relationship mark the beginning of the real work in creating a magnificent relationship.

PERSONAL RESPONSIBILITY IN RELATIONSHIP

This chapter will introduce a group of ideas about love and relationships that challenge these fairytales. They form the bedrock that supports Alice's and my partnership. These ideas are unconventional, maybe even revolutionary in that they don't consider relationship primarily as a connection between two people. Rather, they focus on relationship as an internal process on the part of each partner. The focus is predominately about what goes on *within you* as an individual, as opposed to what goes on *between you* as a couple. Comprehending the rationale for that focus is crucial to understanding the principles behind the Loving Promises.

The following ideas explain and support this concept of the centrality and potency of the individual in relationship. The ideas purport to answer one seminal question, "Why do the Loving Promises require a vow to myself rather than to my partner?"

Just read and take in the concepts. Try not to agree or disagree, prove or disprove. Just follow the logic and hold the validity of the ideas as a possibility. If you lead with an opinion as to the correctness or incorrectness of what is written, you may miss out on the meaning.

OUR LOVE IS MY RESPONSIBILITY

There Is Only Me in Relationship. *You exist for me only in the private world of my mind and senses.*

We start with a basic premise, that all humans are alone. We are separate islands. Each of us is a bag of meat, blood and bone, enveloped by an absolutely impermeable boundary – our skin. Everything within my skin is *I* or *me*. Everything outside is *you*, *them*, or *it*. It is the same for my mind and senses. My thoughts and my sense experience – all are my private universe. No matter how close we get or how well we communicate, you cannot enter my consciousness and I cannot enter yours. Even if we go through the same event together – an auto accident, a hike in the woods or winning the lottery – my experience is totally different from yours, totally my own. I can know *about* you, but I can never truly know you. Everything I can possibly know of you is filtered through my own consciousness. In this sense, my knowledge of you is my own creation. There is *only me*.

Though there is *only me*, it doesn't necessarily mean that we have to feel isolated and alone. It doesn't mean we can't take solace in the knowledge that there is someone "out there" who can grasp a sense of who we are and where we are coming from, someone who may be having similar experiences and feeling similar emotions. This is encouraging and supportive, but it doesn't change the fact that you must experience what you experience alone, as must I.

My Inner State Determines My Experience of the World. *Everything I experience is a reflection of my mind.*

In the Egyptian Emerald Tablet is the mysterious statement, "As within, so without." This means that your own attitude is what you project onto the world, and your own attitude is what is reflected back to you. The Yoga Vasistha, a great Indian philosophical work, states, "The world is as you see it." Your view of the external world comes from your mental percepions.

Your mind is the "lens" through which you view the world. If you see through an angry lens, you live in an angry world, where danger lurks and problems abide. If you peer through a loving lens, even difficult people and situations are perceived in an open and more loving way. That loving vision transforms any encounter, even an uncomfortable one, from negative to neutral or even to positive.

Though it seems logical that the positive or negative events that are happening in your life would determine whether you are happy or unhappy, that is not necessarily so. Your interpretation of those events is much more potent than the events themselves. A relationship breakup could be seen as a catastrophic ending or a potential for a new beginning. A bad investment could be seen as a tragic loss or a valuable lesson learned. An upcoming medical procedure could be seen as impending doom or as an opportunity for healing.

Our enduring inner predisposition to partake of love and acceptance, or partake of fear and contraction, colors our perception. Ultimately our loving or unloving disposition will influence the course of our life.

I Am the Source of Love. *The love I feel is independent of you and originates solely within me.*

Though we each live in our own universe, it seems to us that the love we feel originates outside of ourselves. It appears self-evident that the source of our love is that wonderful person we have fallen for. The qualities they possess – their beauty, their brains, their humor, their radiant personality – these are the things, we believe, that generate the love we feel. This is an illusion. It is easy to see how this confusion can come about. We fall in love with someone and we experience loving feelings when that person is around us and when we think about them. Our loving feelings dissipate when the person is away from our presence or out of our thoughts, and those loving feelings recur when the person reappears. Therefore, it is natural to connect the one we love with the occurrence of our feelings of love, and assume that that person is the *source* of those feelings. In actuality, our beloved is simply the *focus* of our love, the object upon which we have bestowed our love.

It is our inner self that is the repository of love. Love is our own true nature. Our problems, our "issues" – self rejection, rage, jealousy, blame – are merely clouds that obscure the sun of our loving nature. These mind clouds are ephemeral and insubstantial. They come and they go, arise and dissipate as do clouds in the sky. What remains as a constant foundation is the warmth and radiance of our loving nature. That loving nature wants to be and needs to be expressed. Our beloved one is the person we focus our love on. They serve as the catalyst that ignites the love that already dwells within us. In this sense, they, the objects of our affection, are irrelevant. They are precious to us in that they bring us to the awareness of our indwelling love.

This misunderstanding, the confusion of *source* with *focus*, is what drives us in our endless search for Mr. or Ms. "Right" – that magical person we believe has the ability to conjure love in our heart. But if Mr. or Ms. Right is the ultimate source of love, then we are bound to them. We are inextricably dependent on them for love, and unable to fully love without them. It is the same confusion of source with focus that drives us to attempt to fix our partner when our relationship begins to go wrong. Since we believe our partner is the source of our love, if things go wrong in our relationship, then it is they who must also be the cause of the problems. So we try to figure out how, where and why they are wrong. We then attempt to get them to change in order to fix the problem. If our relationship disintegrates, the same misunderstanding provides us with the perfect excuse – they weren't really Mr. or Ms. Right. We made a bad choice or they withheld their real identity from us – and the search for the true Mr. or Ms. Right goes on. As the search continues, we avoid the most effective way of being in loving relationship—doing the inner work that prepares us for love.

If I assume my rightful position as the source of love in my life, I will see my love relationships as dependent on my own ability to be loving. Instead of looking around trying to find the right person to love, my effort will be placed on becoming the right person to love (i.e., a loving and lovable person). Knowing myself as the source of love frees me. I don't need to desperately grasp for the love of others because I can generate my own love – for myself and for others.

The Relationship I Have with Myself Is the Foundation of the Relationship I Have with You. *The way I see myself, value myself and treat myself will strongly influence how I see, value and treat you.*

Since everything you experience is a reflection of the state of your own mind, the issues you have in your mind are similar to the ones you are dealing with in your life and in your relationships. If you are judgmental toward yourself, you will tend to set standards and judge others by your standards. If you are kind and compassionate toward yourself, you will tend toward kindness and compassion in relation to others. If you have areas in your personality that you are blind to, things you cannot see about yourself, you will tend to be blind to those same things in your partner. For example, if you are unable to allow yourself to be vulnerable with your partner, you will tend to be blind to your partner's vulnerability or lack of vulnerability.

The same thing holds for our ability to love. The way we love ourselves is the boilerplate, the map of how we love another. If we do not possess self-love, i.e., know, respect and care for ourselves, how is it possible to love our partner. *We cannot give to another what we ourselves do not possess.*

This points to the essential importance of loving yourself. Many people confuse self-love with selfishness or self-centeredness. Self-love is very different. Self-centered people tend to come from a place of need and try to receive goodies and affirmation from others in order to fill the emptiness inside. Self-loving people are brimming with fullness and are able to easily share their love. They are not dependent on the love of others because they can provide it from within themselves. *A magnificent relationship starts with a magnificent relationship with yourself.*

My Love Is Expressed Through My Behavior Toward You. *The choices I make to act in a loving manner determine the depth and purity of my love.*

Love is usually considered an emotion. Emotions, by their very nature, tend to be transitory and unstable. They can change like the wind. Emotions are thought of as something we passively experience, something that *happens* to us, that moves us and moves through us. Therefore, they are not subject to conscious choice and are thus largely outside our ability to control. The language commonly used to describe love makes this clear. We "fall" in love, we are "smitten," we are "swept off our feet," as if caught in a swift flowing river and helplessly carried away.

This tendency to identify love as an emotion has its roots in the mistaken confusion of *falling* in love, as opposed to *being* in love. The highly emotional experience of falling in love (two relative strangers deliciously opening to one another) is very different from the state of being in love. *Being* in love is what happens after *falling* in love wears off. Yet we assume the high-powered emotions should remain there even long after the initial stages of the relationship have passed. If the emotional roller coaster that often accompanies falling in love – the passion, jealousy, exhilaration, yearning – is not present or is waning, we start to question, "Is it really love that I feel?" We may even believe the intensity of the emotional roller coaster to be the gauge of the strength of our love – the more jealousy and yearning, the greater is our love.

Emotion is an essential aspect of love, but it has been oversold. Responsible loving requires that we see love less in terms of emotion, and more in terms of behavior – less feeling, more action. Love is what I *do* in regards to my beloved. That's the ultimate test. I can feel love, I can think love, I can talk love, but it's not going to be worth a hill of beans unless I *act* loving. And acting in loving ways is something I can control, something I can choose to do. Love is a choice, not just a feeling.

For example, love is speaking to you with respect, being truthful with you, listening attentively to you, refraining from manipulating you, trying to act unselfishly with you. These are loving actions, actions which express love. If I see my love in terms of how I act towards my beloved, I will not be so much at the effect of my emotions. I will have greater power to shape what I bring to the relationship because what I *do* is much more under the control of my will than what I *feel*. I have little control over the love I feel for you, but I have the ability to control how I express my feelings of love. I can choose to speak to you in a respectful tone, choose to tell you the truth, and choose to carefully listen to you. These behavioral choices are powerful and will inevitably have a beneficial effect on the relationship. Changing behavior changes feelings. By making these choices in my behavior, I am making a choice to deepen my love.

The Love I Give You Is Reflected Back to Me. *The quality of the love I receive from you is dependent on the depth and purity of the love I give you.*

We have a friend, a very generous friend who, on her birthday, gives gifts to people she cares about. She derives so much more pleasure in giving to others than by receiving for herself. She basks in love of family and friends.

The law of karma, as popularly understood, is, "what goes around comes around," or, more clearly, "you get what you give." This is especially true in intimate relationship. When you give love generously, love will more likely be returned. If you give selfishly or not at all, that too will be returned to you.

Love is a two-way street that involves both giving and receiving. The emphasis here in this book is almost exclusively about the giving aspect of love. In our culture though, the emphasis is on receiving, on finding love and being loved rather than giving love. A definition of love that is in line with the ideas of the book is, "*Love is your concern for the welfare and happiness of the one you love, and the willingness to commit your time, energy and resources to that end.*" In this definition, love is a verb. It's what you ***do***.

There are many levels of giving. To simplify, I divide it into miserly giving and open-hearted giving. Miserly giving is giving what you don't need or want, or giving in order to get, much like a business deal where you expect something in return, or giving just because it is expected, or giving in order to enhance your social position so that you are perceived as a "good guy." With miserly giving, if you give that which has value to you, you feel that you are giving something away, something you want to hold on to, and in the process you feel impoverished and diminished if your gift is accepted. With open-hearted giving, you give freely. You give the best you have. You give because you derive joy from giving and obtain pleasure from the other person's pleasure in receiving your gift. You give because you are drawn by your empathy and compassion for the need the other person is experiencing. You give open-handedly, from your fullness, and the act of giving, rather than depleting you, enriches and empowers you.

All givers receive back in equal measure what they give. Miserly givers receive miserly gifts, miserly love. Open-hearted givers evoke in their partners a desire to give from the bottom of their heart. Giving in this way sows the seeds of generosity in the relationship, seeds that will unfailingly blossom. When I do things that make Alice happy and content, her happiness and contentment flow back to me. So we spoil each other.

Our Relationship Is My Responsibility. *I am 100% responsible for the state of our relationship.*

Relationship is supposed to be a 50-50 proposition – a shared interaction where each partner has an equal portion of responsibility. This has been said so many times, and in so many ways, by so many people. On the surface it seems so obvious, that it has become gospel truth, not open to critical examination. While this may be a realistic way of looking at each partner's responsibility in relationship, it may not be the most useful way. By accepting this conception of equal responsibility, I give away half of my responsibility and half of my power to love. If relationship is a 50-50 proposition, then I accept only 50% of the responsibility for the state of the relationship, and only half the ability to change it. Human nature being what it is, if things go wrong between us, I will tend to look at your 50% as the source of the problem. Also, each of us will come to expect and demand at least 50% from the other. This will lead to comparisons and examination of each of our performances in the relationship. And it will lead to resentments if we feel the other person is not pulling their weight. We will end up keeping tally of what and how much you and I did or didn't do. Love deteriorates into a bargain we make with each other, and our ongoing efforts to ensure that our partners uphold their part.

I would like to offer a radical concept, one that really puts responsibility on the line. I would like for you to attempt to consider your love and your relationships as your responsibility – 100%. Notice that this is not 100%/100%. It goes beyond that. Whether you give me back 100%, or 50%, or 10%, or 5% is of no relevance. The only relevant factor is the quality of the love I give to you. If you are pleased with how your relationship is going, you deserve the credit. If you are displeased, you deserve the blame.

Does this mean that your partner is not in any way accountable for the state of the relationship? Does it mean that what they say and do will have no effect on the relationship? No! Of course their words and behavior have an effect. They too have 100% responsibility (if they choose to accept it). And, if they choose not to accept it, so be it. You taking responsibility for your love simply means that you focus on your own part... not on theirs. In practical terms, this entails refraining from blaming your partner when things go wrong. It requires you to look inside yourself for your part – what you could have done more skillfully and lovingly. It demands you lead with your love – do the loving thing ...irrespective of your partner's participation. It may entail doing the loving thing with your partner even when you don't feel like it, even when you know they are wrong, even when they are just being stubborn or spiteful.

Some may say this is an extreme position. It is extreme. But I know that if we dilute responsibility even a little, we will tend to dilute it more, and then more. Soon we will be back where we started – bemoaning our unhappy relationship, blaming our partner and feeling powerless. Instead, if we assume 100% responsibility, we will be power-full, filled with power. We are not dependent on our partner for change, but take it into our own hands. This is where true freedom lies.

Any Change I Wish to Make in Our Relationship Is My Responsibility.
I will not expect or demand your cooperation and support if I adopt the Loving Promises.

A relationship is not simply two separate individuals sharing a living space. It is a single unit comprised of two components. It is impossible for one component to change and for the other to remain the same. Any change I make will inevitably affect my partner.

When I recognize the power I have to influence the quality and direction of my relationship, I see that it is in my hands to guide the changes I wish to make. I cannot guide by demanding that my partner change. The most effective way I can improve the relationship is by actually making the changes in myself that I wish to see in my partner. If I wish my partner were more considerate of me, I must be more considerate of them. If I wish them to be more attentive to me, I must be more attentive to them. Appreciative, truthful, dependable, receptive, caring – my partner will find it easier to embody these qualities if I lead the way. And they will certainly will be less inclined if I don't lead the way.

The Loving Promises can entail a difficult path. It would be wonderful if our beloved would join with us so we can tread the path together as loving, supportive partners. This is exhilarating when it happens. And it makes life easier. The truth however, is that the couple's journey is solitary. We must travel it alone. At best, individuals in a couple can be on parallel paths, traveling in the same direction and at the same pace. This is how it is with Alice and me. In many relationships, however, paths diverge or individuals are moving at different speeds. Because it is so inviting to be on the path together, it is tempting to want to pressure your partner – to expect or demand that they support you and contribute in your efforts to progress as a couple at a quicker pace.

When people are obsessed with whether their partner is doing all they can to advance, and are not holding up their part, they end up evaluating their partner's performance and blaming them if they don't measure up. The focus becomes more about them than about you. You give away your power and lose your momentum.

This reason and the previous reasons form the rationale as to why the Loving Promises are promises you make to yourself and not to your partner. Better to look after your own growth. Your partner will be drawn by the peace and happiness you have gained. Trust in the power of love to heal. The purity of your love cannot help but touch your partner. It will in time bring out the best of their love. It will uplift them and empower them to love you with the same purity as you love them.

How I Love You *Now* Determines Our Relationship in the Future. *I can only alter our relationship in the present.*

Your present life is not the result of chance. The things you have done in the past, your behavior thoughts and motivations, have strongly influenced your present condition. Since this is so, it is valid to project into the future. The thoughts you have and the actions you take in the present will strongly influence your future. Your past shapes your present; your present shapes your future. You plant the seeds of your future love in the soil of the present.

So start now with reading this book and contemplating its message. If it resonates with you, bring the Loving Promises into your life. See how powerful integrity, kindness and generosity can be in creating the life and the relationship you desire.

Everything depends on the present moment. You cannot alter the past. The future is the result of the present. If you want a happy life and a harmonious relationship, start here, now. There is no place else to begin. Right now you are creating your destiny.

BEING A RESPONSIBLE PARTNER

The ideas presented in this chapter about assuming responsibility for relationship will be considered by some people as extreme and beyond reason. I agree. One would need to be a saint or a masochist to follow them to the extreme limit in every circumstance. While it is a good thing to be patient, kind and generous, it is possible to be too patient, too kind and too generous, or to offer patience, kindness and generosity to the wrong person or at the wrong time. You could be steamrolled and taken advantage of by a partner who doesn't care. That is why discrimination is required. Some partners are simply not capable of being responsible in relationship because they are irresponsible in life. Sometimes, with these kinds of people, the loving thing to do is to say "no" or make for the exit. Some relationships are just not meant to be.

If you realize the truth of these foregoing concepts, you cannot help but be struck with a sense of the profound responsibility you have for the state of your relationship and for the deep satisfaction you and your partner can derive from it. When you have understood that responsibility, it becomes much more difficult to blame others for the problems you are having and the dissatisfaction you are experiencing in your relationship. No longer are you able to see yourself as an innocent victim. No longer will you have childlike dependency; you squarely face the task of taking care of yourself. In taking responsibility for your relationship, it becomes easier for you to recognize the place to begin making the changes that transform your partnership and your life – your own self.

This involves letting go of assumptions and expectations you hold concerning the power other people can have over your life.

You must let go of the expectation that another person will make you happy.
>Ultimately you alone are responsible for your happiness or unhappiness.

You must let go of the expectation that another person will protect you from the pain of living.
>Along with tears of joy, life inevitably dispenses tears of sadness. Your pain is yours alone to experience.

You must let go of the expectation that another person will provide you with a sense of your own self-worth.
>While other people have their opinions about you, your self-esteem is something you develop on your own.

You must let go of the expectation that you will be the center of another person's universe.
>They are the center of their own universe. If you want to be their center or if they expect you to be their center, you are both in trouble.

You must let go of the expectation that the state of your relationship, your partner and yourself will remain consistently pleasant.
>You don't always like the one you love. As a matter of course, people run hot and cold, feel closeness and distance. You will drive yourself crazy if you freak out every time your partner acts cold or distant.

LOVING PROMISES

This leads us to one last fairytale – the belief in the omnipotence of love. As the song goes, "All you need is love. Love is all you need." We believe if we love our partner and our partner loves us, our problems will evaporate and all our pain will be healed. It is as if love has some magical, mystical power. We believe it will be easy, no sweat, no work. When we find true love we will skip down the yellow brick road into the enchanted Land of Oz and be happy forever after. But remember, the Great Oz was not the all-powerful wizard Dorothy envisioned, and he could not provide genuine courage, heart or brains, nor could he point the way home.

Love is not omnipotent. Love cannot heal all wounds. Some wounds are so deep and so numerous that they are unlikely to be healed in one lifetime. But love is powerful. It can provide an environment within which healing can take place. Love can help us embrace our woundedness and the woundedness of our partner with openness and acceptance. That open hearted acceptance is itself a healing. A gentle, accepting embrace is the way love heals.

Allow me to step back and clarify my thoughts about fairytales of love. I believe, just as the fairytale says, love *can* be magical. Love *can* transform us. Love *can* kiss us awake and bring greater happiness into our life. Love has the potential to do this. I know this to be true because this magic happened to Alice and I. I was the frog that the princess kissed, Alice was the Sleeping Beauty. The difference is that the magic was not the result of some alchemy that took place outside ourselves. When we were awakened by our love for each other, *the magic resided within us*. And it wasn't magic, it was intensive inner work. We made it happen. For years before we met, Alice and I individually did the inner work that created the conditions for love to thrive. We studied, attended therapy and personal growth groups, performed spiritual practices. We prepared ourselves by growing and maturing in mind and spirit. If we had avoided this work, if we had not been prepared, the awakening kiss would have been wasted and I would still be a frog and Alice would still be asleep. When the prince came knocking on Alice's door and princess came knocking on mine, we were ripe, we were ready and able to awaken and give and receive magnificent love.

It is true that love is powerful and has the potential to transform us, but there are forces that dilute its power. Chief among them is fear. We are all born with an innocent, loving nature. A loving heart is every infant's birthright. But, as we grow from infancy, we encounter painful experiences, maltreatment, betrayal, hurt feelings. We become afraid. Fear makes us want to close down and protect ourselves. We go numb, blot out feelings, run away. The open, loving, trusting child that we were becomes wary and defensive over time. To recapture that loving nature requires that we dismantle the walls built by fear. As the 13th century Persian poet, Rumi, wrote, "Your task is not to seek for love, but merely to find all the barriers within yourself you have built against it." Those barriers exist inside you. Finding and removing the walls that hold back your love is the work of becoming a more loving person. It is what the Loving Promises are all about. This work usually doesn't happen on its own. This is your work. It takes courage and self-discipline to knock down and clear away walls that have existed for a lifetime.

Fairytales end on a high note. Happy ever after. The Prince matches the glass slipper to Cinderella's foot, Beauty's tears change the Beast into a handsome prince, the frog transformed, the princess awakened. Then, they marry, and the fairytale ends. But they don't tell anything about what comes after—the conflicts and difficult compromises necessary for enduring love.

A committed relationship requires pushing through uncomfortable places within yourself and acting in ways that promote love – giving of yourself even when you don't feel like it, holding your tongue even when you know you are right, giving up what you want because you must compromise with your partners wishes, confronting your partner even though you are afraid, telling the truth even when you know facing the consequences will be unpleasant. These are all uncomfortable situations that challenge you to push through your inertia and resistance. This is the stuff of real life, not fairytales.

Your mind is the source of your experience of the world. The world you see is a reflection of your mind. If you are unhappy with your world and unhappy with your partner, usually the first thing you do is look to them and blame them and try to change them. "You made me angry. You made me afraid, you made me jealous." Nobody can make you feel anything. They may do or say things that stimulate an *emotional sensitivity* you may have, and their behavior activates the anger, fear and jealousy that is waiting inside you, but they don't cause your reaction and they don't deserve your blame.

Blaming your partner for how you feel and trying to change them is going about it backwards. It is as if you have a camera with dirty spots on the lens and instead of cleaning the lens, you try to remove the spots from each picture you take. Look to your own mind. When you have an emotional reaction, don't immediately blame. Listen to the anger, fear and jealousy you feel. See it as arising from *you*. Look within and wipe your lens clean first before you go about trying to change your world or your partner.

Realize that everything you need for your happiness, the happiness of your partner and for the health of your relationship resides in your own self. If you, your partner or the relationship is not perfect, take on the challenge to make it perfect. Even though you know you have no control, take control, assume responsibility. Of course, if your partner is unhappy that is their responsibility, right? But do you, as their beloved partner, have any responsibility for their happiness? Most people would answer "No! they should take full responsibility for their own happiness." However, being such an important person in their life, you have power. With a powerful injection of your love and appreciation, you can turn their frown into a smile. Your passion can ignite their passion. You can incite their love through the power of your love. If you are able to exert influence for your partner's happiness, why not do it? Don't confuse exerting influence with taking responsibility, though. Ultimately, they are responsible for their happiness.

While the ideas in this chapter about personal responsibility may be theoretically valid, they are abstract and analytical, not of the flesh and blood of a living relationship. As concepts, they can be extremely useful to broaden your understanding and keep in mind when you are working through problems you are having in your relationship, but they have limited practical, day-to-day value. Your relationship is not a theory. It is a living entity. Being with another person is more than just a lonely internal process. In life, what goes on between two people within their relationship has relevance. A relationship is more than just a workshop for your personal development, a process whereby you grow by encountering and overcoming your interpersonal obstacles. Rather, a relationship is a partnership, the purpose of which is to generate love and share love. Ideally, a couple is a team, working together to inspire each other and provide happiness and fulfillment for each other and for themselves. That is what makes a relationship magnificent. If a couple fails to support one another's happiness, this brings into question the very reason why they are together at all.

So, keep in mind these concepts about the awesome power you have to guide your relationship and the responsibility you have to make it magnificent. This is very valuable information. But never lose sight of the idea that you and your beloved partner are a team. If your partner is willing, join together with them. As teammates, the goal of the game you two are playing is to uplift each other, enjoy each other and inspire each other to be immersed in love. Accomplishing this goal is much easier if you and your partner are on the same team.

This game, where the object is to be the most loving and lovable person you can be, is the best game in town. Make it your goal to reach deep inside, to go all out and be the best player you can be.

Part Two

The Promises

Chapter 4

INTRODUCING THE LOVING PROMISES

Relationship is never static. It is a dynamic, unfolding process that ebbs and flows, grows and recedes. Ideally it is a process that moves the couple in the direction of greater depth and harmony. Any relationship that remains frozen, where a couple lacks growing connection and reciprocation risks becoming stagnant. A stagnant relationship is one that is gradually dying. What gives vitality to a couple's partnership is the shared intention to evolve and deepen, both as individuals and as a couple. This has been Alice's and my goal. Our Loving Promises are the way Alice and I have attempted to fulfill that goal and live our relationship and our lives.

The following 39 vows are what has made our relationship magnificent and our lives overflowing with love. While we have not adhered to all the Loving Promises with perfect fidelity at all times, we have set our intention on fulfilling them as best we can. This has been the foundation upon which our partnership is built. It is not as if Alice and I set out to consciously develop and follow a set of vows that would guide our relationship. We simply lived our lives together as best we could. These vows emerged only later from contemplating our relationship and writing this book.

Keep in mind that the order of the Loving Promises and the length of the discussions of each is not an indicator of their relative importance. They are all important and all necessary for a magnificent relationship.

Here they are:

1. I WILL STAND STEADFASTLY BY YOU. I am wholeheartedly committed to the permanence of our relationship. I will not leave or threaten to leave, even during times of great difficulty.

INTRODUCING THE LOVING PROMISES

2. I WILL REMAIN PRESENT WITH YOU. I will abide with you in mind and body. I will not cut myself off from you by withdrawing physically, mentally or emotionally, especially when I am upset or overwhelmed.

3. I WILL BE AWAKE TO YOU. In order to know you, I will take interest in you. I will observe closely and listen carefully to you, with focus, empathy, patience and compassion. I will receive you with an open heart and mind, trying to intuit the feelings and decipher the meanings that lie beneath your words and actions.

4. I WILL SERVE YOUR BEST INTERESTS. I want the best for you in the same way I want the best for myself. I will take care of you, comfort you, encourage you and protect you from harm in ways that empower you and do not interfere with you growing into your perfection.

5. I WILL BE UNSELFISH WITH YOU. I will make it my practice to attempt to give to you unconditionally. When our needs are in conflict I will seek solutions only in terms of our mutual benefit. I will delight in and resolve to consistently do what I can to foster your happiness.

6. I WILL PARTICIPATE IN YOUR LIFE. I will make the ongoing decision to extend myself and choose to participate with you in the interests and activities that you find important and enjoyable. I will reserve time for us to be together.

7. I WILL BE FLEXIBLE WITH YOU. I will always remain open to relinquishing my stance and altering my behavior when it is appropriate. I will aim to do so graciously, without regret or expectation of compensation.

8. I WILL BE ACCEPTING OF YOU. I will not expect perfection from you. I will seek to recognize and appreciate your individual uniqueness and acknowledge your human frailty. I will be patient with you. I will not attempt to change you into my idea of who you should be.

9. I WILL REGARD YOU AS MY EQUAL. I will immediately cease when I become aware that I am judging you to be inferior or superior to myself, believe that my needs are more important than yours, assume I cannot learn from you or expect that I am entitled to better treatment than you.

LOVING PROMISES

10. I WILL EMPHASIZE YOUR POSITIVE SIDE. I will applaud your admirable qualities, activities and accomplishments and refrain from focusing on your failings and imperfections.

11. I WILL INSPIRE YOU TO BE YOUR BEST. I will persistently urge you to strive to be the very best person you can be. I will encourage you to pursue your dreams.

12. I WILL CHALLENGE YOU WHEN NECESSARY. I will not shrink from asserting my power in order to influence you for your benefit. I will confront you and offer constructive criticism when I recognize you are in need of guidance.

13. I WILL BE GRATEFUL FOR YOUR GIFTS TO ME. I will be mindful of the things you do and have done for my benefit. I will not take these things for granted or automatically expect them from you. I will receive graciously.

14. I WILL APPRECIATE YOU. I will honor the miracle, mystery and beauty of who you are. I will keep alive a sense of appreciation of how your presence has enhanced my life. I will not hesitate to express my appreciation for you.

15. I WILL EXPRESS MY FEELINGS OF LOVE FOR YOU. Everyone wants to know they are loved. I will demonstrate my love for you through my words, my touch, my giving and especially through my conduct.

16. I WILL BE FORGIVING OF YOU. Holding on to ill will hurts both you and me. I will look upon you with compassion and strive to let go of my anger, blame and judgments when I feel you have wronged me. I will never engage in any form of retaliation.

17. I WILL BE DEPENDABLE WITH YOU. I will try to the best of my ability to identify and accomplish the things that need to be done for our mutual well-being. I will attempt to always follow through with what I say I will do. I will perform my tasks with care.

18. I WILL BE TRUTHFUL WITH YOU. I will not tell you anything I know to be false, nor will I omit telling you what I know to be true. I will not bend the truth in order to gain advantage, protect myself, or keep peace.

INTRODUCING THE LOVING PROMISES

19. I WILL BE TRANSPARENT TO YOU. I will allow you to know the real me. I will not attempt to protect myself by maintaining a false facade and by withholding my true feelings, thoughts and motives from you – especially when I feel vulnerable.

20. I WILL SPEAK TO YOU WITH CARE. My words have power for you, so I will take care to honor your feelings and your dignity, not only with what I say to you, but also how and when I say it. I will be especially aware when we are in conflict.

21. I WILL NOT MANIPULATE YOU. I will not exploit your vulnerabilities in order to control you. I will not belittle you, blame you, threaten you, deliberately hurt you with words, or intentionally withhold money, favors, information or affection from you in order to get my way.

22. I WILL PROTECT OUR CONFIDENTIALITY. I will not share anything about you, me or us that you would not want others to know.

23. I WILL RESPECT OUR INDEPENDENCE. You are not my possession. I will honor your freedom to think, say and do what seems right to you -- even if I do not agree or understand. I trust you can take care of yourself. I will foster my own independence so that I can be free and autonomous when necessary.

24. I WILL BE CONSIDERATE OF YOUR DESIRE FOR PRIVACY AND SOLITUDE. Periods of interior time are necessary and healing. I recognize your occasional need for privacy, silence and alone time, and I will abide by your wishes.

25. I WILL TOUCH YOU AND WELCOME YOUR TOUCH. I understand that touch is a gift and a healing. I will welcome physical expression of our love for each other through loving caress, in ways that are reciprocally appreciated and at times that are mutually desired.

26. I WILL REMAIN FAITHFUL TO YOU. Sexual fidelity is a bulwark of our relationship. I consider you my exclusive sexual partner and reserve intimate caress for you alone.

LOVING PROMISES

27. I WILL PLAY WITH YOU. An essential purpose of our connection is to create mutual joy. I will do what I can to make humor, entertainment, curiosity, surprise, creativity, imagination, romance, excitement and childlike playfulness vital elements in our relationship. I will make sure to schedule playtime in our calendar.

28. I WILL VITALIZE OUR RELATIONSHIP. A partnership that does not continually grow can stagnate. I will instigate and participate in uplifting activities, learning and adventures that inspire us to evolve physically, intellectually, emotionally and spiritually.

29. I WILL HONOR YOUR FAMILY. Familial ties are complex and binding. I will treat your family with respect and graciousness, ever mindful that my first loyalty is to you.

30. I WILL BE ALERT TO NEGATIVITY IN OUR RELATIONSHIP. I will not allow harmful feelings and destructive situations to persist and fester. I will attend to the first indications of disharmony between us so that minor problems never have the chance to become major.

31. I WILL ASSUME RESPONSIBILITY FOR MY DETRIMENTAL BEHAVIOR. When there is discord, I will curb my tendency to act in ways that create more problems. I will take impartial account of my part and do what is necessary to make things right. I welcome feedback that shows where I can be more loving.

32. I WILL INVOKE THE LOVING PROMISES WHEN WE ARE IN CRISIS. During stressful circumstances, our relationship requires greater loving from me. At those trying times, I will attempt to apply the Loving Promises to the best of my ability.

33. I WILL HONOR MY OWN NEEDS AND MY OWN FEELINGS. When trying to uphold these loving promises, I will attend to the way I feel. I will not disregard my needs and desires, compromise my values or allow others to overstep my boundaries. I will ask for what I want. I will be who I am.

34. I WILL NURTURE MYSELF FOR BOTH OF US. My well-being affects you as well as myself. I will strive to choose wholesome alternatives in my

life that keep my body healthy, my mind positive and my spirit uplifted. I will look after my own needs so that I am not overly dependent on you.

35. I WILL MAINTAIN THE AWARENESS OF THE SPIRITUAL ESSENCE OF OUR RELATIONSHIP. You, our love, and the bond we share are sacred gifts. It is an essential aspect of my spiritual path. That understanding will inform all choices I make.

36. I WILL REMIND MYSELF OF THE FLEETING NATURE OF OUR TIME TOGETHER. At some point one of us will be alone. I will endeavor to keep this in my mind and savor the preciousness of each moment I have with you.

37. I WILL DEEPEN MY LOVE FOR MYSELF. If I do not love me, I cannot give love to you, nor can I be available to receive your love. I will aspire to acknowledge myself as unconditionally lovable. I will adapt the Loving Promises so that they apply to myself.

38. I WILL EXPAND MY LOVE INTO THE WORLD. My love will wither if it is reserved only for you. I will extend my love, respect and care to family and friends, acquaintances and strangers, to nature and to all of creation.

There is a final Promise not listed here which will be considered in the final chapter of the book.

Every religion and every spiritual tradition incorporates a code of ethical behavior that lays the foundation for living a good and upstanding life. The Ten Commandments of the Judaeo/Christian religion, the precepts of Buddhism, the *Yamas* of Hinduism and the Islamic moral commandments set forth in the Koran are examples. Prohibitions against lying, stealing, killing, abusing intoxicants, sexual impropriety, etc. are common behavioral guidelines. There is good reason why these ethical/moral conditions are considered so important as to be included in all major traditions. If a person does not abide by these basic moral injunctions, they cannot live in harmony with others. Moreover, they cannot be at peace in their own mind. One who kills will be ever fearful of retribution. One who lies will be afraid of being found out, one who steals will fear being caught or being stolen from. Conversely, abiding by ethical principles brings peace and harmony to one's life. The Loving Promises is a list of ethical behaviors – a kind of "39 Commandments," designed especially for loving, intimate relationships.

A shared life built on virtue is the foundation of a magnificent relationship. The idea is simple and self-evident. A generous couple, a patient couple, a kind couple will have a happier life together than a stingy couple, an impatient couple and a couple who are unkind to each other.

Buddhism says that the causes of all human suffering are "the Three Poisons" – greed, anger and ignorance. Alone and in combination, they are the source of all the problems we have as individuals, as a couple and as a species. "I want," "I hate," and "I don't know or care" are thoughts that lead to behaviors that poison all human relationships. The Loving Promises are antidotes to those three poisons. The Promises work by diluting the power of the poisons and providing positive, loving habit patterns. The emphasis on acquiring and practicing new, virtuous behaviors or eliminating old un-virtuous behaviors are two sides of the same coin. Both will make you a more loving and lovable person.

One way of understanding the Loving Promises is to see them as an extremely detailed and comprehensive set of marriage vows. When you marry and repeat vows to each other, you and your partner are undergoing an initiation. Initiations are events or ceremonies that mark the transition from one state to another. Graduation from school is an initiation. Becoming a parent is an initiation. Retirement is an initiation. The marriage ceremony and vows contained therein initiate you from being a single individual, into being a couple. After wedding, no longer are you responsible for only yourself. You have taken upon yourself the awesome task of caring for the well-being of another person. You are no longer two separate individuals. You are one. Cementing and purifying this oneness is the intention of the Loving Promises. Adopting these Promises initiates you into a relationship bond of expansive scope and fathomless depth. It is a true initiation into the deepest levels of love.

It is obvious that the Loving Promises are no popular self-help quick fix, no neat, comfortable formula ("39 Easy Tips for A Magnificent Relationship"). The Loving Promises are ways of being, ways of living. They are a lifelong practice for living a pure life. Though presented here in the context of relationship, they have much wider application. They define a way of being in the world with integrity, kindness, patience, presence and compassion. These are the qualities that are essential for love to survive and to thrive. In the first chapter, I described *Necessary Conditions* that allow love to survive. The Loving Promises fulfill those

INTRODUCING THE LOVING PROMISES

conditions. They allow love to survive because the promises embody safety, appreciation and connection. And, the Loving Promises also fulfill the *Optimal Conditions* to allow love to thrive because they are actually a more detailed and behavior-based expression of those conditions. There is a major difference. Unlike the Optimal Conditions, the Loving Promises are not written as if to another person. They are not an agreement you make with that person. In line with the ideas in chapter 3, they are promises you make to yourself. *You are bound not by the commitment you make to your partner; rather, you are bound by a commitment you make to your own integrity.*

Because of this, the Loving Promises differ from a contract. Contracts are based on distrust. They stipulate rights and obligations, more the language of the law rather than the heart. A contract is a binding agreement made with another party and enforced by sanctions. Fail to abide by the agreement and negative consequences will ensue. The Loving Promises is an *internal agreement*, a private choice made by one individual that states how they will govern their behavior in the relationship and in their life. The Promises are enforced not by negative consequences, but by recognition of the truth and goodness of the Promises and recognition that life and relationships will be greatly benefited by following them. The motivation behind the Promises is a drawing towards the positive, rather than avoiding the negative.

The only enduring way you can guide a relationship is through your own behavior, your own example. It is impossible to coerce people to be the way you want them to be by force. However, you are able to influence them by your love and your truth and your courage and your goodness. That influence is powered by attraction. Your way of being, the benefit gained by your way of being and the joy that emanates from you as a result of your way of being compels another to emulate the way you are. The Loving Promises act as a catalyst for love. As you incorporate them into your life, you inspire others to love as you love.

Another way the Promises influence your partner is that they create an atmosphere that encourages reciprocation. Your actions encourage corresponding actions in your partner. Your unselfishness, your honesty, your dependability and all your other positive qualities will tend to bring about those qualities in your partner. It is a natural consequence – be generous with your partner and an atmosphere of generosity is created in your relationship that invites generosity from your partner. Be honest and an atmosphere of honesty is created. Kindness, patience and dependability will be the environment both of you will live and breathe in. The effects of that atmosphere are subtle. They are indirect. The changes you desire in your relationship may not occur immediately, and they may not occur exactly the way you want, but they are bound to occur.

LOVING PROMISES

Your behavior has an incredibly powerful effect on those you love. That effect is additive. As you love more, your love accumulates. Think of your loving behavior with your partner as if it were a bank account. The goodwill generated by your acts of kindness and consideration toward your partner accrues every day and will eventually lead to a surplus of your partner's feeling loved and feeling greater love for you. They in turn deposit their love into the love account. Pretty soon you both will be rich in love. Those abundant feelings of love will characterize your relationship. In lean times – periods of stress, conflict and disappointment, you both will be able to draw upon the bountiful love account.

As you read through the Loving Promises, you will see that, with the exception of two or three, which have to do with expressing love and sexuality, the Promises are attributes of the deepest, abiding friendship. This is the way true friends behave toward each other. Wouldn't a friend who treats you by way of the Promises be the perfect companion? If people treated their partners the way they relate to their treasured long-term friends, there wouldn't be many breakups or divorces. I believe that friendship, not romantic love, is the most complete form of love between adults. My love for Alice is identical with profound friendship. Alice is my best friend, my pal. I truly like her. Liking is simple and pure. It is at the center of friendship. Genuine love and genuine friendship cannot exist without liking.

Besides friendship, almost all of the Loving Promises are characteristic of maternal love. The selfless care that an ideal mother lavishes on her child is the closest humans can come to unconditional love. A mother arrives at these tender feelings almost automatically. This helpless being from her body that she cradles in her arms evokes in her an inborn desire to care for, support and protect. There are often times when I feel this maternal love for Alice. When I see her sweet innocence, I cannot help but want to cradle her in my arms and shelter her as if she were my child.

In addition to friendship and maternal love, the Loving Promises represent the Golden Rule, "Do unto others as you wish others to do unto you." They provide us a yardstick to determine the way to treat others. We use ourselves – what pleases us, what hurts us, what we want and what we don't want, as a way to determine how we should treat others. Each Promise also reflects the way we ourselves wish to be treated – to be appreciated, cared for, regarded as equal, told the truth, etc. Thus, we can reverse the Golden Rule and "Do unto ourselves as we wish others would do unto us." Following this reverse Golden Rule, the Promises ask that we treat ourselves with self-love.

Embodying abiding friendship, maternal love and self-love, the Loving Promises are a comprehensive guide to becoming a loving partner. If you incorporate the Loving Promises in the way you treat your partner, you WILL become a more loving person because the Promises, taken together, define love in its finest incarnation. They define love not in intellectual or emotional terms, but primarily by behavior, by describing how you might act towards your beloved. For example, my love is made manifest by speaking to Alice with respect, by being truthful with her, by listening attentively to her, by refraining from manipulating her, by acting unselfishly with her. All these are behaviors.

Once you understand that the essence of love is behavior, you dramatically increase your ability to alter the quality of your love. Feelings are in the domain of the psyche. For the most part, all we can do is passively experience feelings and involuntarily react as they spontaneously arise. But, behavior is different. It is in the domain of the physical world and the material body and, therefore, your behavior is more subject to the power of will. You can much more easily willfully initiate some action, or interrupt or cease some action, than you can alter your feelings. Intention and will is what empowers the Loving Promises.

To bring will from the mental sphere into the real world involves choice. We choose the actions envisioned by our will. In relationship we are constantly faced with choices between generosity and selfishness. The choices we make determine the nature of our relationship. "Should I serve myself, or serve my partner?" "Should I shade the truth and manipulate, or should I be straightforward?" "Should I try to win for myself or should I help us both to win." Each Loving Promise involves choice and the choice the Promise presents you is noble and sets a high standard. Each asks of you to be the best partner and the best person you can be. The Loving Promises clarify the choices.

Choosing loving actions is a first step. Becoming a loving partner is more than simply making a choice. It is necessary to follow up choice with action. Effective loving action doesn't always occur spontaneously. Often practice is needed. Repetitive practice of the Loving Promises imbeds them in our brain, our gut and in our muscles. Practice increases the probability that a loving response will occur.

The Loving Promises have been described as daunting, and they are. They are even more daunting when you realize there is no cherry picking allowed. To fully engage them, you cannot choose which Promise to include, and which to leave out, which to work with intensively, and which to let slide. They must all be addressed. Every single one of them is essential. Some are more comprehensive, like the Promise of being committed to the permanence of the relationship or of serving your partner's best interests. Some are more limited in scope, such as protecting confidentiality or respecting a partner's need for solitude. But every one must be included.

Whether limited or comprehensive, the Promises are like links of a chain. If there is one weak link, the chain can break at that spot when pressure is applied. The Promises are also interrelated. You cannot be truthful with your beloved and at the same time not be transparent. You cannot be accepting of them, and at the same time try to manipulate them. You cannot be unselfish with your partner, and at the same time not serve them.

The principle underlying the Loving Promises is very simple, *the behavior and emotions expressed by you induce corresponding feelings and behavior in your partner.* It could be a similar or different response, but inevitably, what one partner feels, says and does affects what the other partner feels, says and does. And like a feedback loop, how you respond to your partner's response affects them, and on and on in a cycle of action/reaction. For example, if Alice expressed anger toward me, sometimes I would express anger back at her or, at other times, I would shut down and become mum. Both of these responses would tend to elevate Alice's anger, which in turn would make me want to strike back more or become even more withdrawn. These are not effective ways to improve a situation. However, if I were to quietly listen to Alice, inquire of her as to the cause of her upset, admit culpability if I am at fault, and express a willingness to be of help, her response would be quite different.

The corollary to this principle could be, goodwill induces goodwill, and ill will induces ill will. Every one of the Loving Promises is an expression of goodwill. The Loving Promises set up a positive feedback loop, where the kindness and thoughtfulness of one partner invites reciprocation by the other. Each of us, by exercising goodwill or ill, has the power to make our partner feel better or worse. It feels so much more pleasant, both to them and to us, to make them feel better.

The Loving Promises are not some new, groundbreaking concept. They are as old as the hills. The theory behind them is simple. Instinctively, you already know the Promises and understand how they operate to make relationships magnificent. This book just serves as a reminder–a reminder of the power of your love and the effect of your love on others. When you behave with integrity and generosity you will be admired and loved. Your presence will heal. You will be a magnet. People will want to be around you and want to respond to you with the same kindness and generosity that you exude.

It's not rocket science to comprehend the concepts underlying the Loving Promises and understand how they work. But putting them into practice is not a minor task. It's a monumental undertaking. The Promises are not for "wusses." At times they will require every bit of your strength. At times you will have to be a warrior, a Warrior of Love.

INTRODUCING THE LOVING PROMISES

There will inevitably be times when the warrior in you will be a scared, overwhelmed kid and want to turn tail and beat a hasty retreat. The Promises will seem an impossible chore. It's important to remember that they are ideals. You will lose heart if you expect that you must be perfect. Do the best you can. No one is grading you. No one is going to punish you if you are not impeccable. We are all in this to learn.

When you first encounter them, the Promises seem overwhelming. Don't despair. It's like this with any new endeavor. As you actually work with the Promises, they become more familiar. You get a greater sense of what is involved as the newness wears off. Soon the novel ways of thinking and new behaviors become integrated into your life and become your normal, natural way.

Long-term relationships do not remain the same throughout their duration. As couples grow and mature, their relationship typically evolves and progresses through stages. Each stage of an archetypical couple's journey presents different challenges to be encountered, different tasks to be accomplished, different learnings to absorb. Once the tasks of one stage are achieved, the opportunity to move on to the next stage arises. An initial romantic *Honeymoon* stage often gives way to *Disillusionment,* where reality sets in as partners relax and allow more of their unvarnished self to be seen. This can turn into *Power Struggle,* where partners attempt to force each other to change. The preponderance of relationships reside in *Truce,* where couples negotiate peace and are resigned to "live with" parts they don't accept. For the most part the individuals are happy and are getting their needs met. While things may not be fabulous, they are certainly good enough. This stage can last for a long time and most couples remain content in perpetuity in this non-demanding, relatively comfortable and peaceable phase. This is what many people call a "good relationship." The final stage, the one which is in the domain of Loving Promises, is *Conscious Commitment.* In this stage, the partners undertake a quest to grow. They do what they can, as individuals and as a couple, to further their own and their partner's physical, intellectual, emotional, social and spiritual unfolding. This is a noble purpose. It is toward this purpose that is the aim of all the Loving Promises. This is the stage of magnificent relationships.

The Loving Promises are a path, a profound path. A magnificent relationship is the destination. The path to a magnificent relationship must be trod step by step. You are in unfamiliar territory. You must explore. At times it will be inevitable that you will lose your way, be distracted, and waste time and energy following detours that will eventually turn into dead ends. There are no shortcuts. Working with the Loving Promises is a lifetime enterprise. Don't worry about the destination. Just put one foot in front of the other. Hasten slowly and engage with your heart.

Chapter 5

UNDERSTANDING THE LOVING PROMISES

Underlying all the Loving Promises is a single-minded commitment. That commitment is to the growth, well-being and psychological and spiritual unfolding of your partner and of yourself. So comprehensive is that fundamental commitment that it alone could serve as a guide to creating a magnificent relationship. Each of the Promises can be considered different avenues to this goal. They each delineate specific areas and specific behaviors that move us toward embodying living love. This extended chapter will explore the Loving Promises in detail.

1. **I WILL STAND STEADFASTLY BY YOU.** *I am wholeheartedly committed to the permanence of our relationship. I will not leave, or threaten to leave, even during times of great difficulty.*

This Promise is fundamental. It is a commitment to remain physically present. When one member of the couple is not available to remain in the relationship, there is no relationship. The commitment is not just to be in relationship for the moment, but to remain in perpetuity. All of the Promises are statements about how you will behave in the future. Only this one, however, is unequivocal. With the others I state my intention to be generous, honest, forgiving, etc. with you. These have a measure of ambiguity. But this Promise is black and white. I am either in the relationship, or not.

When I reach out for Alice's hand, and she reaches for mine, it is a relief and comfort to know that our hands will meet and be there – until death parts us. No matter what my emotional state, no matter what the circumstances, if I leave our house, Alice knows and I know, barring calamity, I will be back. This hunger for continuity in a relationship is a most basic desire. It is the answer to the question we all have for at least one person in our life, "When I want you, when

UNDERSTANDING THE LOVING PROMISES

I need you, will you be there?" When the answer is "Yes," there is an inevitable sigh of relief. Here is someone we can trust, who will be solid, who will stay with us, who will take on responsibility for us, who we will take responsibility for. No longer are we alone in the universe.

Each year, thousands of couples make the solemn vow to remain together "until death do us part," and at that moment they truly believe it. Yet, in America, one quarter of divorces occur during the first two years of marriage. Half of couples renege on their commitment within a decade or so. When they made the marital pledge, they may have glossed over the "richer or poorer, sickness and health" part. Over time, circumstances change, people change, there are difficult years, there is a waning of passion and interest. The commitment changes and becomes "I will be with you if it is not too difficult, if I really feel like it, if you don't get fat, if you don't confront me about my drinking, if you don't lose your sexual desire, if someone more exciting doesn't come along." Real commitment though has no conditions, no "ifs." Each "if" weakens the couple's bond until the relationship becomes so fragile that it falls apart.

In the early stages of a relationship, with its excitement and raging hormones, issues of commitment seem far away. Love comes easily, no work or effort is required. You feel as if the bliss will last forever. But when the excitement wears off and the hormones quiet, what seemed like charming quirks in your partner's personality become annoying or unbearable. It is at this time that commitment begins to take on meaning.

In every relationship I was in prior to meeting Alice, I never had a thorough assurance that it would last. It was as if my bags were never completely unpacked. There was always an escape clause, a failsafe understanding that if the going got tough, either of us would have the option of leaving. Because of that uncertainty, there was always a part of me that I held back. I was afraid to make the commitment and afraid to reveal darker parts of myself for fear I would be abandoned. When I met and fell in love with Alice, I knew I had a life partner. I had a sense of home – a safe harbor. I could relax and be me, warts and all, without fear. Now I could feel safe enough to go deep and tackle issues in my life that, by not committing with my whole being, I had previously been able to avoid.

To some, a lifetime commitment to one person is seen as a life sentence – a jail sentence where you are held captive and lose your freedom. In a sense this is true. Commitment is compromise. By committing to one person you are giving up a portion your independence. Never again will you be able to make decisions based solely on your own desires. You must take your partner's preferences into consideration. In a monogamous relationship it is forever forbidden for you to explore the excitement of intimate connection with another person. By committing, you forgo the open road and its dream of freedom, variety and adventure.

There was a time, early in our relationship, where I faced this predicament head on. Though I felt fulfilled and loved being with Alice, I knew that by staying in the relationship, there was a whole exciting world out there that I would be missing. I was mourning my potential unlived life. When I brought up the idea of a temporary separation where we would each go our own separate ways for a while, Alice's hurt and confusion made me reconsider. Could I be so heartless as to wound Alice? Would it be possible, within our relationship, for me to experience the growth and adventure I craved? Was I really prepared to give up our blissful connection in exchange for an unknown and possibly lonely future? After a moment's consideration, the answer was "no way." Though it was a painful few days for both of us, this episode was an important event that deepened and clarified my commitment to Alice and to our marriage. I have never regretted that commitment for even one second.

Committed relationships often demand difficult ongoing work. Look at most of the rest of the Loving Promises. They place restraints and limitations on your energy, time and focus, and they require you to expend considerable effort and self-control. You are pledging to commit for the whole of your lifetime to be forever dependable, to act unselfishly, to monitor how you speak, how you act, how you think, etc. What is the benefit of standing with another person for a lifetime? Is it worth it?

You bet it's worth it! A person can drill many shallow wells and never reach water, but if they sink one deep well, they have the best chance of reaching pure, clean water. So it is with relationship. Commitment to one person and to the permanence of one relationship is essential for enjoying the most profound intimacy. Our primary love relationship is our first source of emotional support and a vital avenue to discover our inmost self. It is the one deep well we drill. It cannot be possible to have multiple partners and still be intimate with all of them. Each relationship takes a commitment of time and energy and each draws on your emotional reserves. Multiple partners dilute both time and energy.

By committing to stay in intimate connection with one person for a lifetime, you are available to allow for undigested issues of your life to arise and be worked through. If you give yourself permission to flit from relationship to relationship, your tendency is to take flight as soon as things get rough, i.e. when personal issues arise that you are unwilling to face, like fear of intimacy, of being controlled, of revealing yourself, or of being abandoned. Growth comes about by dealing with and working through these hard-to-face issues. Hardships, boredom, lack of communication, even betrayal, are all grist for the mill in relationships. When you engage, they can lead to your growth and expand you personally and as a couple. Avoid these difficult issues, and you possibly avoid growing.

Personal problems don't evaporate by ignoring them and sweeping them under the rug or by latching on to another partner. You carry these issues with you wherever you go, and at some later point they will surface – possibly in a different form or with a different partner, but they will surface. With the knowledge that your issues as an individual are similar to your issues as a couple, commitment to be with and grow with your partner is really a commitment to be with and grow with yourself.

When you know you are "stuck" with this person, with no easy exit strategy, there is an urgency to work things out. If you don't, the interpersonal issues you fail to deal with will remain with you. A relationship is like a three-legged race, where two of the couple's legs are tied together and they have to run with that handicap. If one or both do not coordinate their movements and make adjustments to their partner, they will stumble and fall. The commitment is the rope that binds a couple together. While it limits them, it also pushes them to work together to find peace and contentment. In this sense, binding yourself to your partner, rather than restricting you, can be a source of freedom.

Inherent in the commitment to remain together is the idea that, ultimately, the continuity and wellbeing of your relationship is of primary importance and takes precedence over other parts of your life. If there is an unequivocal choice you must make between the alternatives of getting ahead in your career--and your relationship, or a friendship--and your relationship, or some goal or achievement--and your relationship, accommodation must be made that includes the continuation and flourishing of your partnership. A promotion, a raise, a friendship, the satisfaction of a goal, these would be small compensation for the loss of the warmth, love and support if you were to be severed from your mate.

In a monogamous relationship, the accommodations a man must make tend to be greater than for a woman. Career and lifetime goals often hold core importance for the man, and are considered by him to be essential to his identity and sense of self. In a sense, he considers what he does as who he is. There is the almost universal belief that the promise of monogamy is easier for a woman to uphold than for a man. This belief is supported by sociobiological evidence which suggests that a male's instinctive tendency leans toward multiple mates, while a women's tends toward monogamy. It is the male function for the propagation of the species to fertilize as many females as possible. Bonding with a mate is not necessary to perform this function. Females, on the other hand, need to provide a safe, stable environment to raise their young. Having a bonded mate around to help provide protection, food and shelter, supports this function. Though monogamy may be a bit more difficult for a man to maintain, the gratifying benefits of loving, supportive companionship, children and family, happiness and self-discovery make the option of settling in with one partner the choice of most men. Though the accommodations a man must make in the service of his commitment to his partner may seem like ropes that fetter him, they actually are the means to set his love free.

Long-term relationships inevitably go through ups and downs. When partners abide by their commitment to stay and be a solid presence through those downtimes, a feeling of trust ensues. The couple has a proven, solid commitment to each other. With the passing years, they have the perspective of time and the certainty, "We will face all challenges together and we will endure. This too shall pass and we will gain from it together." This certainty creates a powerful bond that is unbreakable. That bond of trust is the fruit of the Promise and the unshakeable foundation of the relationship.

The first and most important question to be answered before a person commits to another is, "Is this person the one for me, the person I will choose to settle with for the rest of my life?" Without having a clear black and white answer, you cannot have a full commitment. The problem is—there is no black and white answer. There are no perfect partners. Mr. Right always has something wrong or Ms. Right doesn't fit in some way. So the choice of a partner is always a compromise. The proper questions are, "Is this relationship workable enough to commit to?" "Is it workable as it is *now*?" Your partner may or may not change in the future, but you are not committing to a partner in the future, you are committing to them as they are now. Ultimately, we are all imperfect people loving imperfect people imperfectly. And so, your choice to commit to a potential mate always contains the element of a leap of faith.

Because your partner is never a perfect match, you always have the opportunity for feeling "buyer's remorse" after you have made the decision to commit. Is he or she really "workable" enough? Could there be someone else who would be a better fit for you? Once you commit, "The Road Not Taken" can seem like the one you should have taken. I think buyer's remorse is often brought about by fear, and the realization of the finality of the choice you have just made. Questions abound, "What if it doesn't last? Does she really love me? Do I really love her?" Without taking that leap of faith, though, you can spend years indecisively bouncing back-and-forth, never really making a stand and putting down roots. On the other hand, factors may induce you to commit before you are ready. The need for security, worry about getting older, societal pressure and family expectations are some of those factors that may induce you to commit prematurely.

Once you do commit, does commitment really mean forever? Are there circumstances where a lifetime commitment can and should be broken? Sometimes a commitment is made by parties too young to truly understand what they are getting into. Sometimes couples grow in different directions. Sometimes people change in destructive ways such as addiction or domestic violence. And, sometimes a relationship just dies and has no possibility of being revived. The truth is that some relationships are not meant to last "till death do us part." Should you grit your teeth and force yourself to stay in such a relationship no matter what? Should you remain if all that is left is a sense of obligation? Is the ideal of commitment itself reason enough to persevere in a destructive or soulless relationship? Maybe you should break off. Or, it could be that problems that you are experiencing with your partner hold a hidden treasure that, if explored, could provide you both with incredible riches?

The choices are many. Stay imprisoned in an unfulfilling relationship? Separate or divorce and move on with your life? Or take the path of commitment – staying, working through problems and exploring the depth and meaning of your existing relationship. There are no formulas and no definitive answers to these questions. The only advice worth giving is, as with any other important decision in life-- think about it, pray on it, feel into it, be conscious of the depth of it. The breaking of commitment is not a minor thing. Neither is committing to stay imprisoned.

I believe commitment cannot be set in stone. I know of couples who have broken their commitment to "not leave or threaten to leave," who separated and then returned, and through the separation have discovered deeper learnings about themselves and the relationship. Ultimately, this resulted in a stronger commitment for them. I don't believe this happens very often. There are circumstances where even the most firm commitment should be broken. Relationships should be rewarding to both partners. When it ceases to be rewarding, when continuing to be together results in misery for one or both, what is the point? Why prolong the hurt and mutual torture? It might be best to move on, or at least change the commitment.

If you are unhappy with your partner, breakup or divorce seems like such a quick and easy solution, like flipping a switch – instant relief. There is the belief that suddenly all the anger and hurt, the frustration and endless arguments will go away. But it rarely works that way. Bonds of former love do not immediately and completely dissolve. The roots of even love that has expired run deep. This is especially true when there are children. Every time you look at them, you will see a reflection of your former partner. And for the rest of your lives you may find yourself sitting next to your ex at school plays, graduations, weddings, even funerals.

When a relationship ends or a marriage dissolves, people often call it a "failed marriage" or a "broken relationship." This is too simple. The success of a relationship should not be measured by the length of its existence. Success should be measured by the quality of their time and by whether it has propelled the partners to deepen and grow. Sometimes the most successful marriages or relationships end in divorce or breakup. Each person has learned all they could from the partnership and now understand it is time to move on to other learnings, other adventures. If they remain together after the relationship is obviously over and beyond the time to move on, then it is truly a failed relationship.

I would state my position on breaking lifetime relationship commitments as follows:

> *I intend with all my heart to be with you for the rest of our lives, no matter what. I will do everything in my power to keep that promise. If circumstances or personalities evolve to the point where it is no longer possible for us to derive benefit from our partnership, and I have explored all possible avenues to repair the rupture in our love, we should consider altering the form of our commitment. This might include living together as platonic friends, being apart temporarily or separating permanently and going our own ways. If we must do so, I will aim to take responsibility for my part. I will seek to forgive, both you and myself. And I ask you to forgive me. Neither of us is blameless. I will strive to let go of any bitterness and resentment I hold. I will proceed in our separation carefully, with highest integrity and impeccable fairness and with abundant loving-kindness towards you. I will undertake to uncover my gratitude. We have shared our life together and learned from each other, and for this I am grateful. I wish for you a happy life. May you be blessed to find sweet enduring love. Ending our commitment is as important as our beginning. If we do not break our commitment consciously, heartfully, we are simply escaping. We cannot come to completion by escaping. Coming apart consciously demands of us the greatest love.*

UNDERSTANDING THE LOVING PROMISES

While this is an ideal, in the real world, hurt feelings and accusations of unfairness, separation or divorce usually carries strong emotional baggage that makes it difficult to mindfully part ways. It can be messy and confusing. Untangling of financial involvements can be a test. Division of possessions can be heart wrenching. If there are children, the pain can be unbearable. Most likely there will be tears. The tears will be greater if only one partner is in favor of the separation. The conscious way of altering a commitment described above is an ideal, rarely achieved but well worth seeking.

I have thought about the extent of my commitment to Alice. Is there a point at which I would abandon her? What if she became mentally ill, or combative or extensively disabled – needing constant care? What if she contracted Alzheimer's and was only a shell of her former self? In these circumstances, it is obviously not possible to derive mutual benefit from the relationship. What would I do? Would I sacrifice my happiness, my resources, my time, my energy for the remainder of our lives only to provide her a few crumbs of comfort? Or would I remove myself – remand her to the care of an institution and then get on with my life? Alice has told me that if she is ever incapacitated like that, I should go on and live my life. However, my commitment to Alice is forever. I will not abandon her. I will provide whatever it takes for her comfort, health and safety. I wouldn't be a martyr and sacrifice my life though. Part of taking care of her is taking care of myself. Should I become incapacitated, I would want Alice to care for me and care for herself in the same way.

Alice and I have strengthened our commitment by renewing our wedding vows numerous times. After our initial ceremony – a traditional Hindu wedding by a Brahman priest in India, we were remarried by Alice's brother in our backyard, had a traditional Native American wedding by an Indian medicine man, renewed our vows in the Christian tradition in a cheesy Las Vegas wedding chapel and finally were remarried by a Jewish rabbi. Each ceremony had special meaning for us. We came away from each renewal with deeper understanding and greater commitment.

You don't need formal vows to be committed to each other. And even with the most fervent vows, if you don't follow up with action, you are not committed. Vows are just words. Commitment is action. Commitment is not a one-time thing. Genuine commitment is an ongoing process. It needs to happen again when you have a child, again when you are going through a rocky period in your relationship, and again when your partner gets sick and needs your care. Each re-commitment strengthens the bond of your love. If you fail your commitment and don't show up when needed, the bonds of love are weakened.

Much of my description of commitment makes it seem as if it is hard work. Must our commitment be such that we capture and cage our partner and are captured and caged in return? Is commitment dry and uncomfortable? Must we effort at commitment? That's not the way it usually works. If love is deep and true, commitment is not an even an issue. A desire to remain together is the natural consequence of the sweetness and comfort of the relationship. Our cat is committed to us. He is free to come and go as he wishes, but he stays because he is loved. The bed is comfortable, the food is good, and he gets his belly rubbed. Why would he want to leave? In the same way, if the relationship is fulfilling and the partners happy, the question of commitment need never arise. *All you have to do is spoil each other with love.* The commitment will take care of itself.

2. I WILL REMAIN PRESENT WITH YOU. *I will abide with you in mind and body. I will not cut myself off from you by withdrawing physically, mentally or emotionally, especially when I am upset or overwhelmed.*

The first Loving Promise, the commitment to not abandon the relationship, is a basic one. However, simply committing to be in someone's presence is just the first step. All ensuing Loving Promises clarify the ways we can be with our partner once we are committed to remain in relationship. This second Promise is about remaining open and present, which here means not cutting off and withdrawing from your partner, especially when you are feeling uncomfortable. Being present with another person is more than just being in physical attendance. You can be face to face, interacting with your partner and still be miles away, roaming in some fantasy. When you do this you are, in essence, abandoning them mentally and emotionally.

My tendency, when I am upset or bored or preoccupied, is to withdraw my thoughts and feelings. My attention drifts somewhere else – anywhere else but here and now. I might play-act that I am in attendance, reflexively responding with appropriate body posture, head nods, facial expressions and vocalizations, but I am not truly present. It is an act, and it rarely fools anyone. By acting as if I am present, I cheat the other person. And I cheat myself.

When the other person is not present for me, I can usually tell. Their eyes glaze over and they glance around the room. Their energy is elsewhere. When they lack presence, it makes me drift away too. That's exactly what happens. It takes two to be present. If one person is not present, soon both are not present, and both people are just going through the motions of communicating. The opposite is true. When you are present for the other person, it draws them into presence with you. The moment becomes alive with the shared energy.

There have been times when Alice has been talking with me and I was not feeling like I was able to fully be with her. Rather than be dishonest and fake the appearance of being present, I would sometimes stop her and say something like, "I am unable to be totally with you now. Let's hold off until I can give our interaction my full attention." Or, if I have had a lapse of attention I might say to Alice, "Please repeat the last few sentences, I lost the thread of what you were saying." This can strike her as off-putting at first, but ultimately, she appreciates it. It is honest, and it honors her, and lets her know exactly where I stand. I appreciate it when Alice does the same for me.

Integral to the concept of presence is the idea of NOW. To be present, I must be attentive to this very moment. I cannot be in the past, which is a memory. I cannot be in the future, which is a fantasy. To remain present, I must maintain awareness of now, the single point where past and future come together. Here lies the difficulty. In some instances, memory and fantasy might be preferable and more compelling to us than what is happening in the present. What we are feeling in the present moment might be uncomfortable for us, or we may be preoccupied, or bored, so we draw our attention away. Drifting our awareness away from the present is an effective way of removing ourselves from an uncomfortable or painful experience. If you are not aware, you cannot feel. However, whenever you dull pain, you also dull pleasure and joy. You dull aliveness by not being present.

Drifting away from time to time is not abnormal. It can even be beneficial. However, if it becomes a common occurrence and serves to avoid genuine encounter, it can be destructive. Recurrent withdrawing can stunt the growth of the relationship by keeping essential areas "off limits." Withdrawing becomes extremely destructive when patterns of escape constitute the normal method of relating. The connection is like two ships passing in the night.

A common method of withdrawing is to defuse intimacy. If our partner has the desire to get more "real," and we are uncomfortable with that level of intimacy, it is not too hard to keep them at arm's length. When conversing, we can change the subject, make light of their seriousness, speak of facts, not feelings. Every time we use these methods that avoid depth, we train our partner, "don't go there," and our relationship remains comfortable, but shallow.

A most obvious way of escape is addiction. Simply stated, addiction is using some chemical or behavior to alter an uncomfortable state. Drugs and alcohol are the classic addictions. However, common activities can be used addictively – gambling, compulsive work, obsessively watching television, viewing pornography, compulsive shopping, and numerous other activities can be used to escape a genuine encounter with the partner and with the self.

The impetus to break presence with your partner is strongest during a time of impasse, conflict or emotional upset. These are times when we tend to cut off feeling, mentally drift away or actually leave. But these are times when our presence is most required. What is needed is a conscious commitment on your part to be awake, stay put, listen, communicate and work things through. Often this is the only solution. Your commitment to be present sends a message that peace, harmony and connection with your partner is vitally important to you, more important than the comfort of temporary escape.

For most of us, when our beloved is suffering, it is especially difficult for us to be present. We feel their pain and their pain causes us discomfort. We may try to stop our pain by cutting off feeling and going into "fix-it" mode with them, coming up with solutions, telling stories of similar predicaments, etc. We attempt to dampen their pain in order to control our own. This is not helpful and not being present. Staying in contact – listening, hearing, sensing our partner's suffering, that is being a healing presence.

Staying in contact is what is needed, yet our partner's emotional storms, and our own, can pull us off our center. Then we can lose contact with them as well as ourselves. The trick is to be sensitive to our partner's feeling state, yet maintain our balance and not be triggered by them. Empathy is a wonderful quality, but not when their anger makes us angry, their fear makes us afraid or their agitation makes us agitated.

What is the action component connected with this promise? The action here is subtle because it lies in the realm of attention. In essence, you must be attentive to where you put your attention. It you allow your mind to roam where it will, it can take you on a wild ride. The only way to avoid being taken for a ride by your mind and your emotions is to practice vigilance. Vigilance in this case is being alert to the first stirrings of the mind's efforts to escape. The sooner you catch those stirrings, the easier it is to place your mind in the present. Once the mind begins taking you for a ride, it is almost always too late. One thought will lead to another, and that will lead to yet another. Pretty soon you are in fantasyland.

The practice of certain forms of meditation can be extremely valuable as a tool to strengthen the ability to attend. In everyday life we are pulled this way and that by our activities, thoughts, sensations and emotions. We can easily get disoriented and lose our moment-to-moment awareness. When we meditate, we are engaged in the practice being present. One form of meditation is ideally suited to bring you into the present moment. It involves sitting comfortably with eyes closed, attending without judgment to each thought, each image, each feeling and each sensation that arises, allowing it to be, letting it go, allowing the next. A structured Buddhist meditation practice called Vipassana moves the practitioner through progressive awareness of sensations, thoughts, positive and negative feelings, intentions, etc. (See the appendix for more detailed instruction.)

As you gain proficiency in this form of meditation through ongoing practice, you see more clearly the activity of the mind and are less vulnerable to its gyrations. You are able to step away from emotional storms and give yourself distance from knee-jerk reactions. You acquire the ability to guide your attention to where you want it to go... and not go. All forms of meditation are best not thought of as a cure – the equivalent of a "happy pill" you take when you are feeling bad. Meditation is a practice. Benefit is accrued subtly, over time, sometimes over years. Progress is usually the result of protracted repetition. It is an effective life changer, but it is not an easy or immediate fix.

When we are lying in each other's arms, (which we often do) Alice and I will sometimes naturally synchronize our breathing. Alice started to do this when we first got together. When our breath is coordinated, it gives us an indescribable feeling of oneness. It seems like we melt into each other. There must be some physiological mechanism behind this. I highly recommend couples try this practice for a powerful sense of shared presence.

Life can be conceived as a series of encounters. With each encounter we have a choice. Do we fully enter each experience, even an uncomfortable one, and become enriched by it, or do we withdraw our presence and thereby become impoverished? Much of our life we have made the choice to break presence by any means in order to numb ourselves to avoid discomfort. Yet, by that very avoidance, we preclude aliveness. The height of joy we are able to experience is limited by the depth of discomfort we are willing to allow ourselves. By cutting out and numbing the lows, we also eliminate the highs. We end up dulling ourselves rather than digging deep into the bountiful richness and celebrating what life has to offer.

We are here to celebrate. We are able to celebrate with gusto by being present to fully embrace all of life, welcoming the discomforts along with the pleasant, the sorrows along with the joys. The choice we make to be present with our self and present with our partner has real significance in regards to the two people we are closest with – our beloved and our self.

This Loving Promise is about being present, with the focus on ourselves. The following Promise is also about being present, but the focus is on our partner.

3. **I WILL BE AWAKE TO YOU.** *In order to know you, I will take interest in you. I will observe closely and listen carefully to you, with focus, empathy, patience and compassion. I will receive you with an open heart and mind, trying to intuit the feelings and decipher the meanings that lie beneath your words and actions.*

The first Loving Promise is a commitment not to abandon you physically. The second is a commitment to not abandon you mentally and emotionally. Rather than what I won't do, the third Loving Promise explains what I *will* do in order to be with you in loving communion. This promise is to *receive* the other, to intuit and understand who they are on the deepest level. When a person is attended to and known in this way, they feel valued. It is not possible to feel valued and loved if you are not known. Likewise, it is impossible to love a person if you do not know them. So, knowing the other is an essential requisite to love. However, people are not always open books. Their words and actions may not convey their inner reality. They might even use their words and behavior to conceal their true thoughts and feelings. What is necessary in this case is to pay special attention, to look below the surface to try to intuit what is really going on. Realize that your partner's every movement is a communication. A sigh, a nervous blink, a held breath, a lifted eyebrow speaks volumes. It is essential for you to be able to read those volumes.

> *You may be laughing and smiling, but I watch the expressions on your face, look closely into your eyes and take the surrounding circumstances into consideration. I sense that behind your apparent jovial exterior, you are feeling anxious and insecure.*
>
> *Overtly you may seem angry and aggressive, but I listen attentively to the tone of your voice and sense that you are afraid inside and lashing out is a way you are protecting yourself.*

By taking what you see at face value, you miss the anxiety behind the joviality and the fear behind the anger.

What blinds us to our partner is not just their reluctance to reveal themselves to us. More often, it is our own blindness that keeps us from knowing them. Especially at the beginning of our relationships, we maintain images in our mind of who we think our partner is. These images have more to do with what we need our mate to be, expect them to be or imagine them to be, rather than who they really are. We become angry or disappointed when we discover the real person behind our illusory, manufactured image fails to meet our needs and expectations.

UNDERSTANDING THE LOVING PROMISES

As with the previous Promise, the key to being awake to another person is to pay attention. However, there are different kinds of attention. Attention is sometimes a passive process where you allow your awareness to rove freely, openly, lighting where interest takes it. This kind of free-floating attention is more like the kind described in Promise #2, where the goal is to be aware your experience of the present moment. Attention can also be disciplined – you willfully place your attention where you want it, or where it is needed. This kind of attention is what is required in order to be awake to your partner. You focus in on them. You use all your faculties to ascertain what is true for them so you can genuinely share in their life. You observe your partner with your eyes, listen to them with open ears, view them with your mind, check in with your gut, receive them with your heart. In doing so, you will be better able to "read their energy" and know what is going on inside.

Open your eyes to your partner. Visually scrutinize your beloved, especially during times of conflict and duress. Watch posture, gestures, and subtle changes in breathing pattern and facial expression. These elements of body language all reveal what words cannot. I have noticed that Alice and I spend a lot of time looking at each other when we communicate, and I notice that we focus in on each other's eyes a lot. A person's eyes have been called "windows to their soul." They are the portals that lead you to better understand what is truly going on within. Eye to eye contact is invaluable for increasing the ability to receive your partner, not only because it gives you more access to their inner state, but also because it enlivens your own awakeness.

Try an experiment for two or three minutes with your partner. Gaze directly into each other's eyes and observe how you both feel. See how this simple process has catapulted you both into the present moment with each other. How beneficial if you could be awake to them in this way more often.

Listen to your partner with open ears. Listening is an act of love. Listening sends the message, "What you say has value. You have value. You are valuable to me." Everyone with functioning ears can hear, but not everyone is able to listen. That takes focused intention. Carefully listen to more than just the words. Listen for vocal inflections, pauses, choice of words. These hold hidden meaning behind the words. Listen to more than just the content of what is said by attending to the feeling tone in the stream of conversation. Listen to hear whether the words and vocal tone match the content of the message.

Being an artist, and very visually oriented, I was surprised at author Helen Keller's response to the question, "What would you rather be ... deaf or blind?" Keller was both deaf and blind from an early age. She answered she would rather be blind. Her reason was that the human connection is maintained most directly through listening to a person's words.

Communication consists of output and input – speaking and listening. People tend to think that speaking is the more important part of conversation rather than listening. It is not. You cannot receive your partner when you are speaking. And when they are not received by you, they don't have a strong impetus to listen and receive you. So listen well to your partner. They will be more inclined to listen to you when your turn comes to speak.

There are many obstacles that prevent you from accurately hearing what your partner is saying. These mostly have to do with following your mind rather than following their words. Obstacles to listening can take the following forms:

> *Analyzing* - trying to figure out in your mind the meaning and, in the process of thinking, missing the feeling tone of the communication.

> *Judging* - condemning, finding fault, criticizing in your mind.

> *Defending* - thinking of ways you can respond if you believe you are being challenged.

> *Irrelevant thoughts* - thinking about other things rather than attending to what is being said.

> *Rehearsing* - thinking about what you are going to say when your partner stops talking.

What these obstacles to listening have in common is that listening takes place within your self-preoccupied mind. They all reduce your ability to receptively listen to others. How can you receive when your mind keeps saying, *"Hurry up! I have something important to say."* The best way to be a receptive listener is to empty yourself. A cup that is full of water has no room to receive more. If you continue pouring, the cup will overflow. Empty your cup. (In Yiddish, *cup* means "head.") Emptying involves quieting your mind so you are a receptive, empty vessel.

Allow your partner plenty of time to speak. Don't interrupt. Your silence is an invitation for them to say all that is on their mind and in their heart. Your silence after you or they finish expressing your thoughts is also an opportunity for you both to digest and contemplate what has just been said. That quiet moment can be full with meaning as you sit and absorb in silence. Your genuine interest and receptive listening is a powerful gift and healing for your partner and the communion this brings about is a gift and healing to you.

When your partner is speaking, there is only one thing you should be doing – trying to take in, as much as you can, the essence of what they are trying to communicate to you. Listen to your partner with such strength of intention as if the next words out of their mouth will save your life. This is not always easy. Listening with intent is hard work. Honestly, I am bored sometimes when Alice keeps complaining about the neighbor's overflowing garbage can, or goes on about something that is not interesting to me, but is important to her. But, I am willing to put my laziness aside and make the effort to be present.

View your partner with your mind. The mind is a fantastic instrument. Most of the time, though, it is involved in incessant, idle chatter. If you are able to focus your mind, you can use it as a magnifying glass to more clearly see and understand your mate. *The key to this whole Promise is curiosity*, so allow your inquiring mind full reign. Be curious about your partner – their thoughts, their feelings, their dreams. Being in conversation is an active process. Rather than being a passive receiver, engage your curiosity and ignite their involvement by actively asking questions, probing for answers, demanding details. Think about their answers. Check the accuracy of your understanding of what your partner has just said by repeating back to them, in your own words, what you have just heard. Ask them if your interpretation corresponds with their intended meaning. Your mental understanding of your partner is an essential aspect of being awake to them.

By far, the thing that blinds you most to knowing your partner is the judgments you hold against them. "She is not a critical thinker. He is a passive person. She is too emotional." Each judgment you have narrows and distorts your vision of your partner. If you have lots of judgments against your mate, you are not seeing them, you are seeing the workings of your own mind. If you were able to silence your judgmental mind and *just see*, without the screen of good/bad, right/wrong, you would be able to view them with far greater clarity.

Check in with your gut to receive a more complete and accurate picture. This involves tuning in to yourself at the same time you are tuning in to your partner. Your inner feeling is where you tap into your intuitive power. We all have this ability. We just have to make space in order to attend to it. Refer to your senses, listen to the silent words popping into your mind and attend to your emotional hunches. Be aware of repetitive patterns of speech and behavior. Watch to see if facial expression matches the words. Attend not only to what has been said, but also to what has not been said, what seemingly is being withheld. Pay attention to breathing patterns – yours as well as theirs. And follow the emotional impressions all this input makes in your belly. These are all sources of valuable insight. Intuition makes use of everything.

"How did what he just said make me feel?"
"Was it just words, or did it come from her heart?"
"He seems sincere, but my gut tells me he is hiding something."

When you attend to your inner feelings and intuition, you gain access to information that might not be available any other way. There is a saying, "First thought, best thought." This may not always be true, but it is valuable to pay attention to those initial feelings that arise in our belly before our mind jumps in to confuse things.

Receive your partner with your heart. You can attend to your beloved through your eyes, your ears, your mind and your gut, but to really receive your partner, *receive them with your heart.* The heart area just to the left of center chest has traditionally been considered the repository of love and of our deepest emotions. This is borne out across time and cultures, in poetry and song. When we pledge allegiance we do so with our hand on our heart. When we are experiencing deep feelings, our hand automatically goes to our heart. When someone we love is going through profound emotions, we intuit it in our heart. What we really want most is to be received through the heart of the person we love. This kind of loving attention is what we all crave.

There are times when I make a practice to experience Alice as if through the area around my heart. I simply look at her or listen to her, or think of her as if my experience of her is coming from the center of my chest. When I focus this attention through my heart, I feel overwhelming love for her. My heart bursts with love. Try this way of experiencing your partner. It really works. Actually putting your hand on your heart as you do this will supercharge the experience. To super-duper charge the connection, put your hand on your partner's heart while touching your own, and both of you send and receive love.

When you use your whole being—your eyes, your ears, your mind, your gut and your heart--you are more able to fully receive your partner.

It is useful to keep in mind that each person has predominant ways of taking in sensory information. Some are more attuned to visual stimuli, others to sound, still others to touch. Alice and I are more visually oriented. Often, if we hear something, it takes several repetitions in order to compute. We have to see in order to best comprehend and retain information. Knowing that our partner has a different way of receiving information than we do can soften our judgments and help avoid misunderstandings.

Sometimes, if we have a problem, we don't need analysis; we don't need advice; we don't need to be soothed. We just want our lover to be fully present with us. Their efforts to help by offering opinions or sharing similar experiences cut us off from what we really desire. We want their undivided attention and for them to be *with* us in their heart, to hear us, to understand how we are feeling. It is as if no one else exists – just the two of us. If they are awake to us in this way, we cannot feel alone. We cannot feel unseen. This is healing presence. By our entering into the depths of our beloved's pain with them, they feel less alone. They have an ally, a partner who sees them, knows them and who will comfort and enfold them in arms of love.

It has taken me a while to develop this presence. My social conditioning as a male in this society made me want to fix things and do whatever it takes make Alice happy if she is unhappy. When Alice was upset or suffering, I tried to remedy the problem, give advice, offer support, protect her – anything to make her feel better. (Also to make me feel better, because when she was hurting, I felt helpless and incompetent.) Alice was clear with me about what she needed and I finally got the concept that I would be most helpful to at first shut up, listen and receive. If there is anything that needs to be done, it is best done in an atmosphere of receptivity.

Those moments in your relationship when your partner is in need of your focused awakeness will require you to consciously alter your ordinary awareness in order to more sensitively receive them. Rather than rushing around trying to figure out something to do, pause, slow down, open yourself to silence. Allow whatever feelings and thoughts that have been gestating to emerge into clarity. This focused silence is essential. When Alice paints a picture, she stares, spending far more time looking at the canvas than actively painting. By being receptive and not *doing*, she gives herself time to tune in and absorb what the painting needs. Then she can take brush in hand and paint. The picture spoke to her and she listened. It is the same process when we tune in to our partner – a silent listening in order to receive. The appropriate response arises as a natural consequence from our receiving.

I was witness to an incident that illustrates this kind of connection. Years ago I attended a meditation retreat. During the break, I observed the leader, Jack Kornfeld, speaking to a blind man and answering his questions. The man never realized this, but while they were interacting, Jack covered his own eyes with his hands so that he could be more in tune with the living experience of the blind man. That is true willingness to reach out and be awake to another.

When you are fully awake to another person, you are as close as possible to empathically feeling what they are feeling and experiencing. To be able to enter another's world like this is a rare gift . . . to both you and to them. Being empathically awake to them goes beyond knowing and understanding them. It is the entree into true togetherness.

Empathy is a wonderful quality, but caution is required. One could be so empathic that they lose themselves in the other person. They don't know where their boundaries begin and the other persons boundaries end. They can be so in tune with the other person that they become susceptible to their changing moods and emotions. When the other person is upset, it infects you and you "catch" it from them.

Awakening empathically to others is a path to peace, not only between partners, but even between enemies. Seeing an enemy as a reflection of yourself, sensing their humanness, knowing that they have the same hopes and fears as you do, cannot help but change your attitude toward them. If on a grander scale, people could awaken to each other in this way, that would be a giant step toward dissolving most of the problems of humanity. People would be reluctant to declare war on those they consider their brothers and sisters.

4. I WILL SERVE YOUR BEST INTERESTS. *I want the best for you in the same way as I want the best for myself. I will take care of you, comfort you, encourage you and protect you from harm in ways that empower you and do not interfere with you growing into your perfection.*

There is a point in many traditional wedding ceremonies that is very powerful and symbolizes the process that is about to take place. The bride walks down the aisle, is met by her parents, usually the father, who accompanies her to the altar, hands her to her future husband and then retires to the sidelines. That moment marks a transition. The future wife has left the family of origin and entered into the orbit of her future husband. They are now free to form their own family unit.

When a couple commits to each other, they enter into a mutual pact to serve one another. It is a pact that supersedes family, relatives and friends. They assume responsibility for the others welfare. Around her neck Alice wears a topaz on a chain. It is called a *mangal sutra*. She received it as part of our wedding ceremony in India. It is a traditional symbol of marital status and also a protective amulet for the husband. By wearing it, Alice protects my health and welfare and assures me a long life. She never takes it off. Maybe it's silly to feel

UNDERSTANDING THE LOVING PROMISES

protected by a mere piece of jewelry, but I certainly feel protected by Alice's intention.

One of the beautiful aspects of committed relationship is that it is a partnership of helpfulness, growth and mutual joy. When one is down, the other one offers support. When one is feeling elevated, the other is lifted up. Where one has weakness, the other has strength. Two working together in loving support of each other can form a powerful unit that is really so much greater than one alone. In this way they serve each other.

The original wording I used for this Loving Promise was, "I will be supportive of you." The word "supportive" however, doesn't accurately convey the depth of my intention to care for Alice. My intention is to serve her and work with her to the best of my ability, in order to promote her best interest. The word "serve" can have demeaning connotations, as if one is a menial servant and "less than." But, actually, to serve someone consciously and with focus and care is ennobling, even enlightening. In India, there is an honored traditional path to enlightenment called *seva*, or selfless service – serving without ego. By attending to another in this way, free of self-seeking, free of needing something in return, the one who serves gains as much or even more than the person being served.

Service can have an opposite connotation – one that is demeaning to the person served. There is an unintended parental tone to some of the language of this Promise – to "take care of, comfort, encourage, protect." Any sense of inequality is not intended. With this Promise you serve your partner from a position of equality, not superiority. You are not meant to be your partner's mommy or daddy. When one partner takes on a parental role, the role that remains is that of a child or a weak person in need of help and protection. Serving another person from that position of superiority is fraught with problems. It invites conflict and power struggles. Or it fosters a sense of inferiority or a helpless attitude on the part of the person being served. The optimal position of service is of two equal adults who have mutual respect for one another. It is inevitable that at some times, one would need support; at other times, the other requires support. Each partner can freely be the provider or receiver of comfort and protection. There is no advantage or disadvantage to either position.

When two people fully support one another, are in each other's corner, are 100% for each other's well-being, they form a powerful unit, a force that is immeasurably stronger that either one of them alone. Alice and I are living examples. Our mutually championing each other has transformed and turbo-charged our entire married lives. It has opened doors to our creativity, brought us closer to family and friends and provided opportunities for our personal and professional growth. By not supporting one another, or worse, actively undermining the other partner by belittling, competing or sabotaging, a couple weakens and can ultimately destroy both parties and the relationship. I have seen it happen and I have had it both ways, and I can testify that it is much better to support and be supported.

With this Promise to serve, my intention is to care for Alice with the same care that I would give myself. This is possible because, in a way, Alice has become an extension of myself. I intuit her feelings. Her pain hurts me. Her joy lifts me. Because I sense her joy and pain as my own, I have a stake in the quality of her life. Her welfare has become my welfare. And so I want and need to support her growth and welfare. It has become my own. Therefore, I will never knowingly do anything to harm her. And I will, without reserve, do everything I can to support and protect her.

I intently care about Alice. My love for her contains an implied responsibility for her. Ideally, if I am to serve Alice's best interests, I should not impose my direction on her; rather, I would respect her own direction and follow her lead. However, assuming responsibility when necessary can be a real problem, especially if Alice is not in agreement. So, what if Alice doesn't want help, or doesn't agree with the way I try to help her? Who is the arbiter as to what is best for another? Who decides what empowers the other person? Who is able to know what another's perfection is? It is hard enough to make choices for our own self. Does this mean that we should, without any limitation, respect our partner's right to self-determination and keep hands off no matter what? Should we avoid interfering, even if we can clearly see they are headed for a fall?

An extreme example to contemplate: Alice's mother, Beulah, discovered a lump in her breast. For whatever reason, she refused to get it checked out. Sumner, her husband, was aware of the growth, but honored Beulah's decision to not get treated. Finally, over a year, the tumor had grown to the size of a small grapefruit and Beulah decided to have it excised. She was treated successfully with a radical mastectomy. Was Sumner right by not countering Beulah's will by insisting she receive medical intervention? What would you do?

If I were in Sumner's shoes, I would try everything short of carrying Beulah kicking and screaming to the doctor. I believe that as a condition of my love for Alice, I have responsibility for her and to her. With that responsibility, I have the right, even the duty, to press for what I believe are positive, life-affirming goals . . . even over Alice's objections. With that right comes a grave responsibility that I do not take lightly. If I decide to interfere with Alice's wishes, I must deeply contemplate what is right for her and how best to communicate that to her.

True, Alice has the ultimate say over her life, but that doesn't preclude me from being a total pest and constantly ragging on her if I see she is taking a wrong path.

Should I always be proactive in taking care of her, comforting, encouraging and protecting? Maybe, but not always. Maybe what Alice needs at times is to follow her path unimpeded, even though it would lead to a dead end and may have painful consequences. Sometimes a bruising she might receive will wake her up and provide valuable lessons, lessons she could not learn any other way. Overprotectiveness on my part could deprive her of a learning opportunity.

An important point to remember is that being of service to our partner is not just taking over and doing things for them. Sometimes it is far more helpful if we would empower them by standing back and allowing them the space to do for themselves. By doing too much, we assume control and power that should rightly belong to them. This disempowers them. We can serve our partner as their needs demand, but always with an eye for them to maintain their active sovereignty. So, as the saying goes, rather than give them fish, supply them with a fishing pole.

It should be obvious that generously serving our partner is not just giving indiscriminately. One must be discerning as to what to give and how and when. Sensitivity to their readiness to receive is also to be considered. This Promise is not so simple as it first seems and the decisions not so easy. It requires thoughtful consideration in addition to a loving heart. The issues that arise from this Promise stimulate more questions than answers.

The reasons why a person serves their beloved can have as much effect as the things they do to serve. In this regard, it is important to distinguish between a genuine spirit of generosity and service, and fraudulent giving based on approval seeking, or bartering for exchange of goods through giving. Genuine service is giving born of compassion for the other's suffering and discomfort, giving from the desire to shower happiness on the other, and giving for the simple enjoyment of the other person's happiness. The source of fraudulent giving is usually fear and greed. The fearful giver gives out of fear of being unloved, being unworthy, being abandoned. These fears lead to a person's need to please others and an inability to engage in conflict or confrontation. The "pleaser" seeks approval and validation. The greedy giver hopes that their gift will bring something in return from the partner. They try to buy "goodies" through giving. These kinds of giving are counterfeit and the receiver can usually see through them on some level.

The last part of the Promise states that I will serve you in ways that "do not interfere with your growing into your perfection." This is a very meaningful but elusive statement. It implies that I can know what your perfection is. I cannot know this. What I can do is not just look and see you as you are now, but also have the breadth of vision to perceive your potential, to envision who you could be if you realized your highest, best self. This doesn't mean that I do not accept you as you are, or that I demand you change or attempt to a guide you to accept and realize my vision for you. It simply means that I have a sense of what a highly functioning, happy and fulfilled human being is like, believe that this level is possible for you, help where I can, cheer you on and avoid saying and doing things that get in the way of your attaining that consummate state.

If you ask for my advice and help, I will be there. If you take a wrong turn, I will guide you. If you stumble and fall, I will lift you up. I will be your cheering section and will shout encouragement to cheer you on. I will not face your demons for you or fight your battles. These are yours to fight. At the very least, my simply holding the vision of your potential within my heart will, by my supporting love, encourage and empower you.

As Alice and I grow older, this Promise to serve each other takes on greater importance. I believe this is so for every couple. Aging brings with it varying degrees of loss of strength, impaired abilities, declining health. Partners are more dependent on each other to help carry the load. Developing a pure sense of service as described in this Promise is a great comfort and a tremendous blessing to a couple in their old age.

Sometimes you just don't know what your partner needs. Rather than being a mind reader, ask. A question that is on target is, "In what way can I serve you right now?" When you get your answer . . . do it.

If you are unclear as to how you can serve the one you love, fulfill the Loving Promises as best you can. There's no better way to care for, comfort, encourage and protect.

5. **I WILL BE UNSELFISH WITH YOU**. *I will make it a practice to attempt to give to you unconditionally. When our needs are in conflict I will seek solutions only in terms of our mutual benefit. I will delight in and resolve to consistently do what I can to foster your happiness.*

The previous Loving Promise, the vow to serve the partner, entails unselfishness. The focus is on your partner – serving them by helping to care for their needs. This Promise is also about unselfishness. However, the focus is on you. It is concerned with working on the inner quality of generosity – cultivating generosity and working through the barriers you may have that prevent you from giving freely. Being able to give freely is a major source of joy and satisfaction in relationship as well as a major source of happiness in life. And giving freely is an essential ingredient needed to implement the Loving Promises.

A key to giving freely is being able to recognize when you have "enough." In a society where "bigger is better" and "more is better," and "better is better," it is a rare person who finds contentment with what they have. This dissatisfaction with what we have is at cross purposes with generosity. When you believe you don't have enough, you will feel like you are being diminished with every gift you give. You will hold on ever more tightly.

Even when your intention is to give freely and not to receive anything in return after you have given, you receive anyway. This is because each act of simply giving openly from your heart eats away, bit by bit, the hard, cold mass of selfishness of which your ego is comprised. So each act of wholehearted giving is a self-healing. When you give . . . you get. As Gandhi said, "The fragrance remains on the hand that offers the rose."

I always loved the story of the man who visited heaven and hell. He entered the elevator, his guide pushed the DOWN button, and they were off. Soon the doors parted and before them was this endless hallway with a vast number of doors. The guide opened a door and inside were hordes of miserable, famished people sitting around an enormous crock of nourishing soup. A delicious aroma filled the room. Attached to the end of each person's scrawny arm was a long spoon. The spoon was so long that they were unable to get the soup into their mouths. And thus they were frustrated and starving. "This is hell," said the guide as he closed the door. The elevator zoomed UP and came to a stop. The doors opened and before them was what looked like the same hallway, the same doors. The guide opened a door and the same delicious aroma wafted out of the room. Inside were many people with long spoons at the end of their arms, but these people were happy and laughing and well nourished. They were dipping their utensils into the soup and gleefully spooning it into each other's mouths. "This is heaven," said the guide.

The key element in generosity, the very foundation – is caring – caring about what is important to another person, what their needs are, what causes their suffering, what they value, what makes them happy. When we care about about a person, our caring blossoms into generous action.

In previous relationships, I didn't really care about my partners. For the most part, I cared only about what affected my own happiness and contentment. I got really good at acting as if I cared. I affected a concerned expression on my face, said the right things with the right tone of voice, but I didn't really feel concern for others. What was a breakthrough for me was a model that could teach me about caring. Alice was that model. She genuinely cares. Living with her, being cared about by her, seeing her care for others, has taught me what it means to care.

In this Promise, I placed emphasis on the word "consistent" because consistency in generosity is extremely important. If Alice reaches her hand out to me, I take it... always. If she makes a bid for my help, I'd respond... always. If she needs my attention, I stop what I am doing and attend to her... always. My consistent response is a clear demonstration that I care. My consistency produces trust. Alice knows I will always have her back. It's not that I am consistent with my generous giving with Alice in order to get her to trust me. I give to her because her happiness and wellbeing are important to me. Knowing that she is cared about and cared for allows Alice to relax in the safety of my loving arms.

Generosity also arises from the quality of letting go, releasing, in our mind, the things and conditions we think we must have. Being able to let go lightly is the basis of inner peace. How can giving take place without letting go? True generosity is expansive, spacious, and abundant. Giving doesn't diminish us, but instead provides us a sense of potency. The opposite – selfishness, stinginess and clinging – impoverishes us. Selfishness is at the heart of every bad relationship, every break up. It is based on fear – fear of loss, fear of not having enough. Selfishness puts us in a world of craving, clinging, and lack.

I know this world well. Unselfishness was not my natural tendency. When I look back at my life, I realize how much time I spent absorbed in me, me, me – my finicky needs, my critical judgments, my petty complaints, my aloof specialness. This had been going on for a long time. Much of my early life was taken up with obsession with what I could get, not what I could give. I do far less of that now. For years, I have been working to cultivate generosity as part of my spiritual practice, pushing the envelope of my comfort zone. "I'm tired; I don't want to do the dishes at the end of the party. I'm lazy; I don't want to make the bed in the morning. I'm busy, let Alice sweep the floor." However, irrespective of how I feel, in situations where giving is appropriate, I observe the stingy, lazy voice in my head... and pitch in and give anyway. Alice has been an inspiration and example for me. I am fortunate to have by my side such a model of generosity. I have learned so much about giving by watching her.

Generosity is the one consistent quality needed to fulfill each Loving Promise. *Unselfish giving is the fuel that energizes and maintains the Loving Promises.* A person simply cannot and will not work the Promises if they are coming from a self-centered, greedy place. But, and this is a very big "but," we human beings are at our core self-centered creatures. We are built so that we seek to satisfy our own needs first – to avoid pain, to obtain pleasure. So, when we act unselfishly, giving the best and the first to another, we are usually going against our human nature.

UNDERSTANDING THE LOVING PROMISES

Even when we act in unselfish ways, there is almost always the element of trying to further our own self-centered ends. We give in order to get – "I will give you a neck massage now, but I expect a shoulder massage from you later."

If people were to give full expression to their selfish impulses, the world would be in far greater chaos than it is now. Therefore, we are domesticated as children, schooled from infancy in the value of generosity. We are told, "Share your toys," "Don't take more than your share of dessert," "Let others go first." Generous-like behavior is enforced by parental injunction, religious edict and social pressure until it becomes almost second nature. Intimate relationship is where the effects of selfishness or unselfishness come into play most directly. It is where your action bears immediate fruit, be it sweet or sour. Normally your unselfish action is rewarded with corresponding unselfish action by your partner. Selfish action is punished with corresponding selfish actions.

I have painted a bleak picture of human nature. It is obviously an oversimplification. There is such a thing as altruism and true generosity. Humans are capable of empathy. They are able to feel another's distress as their own and can have the spontaneous and heartfelt impulse to offer help and provide solace. They will put their own safety at risk in order to prevent harm, even to a stranger. They can and do willingly sacrifice their time, comfort and resources for the good of others. A shining example of this is our next door neighbors, Steve and Elaine. After having five children of their own, they adopted five more from Africa and South America. Several of their adopted children have a serious physical or emotional disability. The last one, Dimasu, an 11 year old boy from Ethiopia, cannot walk and has no use of his right arm. While generosity on this scale is possible, it is the rare exception rather than the rule. I am in awe of such heroic giving. It is beyond my comprehension. When you ask Steve and Elaine though, they say they receive far more than they give.

As I have written previously, in relationship each partner tends to expand their sense of self to include the other. When this occurs, the center of our world ceases to be only our own ego. It expands to include the being of another. That other person's comfort and welfare become our own concern. We receive pleasure when our partner is happy, so giving to them becomes our joy. Buddhists have a name for that form of joy – *mudita* – vicarious appreciation for the happiness and good fortune of others. It is the opposite of envy. Mudita is at its purest when the person receives no direct value from the other person's pleasure. If your life is going well, your relationships are great, your finances in order, it's not that difficult to feel empathetic joy for other people. However, the real test is if your life is in shambles. Then it is much more of a challenge to feel happy for others' good fortune.

LOVING PROMISES

Though self-centeredness may dominate our natural disposition, it is not an immutable quality. It can be worked with and decreased with practice. The intimate bond is the perfect setting to explore and practice unselfishness. Living in close proximity with another person presents endless opportunities for practice. Frequently, moments will occur where you have to make a choice between serving yourself or your beloved. "Do I insist we see the movie I really want to see?" "Do I take the biggest piece of pie?" "Shall I finish scrubbing the pots now or let them soak and have her finish the pots later?" These choice points are key in unselfish practice. I try to be aware of them when they occur – to make the conscious choice to stretch myself and choose the generous alternative.

Here are some of the ways I practice generosity with Alice:

- She asks me to do something to help out; I respond in the affirmative and do it, even though I may not feel like it.
- If I notice something that needs doing, I do it without being asked, even though I may not feel like it.
- I finish completely what needs to be done, even though I may not feel like it.
- In general, if there is something I can do or say or give her that will make her happy, I do it, even though I may not feel like it.

I attempt to do these things without complaint, without seeking acknowledgement or asking for thanks and without wanting anything in return, other than for her to be happy.

Notice that I have made a point of practicing giving "when I don't feel like it." The times I do feel like it or am feeling loving towards Alice – no problem. Giving is easy. The practice of generosity becomes meaningful when I am reluctant to give.

Some relationship experts disagree with the idea of making a practice of generosity. They believe that "real giving" is giving from the feeling of love, and that if you give with reluctance or without feeling love, it is counterfeit. It is merely going through the motions and will eventually lead to resentment and a sense of martyrdom. "Don't give unless you feel it," they say. I disagree. I believe that the quality of generosity is so important and necessary in life and relationships that it is beneficial to do whatever you can to cultivate it.

UNDERSTANDING THE LOVING PROMISES

Some circumstances present especially difficult challenges to giving. These are times when you and your partner are at cross purposes, or when you have given more than what seems like your fair share, or when you are feeling depleted, or when your beloved is being a complete ass and rudely demanding you comply with their wishes. Here's where the real test of unselfishness begins. It is at these times when you feel like digging in your heals, taking an unyielding stand and insist your partner give in and give more. Being generous is the last thing you want to do. Giving at these times may be more difficult, but the rewards are far greater.

Another real test of our generosity is dealing with limitations of our partner's generosity. We fail the test if, knowing their selfish impulse, we insist that our partner return to us, in equal measure, what we have given to them. By recognizing and accepting our partner's limitations in this area, and giving anyway, we will have given expression to our own generosity and strengthened our ability to give. And our generous action can help loosen up our partner's reluctance to give. It is a sure bet that if you were to withhold your generosity in response to their miserliness, they would be even more reluctant to give.

This being said, there are limits to generosity, and the limits vary for each individual. There is a point where you can give too much. If you pass that point, it is not good for your partner, and it is not good for you. Generous people especially need to be conscious of their tendency to give too much. Generous givers need to set limits in giving because takers have no limits in taking. To have limits, you must have the internal freedom to be able to say "no." Without that freedom to set limits, you cannot truly be generous – you give because you are driven to give and are unable to refuse. The narrow edge between reluctantly giving and feeling like you are giving too much is an interesting and important place. It is worthy of conscious exploration.

I found that using affirmations is helpful for me in working with generating the feeling of generosity. Daily, I use the ancient Buddhist *Metta* prayer. It comes in many forms. The one that was taught me begins with myself. (I added the last line)

> May I be happy
> May I be peaceful
> May I be free of suffering
> May I love and be loved

I repeat each phrase several times until I experience a genuine desire for my own happiness, peace and freedom from suffering.

In my practice I expand each line with phrases I use to add more meaning. You may wish to do so too. These are the words I use:

May I be Happy. *May my life be filled with joy and laughter.*
May I be peaceful. *May my mind be serene and untouched by the circumstances of my life.*
May I be free from suffering. *May my body be healthy and vital, and may health and vitality remain till the end of my long life.*
May I love and be loved.

The affirmation then goes on to include people I care about. I also use those additional phrases.

May Alice be happy.
May Alice be peaceful.
May Alice be free of suffering.
May Alice love and be loved.

Then, the affirmations can expand to people I know, then to all people – but this will come in a later Loving Promise.

Let the intent of each statement of the affirmation sink in. There is a kind of click inside when the statement rings true. Then, move on to the next statement. After I have completed this series of affirmations a few times, I experience a delightful sense of warmth and openness.

It makes me happy to do things that make Alice feel good and be happy, so when I am with her, I try to spoil her. As mentioned earlier, a spoiled partner is a happy partner, and a happy partner is a pleasure to be with and will want to spoil me.

6. I WILL PARTICIPATE IN YOUR LIFE. *I will make the decision to extend myself and choose to participate with you in the interests and activities that you find important and enjoyable. I will reserve time for us to be together.*

Every person lives in their own separate universe. When two people come together to become a couple, it is as if the two universes converge. There are private areas where they remain separate, and areas they share experience together. Some couples desire greater amounts of sharing. Some couples desire less. Hopefully, each couple will find balance in the kind and amount of shared experience that is comfortable and appropriate for each partner. This Promise is not as concerned with the quantity of shared time as it is about the quality. A few minutes of focused, undivided presence is worth many hours of "just sorta being there."

A key word in the Promise is "extend." To extend is to reach out, stretch. I push beyond my comfort boundaries when I participate for Alice's benefit. I use the words "choose" and "decision" in the Promise. I make a conscious commitment to extend myself and participate with Alice, and I align myself with whatever makes her happy. For example, when Alice feels obligated to visit friends that I have little in common with and feel bored, I accompany her anyway because she doesn't want to go alone. It's not a big deal and it makes her feel good.

When we choose to do things and go places for each other's sake with purity of heart, we do not expect or demand any favor in return. we do not do it to avoid an argument, we do not do it grudgingly. And we do not carry resentment for our choice. We extend ourselves and participate because we choose the path of generosity and love. Of course I can refuse. But one thing that will influence my decision is the question, "How strongly do you want this?" If I ask Alice and she earnestly answers, "It is important to me if you do this," I will surely take her desire into consideration (and most likely go along with her desire).

If I only join with Alice in the parts of her life I personally find interesting and enjoyable and ignore the rest, I am not really extending myself. I purposely extend myself with Alice because I know these things are important to her. I do what I can to encourage and accompany her in her interests and pursuits, even those that I may not appreciate or understand, because I want her to be happy and engaged. And I do so because this is my spiritual practice, to surrender in order that I may learn to be more generous. As I let go lightly of the things I think I need, I grow spiritually.

Another key word that refers to the quality of our shared experience is "participate." Participation can refer to a wide variety of activities. It can be as minor as stopping what I am doing in order to listen for a moment as Alice recounts a conversation she had with a friend, or as major as spending all day, every day with Alice at the hospital for almost three months awaiting our son Jason's heart transplant. Whether minor or major, the quality of my participation is important. If I simply allow myself to be dragged to some place Alice wants to go and then hang out there in body only, I am not participating. To participate, I must put in the effort to engage. I must choose to be present in mind and in spirit, not just in body. I may not at first be enthusiastic about going someplace and doing something of Alice's choosing, but I find that if I extend myself and make the effort to participate, I usually end up having a good time.

Please understand, however, there is no demand in this Promise that you devote your life to satisfying your partner, or that you have to be together all the time, or that you are compelled to do every little thing together – just share in your partner's life. You already do. In a committed relationship or marriage, there is a commonality of concerns. What affects one partner, affects the other. Their family becomes your family. Your family becomes theirs. If there are possessions they value, you care for them as if they are your own. Their health, their wellbeing, their happiness are intimately tied in with your own. So, by extending yourself and actively participating in your partner's life, you also benefit.

An important way that Alice and I participate in each other's life is that we often check in and share our thoughts and feelings about the happenings in our daily lives. The news, gossip and other tidbits we exchange may not be monumental or earthshaking, but the consistent interchange that takes place daily keeps us current and connected. It demonstrates that we are interested and maintains the sense that we are a part of each other. And it significantly contributes to our feelings of intimacy. We would feel a great loss if we did not have these moments of connection.

This Promise can pose difficulties for many couples. Often times, when you extend yourself and participate in activities you are not drawn to or dislike, you are making a sacrifice. To sacrifice is to give up something you like, something that is valuable to you. This can be difficult to do. But sacrifice always contains a positive. We make sacrifice in order to obtain or achieve something we want. What you achieve through this Loving Promise, besides being a full partner in your beloved mate's life, is a happier, grateful, more loving partner; one who will be willing to extend themselves and eager to choose to participate in the things that are important to you.

7. **I WILL BE FLEXIBLE WITH YOU.** *I will always remain open to relinquishing my stance and altering my behavior when it is appropriate. I will aim to do so graciously, without regret or expectation of compensation.*

I have seen television reports of hurricanes in tropical areas where buildings have been leveled and massive trees torn up by their roots. But there stand the tall palm trees, battered but still upright. Their flexible trunk allows them to bend and sway, but not to break.

UNDERSTANDING THE LOVING PROMISES

Flexibility is water, rigidity is rock. Water freely flows, rock immovably resists. Flexibility is able to yield, and yielding, when merited, can be strength. Rigidity must stand firm, even if it is advantageous to yield. Therefore, rigidity, while seeming strong, can be weakness.

There's only one constant, abiding principle of the universe. That principle is change. Nothing stays the same. Some things change fast, like volcanic eruptions. Some change slowly, like evolution, but everything changes. Humans change, our bodies, our minds, our moods, our likes and dislikes. One day things are nice, the next, everything is screwed. Flexibility is accepting change and moving on.

Flexibility is allowing things to be as they are and not having to control. It is your ability to let go, to not stubbornly cling to ideas, beliefs, behaviors, and to "shoulds" and "oughts." It is readily conceding when you are wrong, freely admitting when your partner is right. It is graciously compromising when compromise is appropriate. Flexibility is the source of creativity. It is difficult to be creative if you are rigid.

Rigidity indicates the presence of tendency to take things too seriously. When you take things too seriously, they become heavy, immobile. If you can't "lighten up," things can turn ugly in a minute. You can feel the heaviness growing more intense moment by moment. A situation is rarely so grave that you can't find the perspective and humor in yourself or your partner. That will take the edge off and allow for more flexibility.

Being flexible is an inner quality, an orientation of "allowing" toward others, toward yourself and toward the events that happen in your life. It is one of those essential personal qualities, along with generosity, patience, presence, perseverance, kindness and humility, which are the very foundation of magnificent love. The easy give and take of a flexible approach to your partner makes the practice of following the Loving Promises easy.

The word "flexible" does not adequately describe the depth of the concept I am trying to impart. "Surrender" is closer, though that word carries the powerful negative connotations of "giving up" and "giving in." Those who surrender are considered losers in competition or war. But in the context of relationship, surrender doesn't involve being defeated. I don't surrender because I recognize I'm losing or I can't win. I don't surrender to avoid an argument; I don't even surrender to another person. I surrender to the "rightness," the "appropriateness" of the situation. If I see that a situation I am involved in requires that I make a change, I amend my position even if it means that I go against my prior beliefs, desires and habits. I do so because it is right.

The difficult part is determining in which circumstances it is right to be flexible or when it's right to take a more rigid stance. There are appropriate times for each. And there are no clear guidelines. I use as my guide whether my behavior is morally and ethically proper, whether it is fair, whether it is beneficial to Alice, to me, to the relationship, and to the issue at hand. I ask myself whether continued pressure and resistance will or will not serve a useful purpose. This is a case-by-case decision. I feel it is important, however, to maintain a *willingness* to let go when appropriate, no matter what the situation.

An example of letting go that was difficult for me but felt appropriate was the following. When I was in my early 20s, for several years I drove around a small motorcycle that gave me a lot of pleasure. About 15 years ago, I noticed a motorcycle on the side of the road with a "for sale" sign on it – same year, same make and model as my old bike. Here was a chance for me to recapture my youth. So of course, I bought it and brought it home excitedly. Alice was not pleased. In fact, she was very unhappy. "I'm afraid for you, it's too dangerous. I am sure you are a good rider, but others are not." I tried every ploy I knew to get Alice to change her mind, but I couldn't convince her that it was safe. She was resolute. I understood that she was genuinely worried and, if I kept the motorcycle, it would be a source of anguish for her. So, not wanting to cause her pain, I resolved to sell the bike. The only concession I asked was that I be able to drive around our property for a little while before I put the ad in the newspaper. Alice watched from the window as I zipped back-and-forth around our property in my leather jacket and bright yellow helmet. She softened. She saw how much fun I was having. "OK, keep the bike if you must, but please don't drive on public highways and don't go any more than a few miles from the house." For years I drove that motorcycle, never venturing very far, but enjoying every minute, until it broke down several years ago. It still sits in our yard. This might sound as if I wasn't being "manly" by acceding to Alice's wishes and not pursuing what I wanted, but for me, it was more appropriate to not have Alice worry than for me to get my way.

I let go for pragmatic reasons – because it felt right in this case to do so. My ego might feel bruised and cry out, "I'm right, she is too fearful, it's unfair, she's won," but letting go is not about winning or losing or about pride, it's about doing the appropriate thing.

The Promise to be flexible describes the optimum ways to surrender. Graciously – in a good natured manner, with ease and consideration. Without regret – no misgivings, reservations or lamentations. And without expecting a payback or something to be given in return. This is a tall order, especially for a person for whom flexibility doesn't come naturally. It is in some people's nature to hold on more tightly than others. They have more work to do if they wish to develop a more flexible approach in their life.

While I have not always been one of those who by nature lets go easily, I have made it my practice to be as flexible as possible with Alice. Unless I have a strong objection, I will defer to her preferences and do things and go places that please her. I do this as an exercise, an experiment, a spiritual practice to see if I can let go graciously, without regret or expectation. This letting go of what I think I would prefer and enjoy, in favor of Alice's inclinations, has been an interesting experience for me. It has helped me live more lightly in the world, and it makes Alice happy too.

By no means has my flexibility with Alice been a sacrifice only on my part. Alice is equally surrendered and flexible with me. This predilection toward letting go of our preferences puts us in a bind sometimes and is the cause of almost all of the arguments we have. Because we want to make the other happy, each of us argues in favor of what the other wants. That's not a bad kind of argument to have. The conversation might go something like this: I would say, "Where do you want to have lunch?" Alice would say, "Wherever makes you happy." I would say "But I want to go wherever makes you happy." And on and on.

8. **I WILL BE ACCEPTING OF YOU**. *I will not expect perfection from you. I will seek to recognize and appreciate your individual uniqueness and acknowledge your human frailty. I will be patient with you. I will not attempt to change you into my idea of who you should be.*

An unhappy person doesn't accept things the way they are.
A happy person accepts things as they are
A truly happy person will accept things however they will be.

Accepting is saying "yes" to reality, to how things are. "Yes" means opening to life as it comes to you.

Accepting is easy if the experiences coming to you are pleasant. It's not so easy if they are unpleasant. Rather than trying to frantically escape from negative experiences like frustration, anger and confusion – (saying "no") –try saying "yes." "Yes" involves welcoming uncomfortable experiences if they come, opening to them, being willing to experience them, maybe even finding them interesting. If you are able to look at any experience with a curious mind, it is possible for the experience to be interesting. In any event, your accepting will allow the negative to dissipate or move on through more quickly. Rejecting an uncomfortable experience does the opposite. The emotion backed effort to push it away makes it solid, makes it more likely to stay.

Accepting is an internal process. It is acknowledging the actual existing condition of a person or situation and not fighting against it in your mind. It doesn't refer to what actions you take. You may be taking strong measures to actively resist what it is that is bothering you, yet at same time you are willing to accept any outcome with equanimity. ("accept things as they are.") When you maintain a blanket attitude of acceptance ("accept things however they will be") your "yes" will be like Teflon and help prevent suffering from sticking. Your "no" will be like Velcro and attract suffering.

If we translate acceptance into a statement about couple relationships, it might go something like this, "I will be more happy and more at peace if I don't demand you think, look, feel, speak and act in the way I believe you should, but rather, allow you the freedom to follow the dictates of your inner urgings." This "hands off" approach is more easily said than done. We have the illusion we can control our partner. It seems so obvious to us that if they would only be different, listen to us and do what we say, we would both be so much happier – or at least that's what we tell ourselves.

Rather than accept our partner, we think, "If only I could badger them hard enough and long enough, or if only I could communicate my complaint about them in the right way, then they would 'get it' and change." Yeah! Like they are going to say to you, "You're right; I'll change that immediately. Thank you for bringing that to my attention." No way! They spent their whole lifetime becoming the way they are. They cannot or will not change just to make you happy, and your harping on them will only get them to resist you.

Of course we love our mate and of course want the best for them, and it troubles us when we see them thinking and behaving in ways that we perceive are harmful to themselves. Often though, there are other, more personal motives why we want our partner to be different than they are. We assume the changes we want them to make will positively affect us. We believe that we will feel more appreciated, supported, attended to, more comfortable if our partner were different. But if we look to them to change in order to make our life better, we will meet with continuous frustration. Usually the source of our dissatisfaction has little to do with them. More often, the source of our problems and the solution lies within us.

Acceptance is just that – accepting the whole package. This means, in addition to accepting the things you like about your partner, if you choose to stay with them, you must also accept the things you can't stand, even the things you know they won't ever change. No one person can ever fit all your likes and dislikes perfectly. There will always be a thing or two . . . or three that will get on your nerves. But these things are part of the package. Choosing to accept them means that you are also choosing to accept your reaction to the parts of them that are not aligned with what you want. Dealing with your own frustration and dissatisfaction may present your greatest challenge.

If you love this person but don't accept what cannot be changed, you are the problem, not them. Your stubbornness may be exacerbating the problem. If you know they are not about to change in the way you want them to – find a way to live with it, adapt to it. Accept the way things are and stop hoping for a miracle. Grieve that you won't get what you want and then move on. You are not helpless; you are not dependent on them. Do what you need to do to take care of yourself. Stop beating a dead horse by arguing and nagging and complaining. If your partner won't spend enough time with you, find friends who will. If they don't appreciate the foods you like, allow them to prepare their own meals sometimes. If they are always late, perhaps leave without them. Most important, don't do these things out of spite or to manipulate or "get back" at them. Simply find a way to accept who they are, take care of your own needs, and move on.

Accepting is not the same as liking. You don't have to like what is difficult to accept, but, –especially since there are so many other lovable qualities your partner has, you can learn to live with it. By "living with" the parts of your partner that are less than perfect, you are content. Being content is "being at peace with." Acceptance helps calm your drive to make things different. Now you can relax.

Of course there are limits to what you should and shouldn't live with. You shouldn't live with physical abuse. You shouldn't live with constant lies. You shouldn't live with betrayal. You shouldn't live with drug and alcohol abuse that endangers your family's safety and stability. If you are in a monogamous relationship, you shouldn't live with an adulterous partner. When you compromise your own and your loved one's security and when you compromise important personal values, you harm yourself and the relationship.

The ability to limit what you accept, to say "no," and to set clear boundaries, gives meaning to your "yes." If you cannot set boundaries and say "NO!" with strength and conviction in the face of offensive behavior, you are at the effect of others. Most of us tend to want to be nice, to accept people as they are, to "cut them some slack," and that is all well and good. But if our tolerance of other people's using and abusing us is rooted in fear, we are helpless and impotent. That fear could arise from many sources; fear of their anger or of our own, fear of confrontation, fear of not being seen as "nice" or kind or "spiritual." When we accept unacceptable behavior from a place of fear and refuse to challenge when appropriate, we give away our power and damage ourselves.

Acceptance is easier in the earlier stages of romance. The burst of new love is exciting. He or she is "the one." They are perfect, and you are perfect, the world is rosy, and there are rainbows and butterflies everywhere. At first the differences are fascinating. He is "the strong, silent type." But after a while, it becomes, "Why don't you communicate?" Then you notice that she yacks on the phone too much with her friends. He doesn't pick up after himself. She nags a lot. He is too finicky about what he eats. She doesn't want sex as often. Around this time you begin to think you made a big mistake. The truth is, this is the point where the work of true love begins. This is the point where you need to start to accept your partner. If not, you are both in for a rough ride.

If you hold strong judgments against your partner, a rift is created, filled with anxiety and defensiveness. Even if not expressed in words, they will pick up your sentiments and react. What is required is a transformation on your part, an internal movement beyond judgment toward genuine acceptance. To facilitate that transformation, we need to alter the way we see our partner and their behavior. We do this by putting our self-interest aside and viewing the person and their behavior from a place of witness. We see them with compassionate eyes, understanding that their maladaptive behavior might come from personal suffering brought on by painful experiences from the far distant past. They may be confused or blind to the negative effects that their behavior is having on us. We remain aware of their present limitations and do not demand of them more than they are able to give at this time. We are patient with them rather than rushing in to try to control or fix them, even though we may be uncomfortable. We are patient with our own discomfort and thus able to be more present with our mate. Approaching a person in this accepting, nonjudgmental way has the best chance of being helpful to them. And our generous and compassionate response allows for the greatest growth on our part.

By evaluating others with the eyes of a judge, we open ourselves to the judgments of those others. It's good to remember the advice of Jesus, "Judge not, lest you be judged." If we fail to heed His advice, judgments will continuously fly back and forth and your home will resemble a courtroom, with each of you being opposing lawyers.

I am not saying here that you should do away with judgments. You cannot do that. The mind judges, judgments will arise, that is a given. Judgments can be useful. And most judgments hold some truth at least. Being non-judgmental has more to do with what you do with your judgments. This includes not condemning, not making others wrong and not seeing them as bad people. It means you temper your verdicts with understanding and perspective and do not take judgments so seriously that they disrupt the smoothness and sweetness of the relationship.

Being non-judgmental doesn't necessarily mean that you withhold judgment. If the judgments you have about your partner are truthful, withholding them could deprive your partner of what could be valuable information. Saying what you see and feel about their errant behavior is a beneficial service to them. It all has to do with the tenacity with which you cling to judgments, the goodwill in the way you hold them and the sensitivity in the way you communicate them.

There were some things that Alice did in the past – her words, tone of voice and other ways that she communicated to me that left me feeling demeaned and drove me up the wall. I understood that she could not easily change these things. They were longstanding habits. She probably didn't recognize what it was that she was doing. Therefore, even while strongly protesting to her, I needed to internally accept what was, or live in discord with her. Constantly complaining or trying to change her, or cringing every time I felt frustrated by Alice, were not options. Luckily, there are so many things I loved about Alice that I could patiently endure those rare things that frustrated me. So I communicated my frustration, worked with my anger and impatience, kept trying to understand and accept. My patience and endurance paid off. She heard what I said and her demeaning ways of communicating are a rarity now. (This freed me up to examine my own part in contributing to situations that were frustrating to her.)

Accepting is a conscious, ongoing decision I make. I have chosen Alice as my lifelong partner. I also choose to live in peace and harmony with her and within myself. This requires that I not cling to my judgments, or at least not to act on those judgments or give them power. What has happened is that my judgments have less force behind them – I get less emotionally caught up in them, and so I feel less frustrated, and for shorter periods of time. Part of the reason for this is that I have come to believe my judgments less. Rather than seeing my way of thinking or acting as correct, and Alice's position as wrong, I am seeing her outlook as simply different from mine – different perspective, different opinion. It is liberating to view differences as simply differences. My impetus now is, rather than trying to change the differences or eliminate them, to appreciate them. In this way, our differences can expand and enrich me.

Alice and I differ in many ways that could cause us problems. Alice is more emotional. I am more detached. Alice is more people oriented. I am more a recluse. Alice likes to go out a lot. I like to stay home. Alice likes to remain indoors when we are at home. I like to be outside. Alice likes to stay up late. I like to go to sleep early and wake up early. Alice likes to keep to the speed limit. I like to drive like a race driver. Alice enjoys spending money. I am more frugal. Each of these differences has the potential to be a major source of conflict, but each of them can also be an opportunity to live, learn and broaden ourselves. It's great that we are different. I would not like to be married to myself. It is not that one of us is right and the other is wrong, or that one is better or worse; but when we accept and incorporate the other's position and viewpoint, we can expand and enrich ourselves. This has certainly happened in our relationship. At the very least, when we can respect the others position as simply another way of seeing and doing things, we will have avoided a major source of conflict.

I think that one of the influences behind my willingness and ability to accept things as they are, is a larger acceptance I have developed, in part because I have worked as a counselor. Having "heard it all" from my clients, I have a sense of the frailty and imperfection of human beings. This has helped me view others with a compassionate eye. I see that we're all just ordinary folks, living our lives and doing the best we can. Seeing others with more compassion has helped me see myself with more compassion. I, too, am frail and imperfect. I, too, am in need of patience and understanding from others. Appreciating my own neediness has given me space to "cut myself some slack" – and Alice, and others too. The less I judge myself, the less I judge others, and vice-versa. In this atmosphere of acceptance, we all blossom.

Acquiring information about your partner can temper your judgments and increase your acceptance and compassion for them. Knowing them more deeply leads to understanding how they came to be as they are. Things like having knowledge that your partner was sexually abused as a child can help explain present sexual issues. Knowing there was violence in a previous relationship might help explain their distress when anyone exhibits anger around them. Were parents controlling? Did they withhold affection? How were conflicts handled? Was alcohol or drugs a factor in prior relationships? Was there a betrayal of trust? These residues from the past are important things to know about your partner and for them to know about you. Such knowledge can provide insight into what automatically triggers them to anger, fear, defensiveness and retaliation. Knowing these things can help temper the tendency to judge and blame them, and allow in the refreshing air of acceptance.

Alice and I have done this. We know almost every important detail of each other's past. We have spent long hours sharing with each other intimate details of our history. Knowing about each other in this detail, besides satisfying our curiosity, has given us a deeper understanding of who each of us is, and this has led to a greater acceptance of each other's quirky thoughts and behaviors.

UNDERSTANDING THE LOVING PROMISES

Letting go of judgments and accepting our partner as they are takes patience and the understanding that everyone has within them a drive for health and wholeness. Positive results will manifest in their own natural rhythm. We need to honor our partner's rhythms, and not demand a change according to our time schedule. They will progress at their own pace, or not progress. Our job is to accept and be patient.

Patience is the key to accepting your partner. Patience is in the same ballpark as acceptance. It is the willingness to abide with what's going on and allowing it to be as it is. It is the ability to sit still and experience confusion, ambiguity and discomfort without having to do something. It turns the old homily on it's head; "Don't just do something, sit there."

Patience is not a passive process, like simply waiting, twiddling your thumbs while time passes, hoping and praying for the changes you want to happen to occur on their own. Patience is an active "being with," a watchful participation, an alert awareness. By being present in this way, you are giving a message to the other person, "I believe you will find your way. I trust you. I am with you."

Patience is allowing even your impatience to be. Not only is patience key to accepting the partner, it is a key to a peaceful life. Patience cannot be acquired when things are quiet and peaceful. The real opportunity to practice patience happens when things are difficult and stressful. Only when you're frustrated can you rise to the challenge of being patient.

Patience with yourself and patience with your partner is a basic quality that is essential to the Loving Promises. I had at one time considered giving patience it's own Promise, but I realized that it is one of those necessary qualities, like kindness, that are diffused throughout all the Loving Promises. If you lack patience, your chance of abiding with Loving Promises is nil.

Patience can be developed. One of the best practices for developing patience is meditation. A common form of meditation is simply sitting and watching the stream of experiences that arise and fall away, not holding on, not efforting at letting go – just watching and letting be. What better practice can there be for acquiring patience and acceptance.

Acceptance is powerful medicine in relationship. To be accepting is to be non-threatening. To be non-threatening allows your partner to feel safe being themselves. If you blame them, punish them, criticize and judge them as wrong and compare them to others, you are inducing fear. Fear perpetuates fear, promotes hiding, actuates defensiveness and dampens love. Fear, judgment and non-acceptance are incompatible with love. The following simple chart shows the effects on a person when their partner is being accepting or non-accepting.

Not Accepting
- ➢ Sends a message they are not okay, not lovable as they are.
- ➢ Creates resistance and defensiveness.
- ➢ You are right, they are wrong.
- ➢ Atmosphere of tension and distance.

Accepting
- ➢ They are okay and don't have to change to be loved by you.
- ➢ Nothing to resist or defend against.
- ➢ No one is right; no one is wrong.
- ➢ Atmosphere of peace and closeness.

Which circumstance do you believe would be more likely to invite change in your partner? Under which circumstance would you prefer to live?

I believe that the basis for accepting your partner is accepting yourself. To accept yourself means that you must also accept your limitations. Some of those limitations, like tendencies toward timidity, volatility or self-centeredness, may be a part of your personality makeup and can remain for the rest of your life. Like it or not, those patterns of thought and behavior are so ancient and buried so deeply that they rarely can be altered, except superficially, no matter what you do to try to change them. What should you do about these unalterable parts of yourself? Should you struggle against them? Should you give up and just accept them and move on? Whether you struggle against or accept, hold back on the self-judgment, it doesn't do you any good to feel bad about yourself or put yourself down. The same advice about accepting your partner applies to you—appreciate and accept the whole package.

Ultimately, we are all in process. We are on a journey and none of us knows the twists and turns even our own road will take, much less the route others will travel. And we can't know where things will end up. Abraham Lincoln's life is a case in point. Up until the latter part of his life, he could be considered a loser by most people. Failed business ventures, lost elections, depression, unhappy relationships – his was a sorry resume. Yet this slow, gangly, unattractive man would come to be one of America's most revered personages. The point is this – never, never, never judge a person for where they are in their journey. Each person's life is a process of unfolding. No one can know another person's path. We can watch, accept others as they are, and wish them a safe, productive and enjoyable voyage.

The 3rd Zen Patriarch in the 4th century wrote "The Great Way is not difficult for those who have no preferences. . . If you wish to see the truth, then hold no opinions for or against anything. . . Do not search for the truth, only cease to cherish opinions." If we are able to see the world and our partner, as the sage says, "Without preferences," we would begin to see and appreciate them and our world world as perfect, just as they are. Even so-called "flaws" become part of the perfection.

In the old days, if Japanese master potters created a flawless vessel, they would not accept it. They believed there was nothing in this world that was perfect. They would purposely put a flaw in the piece. That flaw became part of that perfect vessel.

We are all flawed vessels, perfect in our imperfection.

9. **I WILL REGARD YOU AS MY EQUAL.** *I will immediately cease when I become aware that I am judging you inferior or superior to myself, believe my needs are more important than yours, assume I cannot learn from you, or expect that I am entitled to better treatment than you.*

Love doesn't judge the value of another person. Love honors. That is true equality.

Some of the worst deeds of mankind that one group has visited upon another come from the belief that "we" are better than "them." War, slavery, "ethnic cleansing," institutionalized financial and educational prejudicial treatment are the result of believing my people are superior because we have greater intelligence, strength, wealth, beauty, moral character, etc., than yours.

Maybe I feel more important than you because I have advanced college degrees. Maybe I defer to you because you are a male and I am a woman. Maybe I feel I deserve more consideration than you because I bring home a salary and you are only a housewife. Couples can find many reasons to retain a sense of inequality in their pairings. However, a loving relationship is truly a partnership – a relationship between equals. This assumption of each person's equal value is an absolute necessity. Of course, no two individuals are equal. People vary in intelligence, maturity, physical attributes, creativity, etc. They have different strengths and weaknesses, and different acquired skills. But in spite of divergent characteristics, no one should be considered an intrinsically better or worse, higher or lower human being. We humans are a community of equal souls.

A couple's differences are valuable. Differences make their partnership more whole, add variety and spice, and challenge them each to incorporate new ways of being. How monotonous and limiting it would be to marry someone exactly like yourself. Relationship will suffer, however, if one partner criticizes and evaluates the other's differences and consistently takes on the superior position of teacher, guru, therapist or parent, i.e. the person whose job it is to lead and correct their mate. The partnership will also suffer if one partner consistently assumes the opposite position of student, disciple, patient or child. In either case, each partner becomes locked into a role. The roles are mutually exclusive – assuming the role of the teacher forces the other into a role of student. Assuming the role of student forces the other into the role of teacher. The partners' options narrow and harden, and each becomes less free to manifest their fullness.

What about circumstances where partners really are unequal? One has special knowledge or skills, or is more developed in one area than the other. What then? Equality in this Promise refers to believing that each other are beings who are essentially equal in *value*. A person who *knows* deep down that they are equal to their mate will have no qualms about letting their partner take the lead if they are more skilled or knowledgeable. Their understanding that they truly are equal takes away the desire to control or compete with the other. He or she can then become a supportive follower.

Equality is stable. Inequality is unstable. It's a rare occasion when both partners are in complete agreement for long about their inferior/superior positions. What often happens in this case is the person in the superior role, believing their needs are more important, their decisions more relevant, may begin to demand more "goodies," expect the other to defer or start treating the other in demeaning ways. The person in the inferior position begins to harbor resentments and insist on fair treatment. In this state of flux, the stage is set for conflict and power struggle. Many arguments these couples have are not about the issues at hand, but about "pecking order," the person in the subordinate position trying to prove that they are as good as or as entitled as the other, and/or the superior partner trying to maintain their elevated position.

The question of who wields more power in decision making can be the source of many divisive conflicts and it is in this area that extreme caring must be exercised. It's often not easy for the one who feels entitled to greater control to let go and relinquish that control. The writing of our book, "THE ART OF AGING: Celebrating the Authentic Aging Self," is a perfect example of how I learned a lesson in equality. By virtue of my degrees in psychology, therapeutic experience and my supposed superior writing skills, I felt that my input should carry more weight than Alice's. I became impatient with her comments and tried to bulldoze my judgments over her objections. Alice was buying none of it. She considered the book a joint venture and insisted in having an equal say. Numerous arguments ensued, but Alice refused to back down. I'm so happy she resisted because, in taking a strong stand for herself, she helped me to release my sense of entitlement and honor her strength and wise counsel. In the end, the book turned out to be a melding of both our voices and was much better for it. I realized that if I had written it the way I wanted, the book would have been tedious and boring. Also, by sharing our writing equally, the book truly became ours.

The higher/lower game gets played out in different ways, often with the element of gender bias. In the old days, couple's roles were rigid. Men were the ones in control, but a woman could get her needs met by assuming the inferior position and, from that position, manipulating her man. In some cultures, this is still the case, but here in the U.S., things are gradually changing. The Women's Movement of the 60s empowered women and enabled them to begin to meet men eye-to-eye as equals, thus forever changing the landscape of relationship. This was after my time. I was brought up in a household where my mother did the housework and my dad did the "important" job of bringing home the bacon. I adopted this attitude.

For me to fully embrace this Promise I have had to relinquish some of the luxury of male privilege. In previous relationships I felt domestic duties, like cooking, cleaning the house and washing clothes were "women's work" and thus, below me. I would deign from time-to-time to pick up a broom or wash a dish, but cleaning, washing and cooking was not my business. Not now. With Alice, I don't just "help her out." I am a full partner in taking care of the house. While I don't consider these activities fun, I am eager and willing to do them, in large part because I am so grateful for what Alice does for me that I look for opportunities where I can share the load.

Simply by being a male, I tend to automatically be treated with slightly more deference and respect by many women friends and strangers – my words are given a bit more credence, I'm accorded the luxury of being served. It's just the way it is. Part of me secretly enjoys this special treatment and being held in higher esteem, but it goes against my own principles, so if I could wish it away, I would. (I still would want to retain the perks of being an elder though.)

While gender bias is not so blatant as it was past, it is still rampant in subtle forms. Many men still speak about and treat women in demeaning, sarcastic and dismissive ways. And many women consider men to be foolish, helpless, unfeeling oafs. There is hidden cultural pressure to maintain these prejudices and it takes awareness and courage to oppose that pressure, examine personal biases and treat the opposite sex with the equal respect they deserve.

It is essential to not just treat the opposite sex as equal, but to *know* them as equal – not just equal, but as having valuable characteristics that are worthy of deep respect and emulation. If men don't honor their feminine side – the receptive, feeling, care-taking aspects of their personality, and women don't honor their masculine side – the active and assertive parts of themselves, they will be out of balance. And they will judge and not honor the masculine and feminine in their partner. There is no such thing as 100% male or 100% female. We all have these opposite poles in our personality, even if they are not overtly expressed. It will serve us well to recognize and develop them. If we fail to do so, we will be unable to realize true intimacy and experience our full potential as individuals and as a couple.

In addition to wanting the perks of better treatment and greater control, some people have a need to feel superior. Most often this is a consequence of actually feeling inferior. By maintaining a prejudicial attitude and keeping others below you, you seemingly stand taller by contrast. But you also alienate and stay separate from others, a prescription for loneliness. This was the dynamic by which I operated for years. Over time, as I became more able to see myself as the vulnerable, limited, imperfect being that I was and accept that part of me, I gradually let go of the need to present myself as someone who is better than others. By admitting my humanness and becoming more humble, I was able to join the community of other imperfect humans as an equal member.

The importance of the virtue of humility cannot be overstated. I would define humility as not being overwhelmed by your own importance, not thinking you are superior to others, not being prideful, conceited, and arrogant. Traditional definitions emphasize the negative aspects of humility – lowness, meekness, submission. This is not a full or accurate description. One can be humble and still be a powerful and worthy individual. The ideal is to engender superior qualities, but not to think of yourself as superior or to act superior to others, especially your mate.

In Proverbs there is a saying, "Pride goeth before a fall." It's true that the bigger you think you are, the harder you can fall. As you make progress on the path of love, the issue of humility can come to the foreground. It may be necessary for you to monitor your pride in your accomplishments. The thought, "Look at me, I'm more loving, more spiritual than others," can find it's way into your mind. It is a subtle trap that is easier to to get caught in than you think. The further you advance, the more of these traps there are.

Humility is an important aspect of spiritual practice, especially in Christian and Eastern religious traditions. The work of whittling down my pride and arrogance has been an important part of my spiritual path and a focus of those who were trying to teach me. The first time I visited my teacher's ashram in India, I arrived with an inflated ego. I was the manager of a thriving spiritual community in Los Angeles and assumed I would be welcomed with open arms and treated as an honored guest. My expectations were dashed when I was assigned to a bed in a large dormitory and given the job of cleaning toilets. After a while, I was promoted to washing dirty rags. Needless to say, I returned to America a lot more humble than when I left.

This issue of equality can be viewed in a more enlightened way. The Buddha spoke of "three conceits" – arrogance in the way we consider ourselves and others. The first is, "I am better than you." The second is, "You are better than me." What's left is the third conceit which is, "We are equal to each other." The error in this third conceit is, like the first and second – it depends on comparing ourselves to others. But if I am able to refrain from any form of comparison and simply see you, be with you and appreciate you just as you are – not higher, not lower, not even equal, and know and appreciate myself just as I am – how simple, how uncomplicated.

However, we can go beyond the "I am better than you," or "You are better than me," or even "We are both equal" judgment. We can even go beyond the judgment-free position of no comparison. To do this, expand your conception of a human being. See yourself, your partner and all humans as not merely individuals consisting of bodies, minds and personalities, but as souls, as a part of the Creative Consciousness. On this level we are all the same, made of the same divine stuff. One divine soul cannot be better or worse, higher or lower, more valuable or less valuable than another divine soul. When you see and honor the divinity in your partner, you will treat them with utmost care and consideration, as if they are a precious, sacred treasure. They are.

10. I WILL EMPHASIZE YOUR POSITIVE SIDE. *I will applaud your admirable qualities, activities and accomplishments and refrain from focusing on your failings and imperfections.*

Brook is the daughter of a family friend. She is beautiful, intelligent, warm, talented and creative. She is also my treasured friend. This was not always so. For a long time, there was minimal connection between us. Then one evening I felt the urge to call her on the phone. I told her how much I deeply admired her for the very special person she was. She was taken aback and overwhelmed. That one brief phone conversation opened the doors to our friendship and forever changed how we felt about each other. It demonstrated to me the awesome power of praise.

Of course, like everyone else, Brook also has some imperfections. I chose not to go there. If your interest is to look for negativities in your partner, you will find them. Everyone has their imperfections. Invariably, the harder you look and the more you analyze, the more you'll discover. When you start adding up all the negatives, doubts will creep into your mind and you'll wonder if you made the right choice of a mate.

Several times during a previous relationship, my partner provided me with a neatly typed, detailed list of my shortcomings. She thought it would be helpful to me (and more pleasant for her) if I knew what exactly was wrong with me. It wasn't helpful. I began focusing on my negativities and shut down. I attempted to hide things about myself from her that I was ashamed of, trying to earn her approval. It wasn't real. I was just acting. Often I would attempt to dispute her and argue that she was wrong in her evaluation of me. Whether I accepted her criticism or rejected it, either way, I was automatically trying to dig myself out of the hole I found myself in. I lost before I began. Her focusing on my negative parts put me on the defensive and caused both of us pain.

What a relief it was for me to join with Alice, who has always been so free with praise and encouragement. Instead of a list of my negatives, every day I am told of my virtues. Coming into this healing environment has allowed me to flourish.

I think it works this way energetically. Once you place your attention on what is wrong with your partner, you invite in the negative energies. Our harsh and critical words, even our nonverbal communication, can cause them to wilt. Your words cause his or her shortcomings to become present, right in front of both your faces. Negative criticism can immediately bring on fear and defense. Fear takes us out of our heart and puts us into our mind. We start questioning, "Is it true? Where did I screw up? Am I a bad person?" Along comes shame, blame, hiding, justification.

On the other hand, praise motivates. When you emphasize your focus on the positive, on what is good, on what is right with your mate, those behaviors and qualities are reinforced. The energy of the negative will weaken and dissipate. Positive praise, appreciation and encouragement will empower your partner, strengthen them. They will feel better about themselves and feel better about you. Focus on the negative, and they will feel worse about themselves and about you. Which do you want?

In the past, I only used praise when I felt praise was clearly deserved (lots of judgment in that.) But if it serves others to complement their qualities and activities that might not quite yet be praiseworthy – what's the harm in that? Is it technically dishonest to commend someone for performance that is less than perfect? Who knows? But it is helpful. Praise motivates and energizes. I am not advocating lying. Complements and praise must have a source in reality, or else it can cause the person whom we complimented to distrust us. But it is disheartening to a person if we withhold praise and compliment them only if they perform like a professional.

Looking for and expressing the positive has no depth and meaning unless we are able to openly express the negative. We must be free to be able to give and receive honest feedback without fear. Part of our job as a loving partner is to be clear about what can be helpful to them and not hold that back. I am liberal with my praise of Alice, and spare in my criticism. I don't have to be Alice's professor or disciplinarian. She is aware when she has made mistakes and my echoing her self-criticism will only be a distraction and not serve any useful purpose.

One may ask, "If I focus on the positive, I am not always acknowledging reality. What if I have legitimate, constructive criticism? Wouldn't it be dishonest for me to withhold it?" Emphasizing the positive is not about turning a blind eye, or lying or remaining mum about negatives. The key words in the Promise are *emphasized* and *focus*. It's a matter of what you accentuate. Emphasize the positive, keep attending to the good that is there. Be aware of the negative, but don't focus your attention on it. If you feel legitimate criticism is necessary, do it with the full intention to benefit. The surgeon cuts with a sharp instrument. So does a warrior. One intends to heal, the other intends to harm. Use a scalpel, not a sword, and wield it with kindness and sensitivity.

Emphasizing the positive encompasses more than what you say. It begins with your attitude, your desire to see the good that exists in your partner. It's so much more productive and fun to focus on their light, and celebrate, than to focus on their shadows, and complain. As you place your attention on your partner's positive qualities and worthy accomplishments, these will become more solid for you and your love and admiration for your beloved will blossom. Also, that positive focus will make you a more loving and lovable partner in their eyes.

So I suggest you take upon yourself a simple but powerful exercise. Make a list of the positive qualities of your partner. Include all the wonderful things that make them special and add joy and beauty to your life. You might want to share the list with them.

There are few greater contributions you can make to a person's life than to show them how good, how precious, how beautiful and how loved they are.

11. I WILL INSPIRE YOU TO BE YOUR BEST. *I will persistently urge you to strive to be the very best person you can be. I will encourage you to pursue your dreams.*

Promise #8 is about accepting your partner just as they are. Promise #11 is about seeing your partner, knowing your partner, accepting your partner, and at the same time, *envisioning what they could be if they reached their highest potential.* Because you love them and know them differently than they know themselves, sometimes you are able to see their potential more clearly than they can. Your vision for them can inspire them. It is not your vision of what they should do or how they should be. It is your intuitive insight into their unique potential, a potential that, if realized, could bring them greater joy and aliveness.

Each person's potential is unique unto themselves. One discovers their capacity through living experience, through exercising their gifts and overcoming their deficits. Potential implies a view into the future. However, an important part of their potential is the way a person lives their life *now*. To live as the best person you can be means conducting all your interactions with integrity – being of sound moral character and overcoming obstacles in life with toughness and persistence. Being your best also means living with generosity – behaving toward yourself and others with kindness, patience and sensitivity, and doing so with joy and aliveness. We cannot force our partner to live with integrity and generosity. We can congratulate them when they do and enthusiastically cheer them on. We can support them by holding their vision and reminding them of their vision if they lose their way. Most important, we can stand as an example by the way we ourselves live with integrity and generosity. There is no more powerful way of inspiring our partner than by standing as an example for them.

People are at their best and feel most alive when they are fully engaged, when they are enthusiastically pursuing something that has captured their interest. It could be as mundane as making quilts or researching ancestors for a family tree, or as lofty as ministering to people's spiritual needs or serving the sick and homeless. Even more engaging than pursuing an interest, is pursuing a dream – some project or undertaking that takes energy and involvement over a period of time. A dream holds passion. The goal of a dream is to produce a result for which one has a profound yearning. Human beings feel most energy and aliveness when they are in pursuit of their passion. And when they lack things in their life about which they are passionate, they lack energy and aliveness.

To follow your true calling is an act of self-love, often a courageous act. The middle-aged corporate executive who deserts his well-paying but boring job in order to pursue his dream of world travel, the mother of two children who reorganizes her life so that she can take art classes, the young man who defies his parents by rejecting the restrictive life course they have set out for him – all are performing acts of self-love and, in the process, courageously jumping into the unknown and choosing aliveness over deadness.

Few things reveal more about ourselves than our hopes and dreams. Our dreams indicate what is important to us. They are a window into our future. Our passions tell not only what we are like now, but also what we intend to be. That is why it is important to be clear about what you hope for. Not only will that clarity make it easier for you to realize your dreams, defining your dreams will help you know if you and your partner's dreams are in sync. If they are significantly different and in conflict with each other, divergent aspirations can pull the relationship apart. If one partner's dream is to buy a boat and travel around the world for years, and the other's is to enter college and study for an advanced degree, it just won't work. A dream that that will work for both of you is to keep the ideal of maintaining the excellence of your relationship.

Do what you can to bolster your partner's involvement in their pursuits. Encourage them to realize their dreams and to share their dreams with you. If they don't have any, urge them to find something that engages them. Realize that your partner's interests and dreams are deeply personal and are to be treated with great respect. Provide encouragement but don't try to impose your vision upon them.

Your inspiration and support is a great service you can provide for your partner. By encouraging them to "follow their bliss" you help set them on a path to joy and aliveness.

12. I WILL CHALLENGE YOU WHEN NECESSARY. *I will not shrink from asserting my power in order to influence you for your benefit. I will confront you and offer constructive criticism when I recognize you are in need of guidance.*

Some couples make an unstated agreement with each other. "I won't make waves in our relationship if you won't. I won't press you to look into sensitive and uncomfortable areas of your life if you won't press me." A pact like this keeps both partners from realizing their full potential. Individuals in a couple relationship can have a powerful, positive impact on each other. However, if they collude to avoid growing by staying within safe boundaries and evading challenges, they insure the mediocrity of the relationship . . . and of themselves. By tolerating their partner being less than their best, such a relationship becomes a cozy cocoon where little real growth can take place.

Most of us tend to seek partners who agree with us, who give us the benefit of the doubt, who see things the way we see them. Because they are in alignment with us, there is a limited amount we can learn from them. Sometimes our best teacher is our opponent or our enemy, one who opposes us and challenges us, one who tries to find where we are wrong and searches for where we are weak. If you listen to your opponent and are open to learn from them, they can be considered your ally.

This is not to say you should take on the role of being your partner's enemy. However, if you become aware of their straying from integrity, abandoning their dream or departing from the path of their life's purpose – speak up, be honest, don't let them off the hook. Challenge their choice for mediocrity. By simply telling your truth, with strength and kindness and with sensitivity to their feelings, you serve as a mirror for them. If your reflection is clear and accurate, your input can wake them and help get them back on course.

Sometimes this can lead to arguments. I'm not referring here to the kind of arguments where one partner is trying to win for themselves, trying to get their way for their own advantage. I'm referring to the kind of argument where one partner is trying to wake up the other to their unconscious, self-defeating behavior and provoke them by rattling the cage of their complacency. It could be very uncomfortable when their laziness is exposed and a part of themselves they want to remain covered is revealed. If done in good faith and with love, your challenge can melt defenses and allow them to take in the messages they need to hear.

It is important to be sensitive to your partner's needs in the moment. At times your partner might be feeling fragile and will require your protection. Pressure from you at those times is the last thing they need. At other times they might be blind and in need of guidance from you. Still other times they may be stubborn and the action demanded is a kick in the ass. It can be difficult to tell the difference and discern what is really your most appropriate action, and even more difficult to administer the kick if that is what is needed.

Everyone has an edge, a comfort zone, and when they are pushed beyond their edge, fear and stress begin to take over and they can become immobilized. If they don't even approach their edge, they can become lethargic and fall into a comfortable, secure deadness and stagnation. The edge contains depth and aliveness, but also risk. The trick is to be sensitive and know when to push your partner, and when to withdraw.

It takes courage to stand up for what you believe is best for your partner, especially in the face of their opposition. You may frustrate or disappoint them or arouse their anger and resistance. Most likely they will become defensive. Fear of these reactions may make you inclined to withhold your opinions and sugar coat what you tell them. Saying your truth means silencing your fearful "Mr. Nice Guy" or "Ms. Nice Gal." It requires of you a willingness and readiness to stand up and wound your partner if it serves them. Sometimes their feelings might be hurt, or their ego punctured. Occasionally though, these are the consequences of truth.

UNDERSTANDING THE LOVING PROMISES

Our reluctance to challenge our partner may have more to do with ourselves than with fear of our partner's reaction. If we were to challenge them to be their very best, would it not require us to be our very best? How can we throw stones when we, ourselves, live in a glass house? Do we have the right to tell anyone how to live their life if we lounge around on the couch, drinking booze and watching television? Why would they follow our urgings if we don't have the wisdom and discipline to correct our own shortcomings and mistakes? Why would they want to emulate us if we don't have the courage to live up to our highest ideals? So, the most potent way to encourage your partner to be their best is for you to be your best. Practice what you preach.

As part of the function of challenging your partner to be their best, this Promise may require you to take on a grave responsibility at times, one that is especially difficult to assume in an equal partnership. If you have special skills and understanding, it asks you, when needed, to be your partner's guide. You already teach informally through your day-to-day presence in the relationship, but this Promise will make manifest this position as one who offers guidance. To take on the role of a coach, even if in a limited sphere, can be uncomfortable for you and for your partner. It may require you to criticize and confront as well as educate. If not handled right, if you treat your partner with righteous superiority rather than as a loving friend, it can potentially unbalance the sense of equality that has developed between you. But, if you can serve your partner in this way, it is worth the discomfort. Being available to guide your partner by offering advice and imparting information when needed is a valuable and, at times, necessary function. It will be greatly appreciated by your partner, especially if handled with sensitivity and tact. However, if you refuse to challenge or offer criticism when needed, you are shirking your responsibility to inspire your partner to be their best. Failure to confront when necessary is a failure to love.

Be especially sensitive to the way you confront – the wording and the timing. Inherent in a situation where you are being critical is the position, "You're wrong and I'm right," which reeks of superiority. You are correcting them; therefore, be gentle. The wrong word in the wrong manner at the wrong time can be interpreted as disapproval and can easily lead to defensiveness. If they feel you are trying to blame them, their defensive hackles will come up. An important key to defusing defensiveness is to criticize the action, not the person. It is not *they* who were wrong or bad. The fault was in their behavior. It was what they said or did that led to unwanted consequences, not who they are.

Timing is important. It's probably best not to confront or offer criticism at times when feelings are intense between you and your partner. You can wait until the storm is over and things calm down. Choose the right place and time. In public, at a party, is not the right place. The minute they return home from a tough day of work is not the right time. Keep specific when expressing disapproval. Don't use a shotgun when a flyswatter will do. Don't pile on loads of past criticism you had previously held back. That's overwhelming. Be gentle, don't clobber. If you see the conversation is not going anywhere and your partner is becoming defensive, there is no profit in forcing the issue. Tactfully break off the conversation and take up the issue at another time.

More important than the way you confront is your motivation for confronting. Is your challenge to your partner based on goodwill and desire for their best interest and the best interest of the relationship? Or is your real motivation to manipulate, control, retaliate or put them down? These are important questions to ask yourself. Your motivation must be "clean." If you are not motivated by goodwill, your partner will likely pick up your true motives and respond accordingly.

If you occasionally take on the function as your partner's guide, it is very different from being their therapist. Don't try to be their psychotherapist, which is an unequal alliance. That is not your place. Always remember that when you instruct your partner, you are equals. You will probably take instruction from them sometime in the future. The therapist/patient relationship is quite different. Don't go there. As the saying goes, "A smart person does not try to repair their watch."

To challenge your partner to be their best is an expression of your love. How better to serve them than to ask them to live with integrity and generosity and encourage them to pursue that which will bring them alive.

13. **I WILL BE GRATEFUL FOR YOUR GIFTS TO ME**. *I will be mindful of the things you do and have done for my benefit. I will not take these things for granted or automatically expect them from you. I will receive graciously.*

The German mystic, Meister Eckhart wrote about gratitude. "If the only prayer you ever say in your entire life is 'thank you'-- it will be enough."

A while ago Alice and I had friends over for dinner and before we began our meal, as is our tradition, we all held hands around the table and someone offered a prayer of thanksgiving for the food. Someone else chimed in with another benediction, and then someone else. It became a joke as we went round after round, giving thanks for minute details. "I am thankful for the workers who picked the grapes for this wine. I am thankful for the wine bottle maker, the printer that printed the label, the ink manufacturer . . ." While we had great fun, after a time the realization dawned on us that thousands of hands had contributed to make this meal a reality. Without their concerted effort, it never would have happened. How mind expanding it was to see this and be grateful.

Thanksgiving is our favorite holiday. We have been hosting the celebration at our house for over thirty years. On our most recent Thanksgiving we had over eighty friends and family for dinner. The highlight of the evening is our "thankfulness ceremony" where we form a large circle. Everyone takes a moment, reflects back on the past year and expresses their gratitude. By the time we complete the circle, the sense of thankfulness permeates the air. Then, with full hearts, we fill our stomachs.

When it comes down to it, gratitude is a choice of where you want to put your attention. You can attend to all the positive things in your life and be grateful and happy. Or you can focus on all the negative things and feel frustrated, angry and miserable. I choose to be grateful.

Gratefulness is one of those global qualities, like patience, kindness and generosity, that applies to your whole life and not just to your relationships. It is highly unlikely that you would be grateful only in regards to your partner. When you work to cultivate an "attitude of gratitude" in all areas of your life--your work, your family, your friends, your health--you are automatically cultivating gratefulness for your mate.

Day after day we live with our partner. We get used to each other and comfortable with them. We lazily trust in the durability of our relationship. Familiarity takes over and it becomes easy to take them for granted. We can expect things from them without thinking, neglecting to pause and respectfully make a request. We can be oblivious to their boundaries. We can forget to be gracious in accepting their generosity. We can neglect to offer our help to ease their burden as a gesture of our appreciation. These kinds of behaviors kill love. Love requires ongoing vigilance. Love requires gratefulness for what is given. We need to always remember that when our partner gives to us, it is a gift we are privileged to receive, not a right we are entitled to.

Gratitude is an essential part of a magnificent relationship. It is a reminder of how fortunate you are to have this generous partner in your life. With gratitude, the seeming importance of their blemishes, defects and deficiencies melt away. Gratitude gives you perspective, your problems seem to shrink when you focus on what is good in your life together. When your partner knows you appreciate them and knows that you are grateful for their generosity, they know they are loved.

I am grateful for all the things Alice does for me. She does most of the cooking and shopping for us, brings flowers to the house, takes care of me when

I am sick, plans our trips, makes me laugh, listens to my complaints, makes sure I take a jacket when it's cold out, attends all my musical performances, cuddles in bed with me at night and on and on. Alice has created a space for me to be myself, to be taken care of, to be safe and snug, to be appreciated, to be loved. I could fill this whole book with the ways Alice serves me, and I am not even fully aware of all that she does. Bills get paid, leaves raked, clothes washed, food bought, put away and on and on. Just thinking about how she takes care of me fills my heart with love for her.

What I have just written in the previous paragraph is an important part of the action component of this Loving Promise. That is--simply take time to periodically contemplate the gifts your partner gives you. Make a written list if you want to make it more tangible. Luxuriate in the warm, appreciative feelings that result. Those feelings are love.

Another thing that generates gratefulness for your partner's acts of service for you is to try to be consciously aware of those moments when your partner is extending themselves for your benefit. Don't reflexively expect favors. This would denigrate the gift and denigrate the giving. Express appreciation when you are gifted. This is receiving with graciousness and is an act of generosity on your part. It's not that your partner needs or even wants validation for their acts of generosity. However, it would probably bother them to know that you expected, or didn't appreciate, or possibly didn't even recognize when you had received their gift.

It may seem odd to speak about improving your ability to receive in this book whose theme is predominantly about giving. However, paradoxically, your receiving graciously is a generous offering you give to your partner. Some people have difficulty receiving. They reject offers of support, minimize their partner's encouragement, brush off compliments, spurn an intimate gesture or criticize a gift. The origin of this "I don't need anything from anyone. I can manage it myself" attitude probably has its roots in childhood. Whatever the source, if you continue with this behavior, you will dampen your partner's joy in giving and this will eventually turn off their desire to give to you.

Alice gives easily and generously. I find that for me, the most valuable part of her generosity is that it opens my heart to gratitude and makes me want to give back to her. It is not in the sense of trying to even the score, but a giving that feels free and creates a sense of oneness between us. Her giving has freed up my giving, not just to her. but to everyone.

You want to do things that will make each other happy. How can you best do that? You train each other about what it is that makes each of you happy. How? Very simple. You express appreciation and thanks. Your mutual expressions of appreciation serve as a guide that lets each of you know the ways you can please each other.

14. **I WILL APPRECIATE YOU**. *I will honor the miracle, mystery and beauty of who you are. I will keep alive a sense of appreciation of how your presence has enhanced my life. I will not hesitate to express my appreciation and admiration for you.*

We can have the most wonderful person in our life, possess limitless wealth, be surrounded by the most beautiful objects, but if we don't appreciate them, we have nothing. Joy arises not from having, but from appreciating what we have.

Alice and I awaken each morning in gratefulness. We give voice to our appreciation for our life, our home, our health and, of course, for each other. Appreciation, I believe, opens the door to bounty. Our appreciation is like an affirmation that says, "I give thanks to the universe for the gift I have been given and I am open to receive more." That openness makes it more likely that the universe will provide.

When my heart is closed--when I judge and blame and find fault--I cannot appreciate. When my heart is open and grateful, my appreciation for my partner flows freely, even in light of their failings and imperfections.

With the previous Loving Promise, I am grateful for what my lover does for me. With this Loving Promise, I appreciate and am grateful for the person they are. The person they are is their gift to me. Similar but separate from appreciation is admiration. Admiration has the flavor of respect and holding in high regard. When I appreciate and admire my partner, I treasure their smile, their walk, their voice, their integrity, their humor, their tenderness, their deep feeling. I will even cherish what could be seen as negatives—their less than perfect physical features, their quirkiness, their weakness, their foolishness, their stubbornness – the whole package that comprises this amazing human with whom I am privileged to share my life.

Appreciation of our partner's qualities also extends to their physical appearance. Even if a partner is not an Adonis or a beauty queen, our love will make them so. *Love and appreciation can actually transform perception.* With most people, the more intimately you know them, the more lovable they become. By the light of your love, you are able to see beneath the surface beauty, the first few millimeters of skin, muscle and subcutaneous fat, and are able to appreciate their inner beauty. Their inner beauty is so much more captivating and so much more enduring.

LOVING PROMISES

A stranger viewing Alice walking down the street will just see an elderly, gray-haired woman. I see a strikingly beautiful creature. Love is blind. It does not register and is blind to all in our partner that is not beautiful. My love has allowed me to take my blinders off and see the true beauty that resides in Alice. Alice has no idea what I see when I look at her. I see incredible beauty. I see beauty because my eyes are saturated by my love for her. When she looks in the mirror she only searches for new wrinkles or flaws or makes sure her hair and makeup is right. When I look, I see the reflection of her soul.

This speaks to the fear many people have concerning the acceptability of their own and their partner's physical appearance as they grow older. Yes, surface beauty fades, hair turns gray or disappears, breasts fall, skin wrinkles, bellies expand and with each passing year, our appearance transforms into the likeness of our parents and grandparents. The question arises, "Will you still love and accept me when I'm old and have lost my looks?" Or, correspondingly, "Will I still love and accept you?" Self-love and love for our partner can help temper that fear. When I kiss the loose skin of her upper arms or run my fingers through her grey hair, Alice knows she is appreciated just as she is and this helps her love herself, even through those times when she may be inclined to judge herself.

An action component of this Promise is to consciously seek to experience the beauty in myriad forms in your partner. It is there. You will find it if you look for it. Look for it beyond the visual. See it in the beauty in the sound of their voice, the way they smile, their joyous laugh, the way they walk, how they do the dishes and make the bed. There is beauty in their loving embrace, in the movements of their mind in a deep conversation. There is even beauty in the energy of a flash of their anger. His or her beauty is there if you just take the time and make the effort to open your eyes and look with your heart.

A key element in our experience of love is the appreciation and admiration we hold for the awesome human essence of the person we love. When we feel that appreciation, we cherish our beloved, treat them as if they are a precious jewel. Loving Promises manifest spontaneously, a natural response to the appreciation we feel. It is not a burden, but a joy to engage the Promises. The Promises are not a struggle. They are an easy, natural outgrowth of our feeling. This all arises from appreciation.

Another action component of this Promise to appreciate is to simply count blessings, the blessings of your partner's presence. Focus your thoughts on your partner and intentionally contemplate those qualities that make them adorable, appreciate them, ponder the ways they have enriched you just by being in your life, experience the gratefulness you feel for their presence . . . and, of course, express that appreciation to them.

UNDERSTANDING THE LOVING PROMISES

A way Alice and I can intentionally manifest appreciation is to look back at the history of our relationship. We often bring up memories and speak of the good times together. We have shared so many beautiful experiences in the past. We are filled with gratefulness that we are blessed to have spent this precious time together. It's not only the good times we appreciate. We equally value the sad and difficult times we shared, times when we needed and received each other's love and support. These times have also enriched us and are deserving of our appreciation.

The walls of our home are filled with photos depicting important events and great times we have had together. Scattered around our house and garden are objects we have collected that hold sweet memories for us – our marriage certificate hanging on the wall in our office, the painting in our bedroom that we bought in New Delhi, the coral in the garden that we found at the beach.

All those objects are containers that hold appreciation. The energy of appreciation can be released by just glancing at them.

My appreciation for Alice expands exponentially when I keep in mind that time is fleeting and can never be recaptured. This attention to the ephemeral nature of time is something that is always in the back of my mind, especially at our age. It makes our past and present moments together incredibly precious.

Appreciation is not a vast enough word to describe how I feel about Alice. I feel she is a blessing and a gift that has been bestowed upon me, as if it were by Divine grace that Alice has come into my life. At the same time, my appreciation is not unbalanced by reality. Though I consider her my queen and my goddess, I also know her as a grumbler, a glutton, as righteous, as pushy and impatient, and as an occasional pain in the ass. She is all at once an enchantress, a vulnerable child and a frumpy elder. She is saint and sinner, angel and devil all rolled into one. I can encompass both divergent visions at the same time, and that expanded view that includes both sweet and sour is closer to the truth of who Alice is. Even in the rare times when I get frustrated with her, I am aware of her as a blessed presence in my life.

With any relationship, time can remove some of the sheen that was originally there. Dirty clothes left on the bathroom floor, dishes in the sink, smelly farts, petty arguments, the same routines, these things make us wonder if the person living with us with is the same one we first fell in love with. How can we regain the spark that seems to of gone out? Rather than trying to change your partner or yourself, the spark can be rekindled by opening your eyes and changing the way you think you know them.

Even if you think you know a person like you know the back of your hand, there will always be more to find out. Retain uncertainty about who your beloved really is. When you are sure you know your partner, you are not open to learning. Discovering the mystery in your partner requires you have curiosity about them and a "don't know" attitude. This demands you to drop assumptions, drop beliefs, drop expectations, drop history. Getting to know this person you live day-in and day-out with is not an event, it is an ongoing, unending process of exploration and discovery. When you understand this and approach your partner with genuine unknowing, you will continually uncover new facets in your relationship. There is always more to learn, depths to be plumbed, always more to be revealed. A whole lifetime is not time enough to know them. This attitude can keep even a long-term relationship an ever new and exciting adventure.

However, most of us, if we are honest with ourselves, will admit that one of the things we want in our relationship is certainty and control. We don't like surprises. We would like our partner to be the way we want and respond the way we expect. Well, there is no such thing as certainty in relationships and in life, (except death and taxes.) The more we try to insure certainty, we will fail and will suck the life out of the relationship. What makes life with our partner interesting is that they are not automatons. They are free to surprise us and sometimes frustrate us.

No matter how long I have lived with Alice and how much I think I know her, she will sometimes do something or come up with some totally unexpected, off-the-wall response that has my mind stopped, my head spinning and my jaw dropped. I love to be surprised by her in this way. It reminds me that I "don't know" her completely, and never will. In truth, I can only know Alice from the outside, just as she can only know me from what she can hear, see and infer. The rest is mystery, enticing mystery, mystery beyond the reach of the rational mind.

Appreciation cannot be a significant factor in relationship unless it is expressed. The next Promise speaks in more detail about expressing love and appreciation.

15. I WILL EXPRESS MY FEELINGS OF LOVE FOR YOU. *Everyone wants to know they are loved. I will demonstrate my love for you through my words, my touch, my giving, and especially through my conduct.*

An essential aspect of every person's happiness and wellbeing is to be able to feel good about themselves, to appreciate their positive qualities and not be overwhelmed by their negative ones. Being loved by someone special who appreciates us is an affirmation of our worthiness. Our partner is our mirror, whereby we can look and see our beauty reflected back to us in the love from their eyes, hear it from their words, feel it from gentleness of their touch. In

UNDERSTANDING THE LOVING PROMISES

order for us to really know our worthiness without the shadow of a doubt, we must see it, feel it and hear it from one who loves us.

My dad was a product of the older generation where men didn't readily express their feelings, so he felt uncomfortable when I (his hippie son) kept trying to put my arms around him and embrace him. For a long time I felt rebuffed by him and was uncertain of the depth of his love for me. There was one moment, however, when I recognized that my father truly loved me, but was limited in the way he could express his love. One day, after a family visit, I was standing at the doorway of my parents' home saying goodbye. My father was holding Snoopy, the pint-sized family dog, in his arms. As I was about to leave, dad lifted Snoopy to my face to have him lick my cheek. I was confused for a moment, then I realized, by that act, dad was having Snoopy do what he himself could not – show physical affection. With that realization, I came to greater acceptance of my father's love for me.

Everyone has their own style of expressing love and appreciation. Some do it with gifts, some with words, some with touch, and some with caretaking or with comforting actions. One thing is for certain; just about everyone wants to know they are loved. Alice and I use many ways to demonstrate our love for each other. I know Alice likes flowers, so I cut some roses from the garden and place them in a vase near her side of the bed or on her bathroom sink. I open doors for her and bring her a drink when it is hot out. She enjoys being massaged, so, many times I will rub her neck, shoulders or feet. When Alice makes me a bag lunch, I will always find a love note or a lipstick impression of her kiss on a piece of paper in the bag. When I divide up the chocolate bar, I always give her the piece with more almonds. Often she will grab my hand and kiss my fingers, or will cook my favorite meal. When we walk arm-in-arm, I slow down and she speeds up so that neither of us is uncomfortable with the pace. I always make sure Alice is seated in her favorite location when we are out, back against the wall so she can watch people. Sometimes, on cold nights, I will climb into her side of the bed first so it will be warm when she gets in. We both understand all of these actions as expressions of love.

There is no "proper" way or "best" way to express love. Is writing a heartfelt love poem to your beloved any more loving than going to work every day to a difficult job in order to support your family? Is saying "I love you" any more loving than helping carry groceries from the car? Whatever form you use to express what is in your heart, if you aim that expression in a way that your partner can best receive and appreciate it, your expression will be a sweet, loving message from heart to heart.

LOVING PROMISES

Expressing love is more than just a sweet message. It is an integral part of loving relationship. Expressing your love to your partner greatly enhances your experience of love. It also greatly enhances your partner's experience of love. It brings the feelings in your heart from a vague, nebulous place, into the solid here and now, where that love can be seen and felt and tasted by both of you. Expressing love makes everyone's experience of love more real.

If we fail to express our love to our mate, even if we feel it deeply, our love will dwindle. Expressing love is essential for love to stay alive. "She knows I love her. I don't have to say it," is no excuse. Don't assume. Say it! Express it! Everyone wants to hear the words *"I love you"* spoken by the person they love. However, if it's only words, it's not enough. Love needs to be proven by action through kind and generous behavior. Only then will it be a full expression of love.

Expressing love is just that – expressing – bringing out what is inside, a communication of inner feeling. The purpose is not selfish. It is not to make your beloved feel better about you, or to gain points, or to try to manipulate, or obtain something in exchange. Demonstrating love is simply and honestly communicating your loving feelings. However, understand that when you desire to receive expressions of love, some people, like my dad, may have limited techniques for articulating their feelings. If your partner is one of those people, you should have forbearance and understand that your beloved may be incapable of expressing or receiving love in ways you desire. If love is present, it cannot help but be expressed. The expression may be subtle though, and you may be required to search hard in order to find it. It might serve you to become an expert at deciphering when and how love is given in more obscure ways by your partner – like dog kisses.

There are two moments when the expression of love is especially called for – leave-taking and re-uniting. These are moments where it is important to stop, feel and make contact. It could be just an hour or so absence, but when Alice and I come back to each other's presence, we are happy to see each other and express our greeting with a big smile and a hug and kiss. There is the same loving acknowledgment when one of us departs. How anticlimactic it it would be to come home from work, grunt "Hi" and immediately rifle through the mail, or to be greeted with "You're late" as you come through the front door.

The prerequisite for expressing love for your partner is feeling that love. You can bring out your loving feelings through a process similar to the one described in Promise #3. This time, instead of receiving your partner through your heart, radiate love to them *from* your heart. Imagine as if love energy is flowing from the center of your chest to your beloved. Maybe even visualize that energy as light and see it connecting you with your partner. This also works well if you feel love radiating from your eyes when you are looking at your partner. You can also hold your hand on your partner's heart and feel love streaming from your hand to their heart, or more directly, from your heart, through your hand, to their heart.

Sometimes I feel a craving for Alice, like a hungry person craves food. And sometimes when I'm with her, I feel so full of love that I can burst. Feeling that love and yearning makes me vulnerable and strong at the same time. I'm vulnerable because I am defenseless against that yearning, and I am strong because my love for her is true and unadulterated and flows unhindered, spontaneously, from a deep place inside me.

Love like that must find expression. What better way to start off a day than with a love fest. Every morning when we awaken, Alice and I cover each other's face and hands and shoulders and neck in joyful, appreciative kisses. A hearty breakfast of morning kisses sets the course for our day.

An evening candlelit dinner in a private booth in a charming French restaurant is a romantic way to say "I love you;" however, you don't have to wait for the perfect time or the perfect place to declare your love. Any time is the perfect time. Any place is the perfect place. Don't wait till you have the perfect words. The words in your heart are the perfect words. Don't put it off. Do it now. And do it again and again. You never know what your next moment will bring. Speak, write a letter, send an email. Don't wait for a serious illness or death before you tell your partner how important they are to you. Too many times a person who I cared for died or left, and I never took the opportunity to say "I love you."

If you are unclear as to how to express your love for your partner, here is a question to contemplate. "How can I let you know that you are completely loved?" This is not something you would ask of your partner. It is something you discover on your own. It has more meaning if you explore the question yourself and delve for your own answer rather than receive one from your mate. When you find your answers to this question, you will have found a key to your partner's heart. In order to use the key and open their heart, take action based on what you have discovered. Do what it takes so they will know without a shadow of a doubt that they are loved.

As I noted before, there is no one proper way to express your love to your partner. However, there is a complete, all-inclusive way to communicate love, one that will be forever welcomed by every partner. That way is to embody the Loving Promises. The Loving Promises are a clear, authentic, comprehensive communication of love.

(At this very moment, just as I wrote these words, I glanced out the window at the rosebush in the garden and noticed a pink rose, the first of the season. I'm putting my pen down now, to get the shears so Alice will have a flower on her bathroom sink when she gets home.)

16. **I WILL BE FORGIVING OF YOU**. *Holding on to ill will hurts both you and me. I will look upon you with compassion and strive to let go of my anger, blame and judgments when I feel you have wronged me. I will never engage in any form of retaliation.*

Alice and I do not hold any unresolved issues from the past against each other, no unexpressed anger, no resentments, no withheld considerations of unfairness – absolutely none. If those thoughts and feelings arise, we deal with them right away. If one of us has been hurt by the other, we acknowledge the hurt, deal with the issue, then forgive and move on. Even better than having to forgive or ask for forgiveness, Alice and I put our effort into always behaving lovingly with each other. When we do so, there is no need for forgiveness because nobody has done anything wrong to be forgiven. We remain clean and light about each other.

Forgiveness is relinquishing demands about how the past should have been. It is letting go of insistence about the way another person should have felt, spoken or behaved. It is releasing your anger, resentment and righteousness, and relinquishing the desire to punish or gain compensation for your pain. The events that triggered the pain occurred in the past. The past cannot be undone. However, you are experiencing your anger and frustration in the present. Through releasing painful memories from yesterday, you are able to live more lightly today.

Forgiving another person who has hurt you is an act of kindness toward them. It helps release them from guilt over their misdeeds and unbinds them from obligation. It restores balance and equanimity. It helps them be around you without shame. Forgiveness is also an act of kindness towards yourself. It releases *you*, because holding on to festering anger and resentment is a painful, self-imposed prison. The heart shuts down and the hurt and anger are walled up inside where they fester because they cannot be freed.

If we have been demeaned, frustrated, let down, hurt or treated unfairly by our partner or anyone, it is an instinctive emotional response to want to strike back, to retaliate. This is especially true if we perceive the offense to be deliberate. We want to give them a taste of their own medicine. We want them to realize "Now you know how it feels. How do you like it?" The Old Testament even recommends "an eye for an eye, a tooth for a tooth." However, this leaves both parties blind and toothless. The Buddha drew a beautiful analogy about holding on to judgment and anger and doing what you can to try to get even. He said it is like reaching into a fire and grabbing a glowing ember to hurl at the person who has offended you. You burn yourself.

Retaliation is usually more than a simple unconscious response to being hurt. It contains elements of manipulation. If you know I will seek revenge if you mistreat me, you will be afraid and be reluctant to repeat that hurtful behavior. While the threat of punishment and retaliation can be an effective (though brutal) technique for enforcing obedience, it introduces an element of fear, and fear is a major barrier to love and intimacy.

Retaliation is essentially a declaration of war. If it doesn't result in capitulation, is almost certain to invite escalation. So while you may feel justified to inflict discomfort on your partner in order to "get even," you cannot do so without violating the Loving Promises. You should not attempt to even exact revenge covertly, such as by undermining them behind their back. Passive aggression is still aggression, and the intention is the same—to hurt. Retaliation must be removed from your behavioral armory. The joy of getting even is not worth the disruption of love.

Should we "turn the other cheek" instead? Ignoring another's offense is risky because it might invite further mistreatment. Instead of a *passive* response, like ignoring or turning the other cheek, or an *aggressive* response, like accusation or retaliation, a viable alternative is an *assertive* response. This is where you directly address the person and confront their offending behavior. If you feel wounded by your partner, what is required is a vocal "ouch," followed by an earnest discussion of the behaviors that have caused you pain, airing of your genuine feelings in response to those behaviors, and firm demands to cease, if they have not done so already. Sometimes an apology, amends or restitution by the offender is required in order for forgiveness to be complete. This is as much for the benefit of the person who is the cause of the pain as it is for the one who was hurt. It allows them to air their remorse and bring things back to balance. Once you have been heard and understood, and your concerns heeded . . . then, forgiveness.

There are lots of things we tell ourselves in order to avoid forgiving. "I am the right one. I am the injured party. I am the one who has suffered through your actions. It is only fair that you should suffer for what you have done to me. You haven't even admitted your part in it. Why should I forgive first?" We tell ourselves these things and feel the pain of the Buddha's "glowing embers" – our anger, our judgments, and our righteousness.

LOVING PROMISES

These arguments against forgiving come from our mind that clings to the past, to a time which is gone and cannot be changed. Forgiveness comes from our heart that looks to the present. How do we open our heart and release our burden? I think it helps to view the harmful behavior of another with a larger perspective and with compassionate eyes. The person who has hurt you is, as you are, and as we all are, a flawed, wounded human being. When people you care for hurt you, most often they are acting out of their own pain and ignorance. So much of people's belief and behavior are "knee jerk" reactions. They are not thought out. They may be inherited responses, passed down from parent to child, adopted as a youngster from friends and classmates, or picked up from the cultural norms or the media. These patterns are so ingrained that a person is not able to see or understand their own process. Are we to heap blame on one who is so blind?

Take an extreme example. Say, for instance, you are a victim of a home invasion robbery. A man broke into your house at night, brandished a gun, stole from you, terrorized you, terrorized your family. It may be of some help to understand that this was not a man who did this, but a wounded boy within the man. Let's assume this was a boy whose father abandoned the family when he was a toddler, whose mother was a drug addict who turned to prostitution to support her habit and her family. This was a boy who grew up in a dangerous neighborhood, who sought protection by joining a gang, whose only solace is drugs for which he now needs money. Imagine yourself in his place. Would you think differently, act differently? Would seeing the pain and ignorance in his life and knowing the difficult circumstances in which he lives allow you some measure of compassion, some understanding of his actions, some place in your heart where you might forgive?

To see the causes of another's hurtful actions can bring on compassion and make it easier for you to forgive. It does not, however, excuse their actions, and it does not allow them permission to keep on hurting you. Transgressions that go unpunished will tend to be repeated. Evil is real and dangerous, and judgment, punishment, incarceration, and maybe even a death sentence for heinous acts is necessary. But compassion and forgiveness remove some of the sting of anger and the voracious hunger for retribution. That anger and hunger is *your* pain.

Forgiving is not complete without forgetting—putting the incident or situation out of mind so you don't keep chewing on it. Forgetting wipes the slate clean. Forgetting is the only circumstance where having a bad memory is an asset. Without forgetting, we still hold on to remnants of anger and blame. Drop the blame, let go of ill feelings if you can. Wipe the memory from your conscious mind, but don't be stupid. Don't close your eyes to the possibility that you can be harmed again. Protect yourself and avoid persons and situations where you are exposed to harmful influences. Don't swim in shark infested waters.

Forgiving begins from the inside. It is more than just words. The words are the easy part. Letting go is hard. There is no blame if you are not willing or ready to forgive. If you are not ready, you are not ready. Mouthing the words when you don't feel them would be a lie. If you are still feeling the sting of hurt and the heat of anger, don't be too quick to forgive. Don't cut off your true feelings. If you are angry at the person who hurt you, you deserve to have your anger and they deserve to have your anger too. But don't carry it around too long. Anger internalized can eat you up inside and cause physical and psychological harm. So, if you really feel you are ready to forgive, don't wait. Do it now. But if you are not truly ready, don't do it. If you rush the process, you are being unkind to yourself.

Forgiving when someone close to you has hurt you is not instantaneous. It is a process that can take a long time. Once a loved one has been unkind or hurtful to you, the residue of caution and distrust you hold in your mind can remain for years. Though it may recede from your consciousness, it may never go away.

Is it possible that your partner has done something so drastic, so hurtful, so unforgivable as to create damage and pain which is beyond forgiving? I suppose that is possible. But I know that it is rarely impossible to put the past behind you, attempt to clear the air and perhaps begin anew. Believing this to be true can be enough to open a dialogue. If both partners feel the relationship still has value and is to endure, opening to forgiveness must occur.

Forgiveness is not just for others. We, too, need the soothing balm of forgiveness. We too are in need of being forgiven. The Lord's Prayer says it clearly. "Forgive us our trespasses, as we forgive those who trespass against us." We have all failed, hurt others and ourselves, done things we were ashamed of. This recognition of our own human frailty is the beginning of being able to forgive others. The willingness to forgive ourselves and openness to be forgiven makes the task of forgiving others easier. Forgiving others starts with turning our compassion inward and forgiving ourselves.

Healing energy is released by forgiveness in all its forms – forgiving others, forgiving yourself, being forgiven by others. Forgiveness has no time limit. Unresolved feelings from being hurt or hurting others can last a lifetime. Even now, feeling incomplete, I have spent hours recently trying to track down several women that I had treated badly, some from relationships forty and fifty years ago. (Ladies, if you are reading this, I'm sorry. Please forgive me. You deserved better from me.)

I recently felt the liberating effects of being forgiven. Years ago, when a previous wife and I divorced, I was in control of our finances. I forced on her what I thought was an equitable settlement, 50/50. She did not think it was fair, but I persisted. The amount of our assets was too paltry to adjudicate. So we went our own ways, she feeling cheated and I feeling righteous, but stingy, both of us with the unresolved issue an undigested rock in our respective guts. Though we reconnected and began corresponding again after a decade of silence, the rock remained, still undigested, still not talked about. Then, not long ago, I received an email from her. She recounted all the support, financial and otherwise, that I had provided her throughout our marriage, and she thanked me for my generosity with her. Those few words were a powerful emotional release for me. Unknown to me, I needed her forgiveness. I received it and, with a feeling of relief, was able to dissolve an invisible barrier between us, complete an unfinished chapter and move on.

Though forgiveness is a good thing, it may contain booby traps. Our extending forgiveness can sometimes contain the flavor of ego and superiority and righteousness. Maybe there is even an effort to avoid responsibility for our part. We all have the natural tendency to look for fault outside ourselves. "I, who am right and blameless, deign to bestow my forgiveness upon you, the culprit." With this attitude there is no room for personal responsibility. Rarely is there an issue where the fault is so totally one sided. We need to remain aware of that and remember that relationship is a dance that requires two partners.

We have a choice; we can use another person's bad intention or bad behavior as an excuse that we give ourselves to find fault, shut down, reject or become defensive, or we can use it as an opportunity to open and practice love and forgiveness.

There are many different ways of attributing fault, but only one way of extending forgiveness—do it. We could blame the person. "You did a hurtful thing and your intentions were wrong—and I forgive you." We could blame the act. "It was a hurtful thing you did—and I forgive you." We could take on the blame ourselves. "You did a hurtful thing, but I contributed to your error—and I forgive you." We could minimize the act. "You did a hurtful thing, but we're all human—and I forgive you." However we do it, the main thing is to let go of our hurt feelings and forgive. Forgive as one sincere and respectful person to another. Forgiveness releases us as it releases them.

17. I WILL BE DEPENDABLE WITH YOU. *I will try to the best of my ability to identify and accomplish the things that need to be done for our mutual well-*

being. I will attempt to always follow through with what I say I will do. I will perform my tasks with care.

Being dependable is the willingness to be depended upon. It is assuming responsibility for what needs to be done. It is saying what you will do and doing what you say.

Alice and I have certain responsibilities for maintaining our lives. Some of mine include picking up after myself, taking out garbage, helping prepare food, doing the majority of the dishwashing, pot scrubbing and clean up, overseeing maintenance of house and auto, cleaning the mess after the cat has slaughtered some small animal and (as a convenience for Alice) always leaving the toilet seat down.

Who does which tasks for maintaining home and hearth has evolved naturally for us. We do what we are best physically suited for (I do the heavy lifting and reaching for objects on the higher shelves), what we are skilled at (Alice is a good cook), what we enjoy (Alice loves to arrange flowers and work in the garden), what circumstances force us to do (I'm "the man" so I get to clean up the cat's mess, fix things and kill bugs). The responsibilities we take on are pretty evenly divided so we don't feel either of us is doing too much or too little. We're flexible. If one of us is not feeling well or doesn't feel like doing their usual task, the other will step in and take over. These arrangements we've made seem even-handed and have worked well for us over the years.

These chores we do to help each other, even the minor ones, are important and not to be minimized. They indicate that I am a full partner and helpmate to Alice. In doing them, I show that I respect our living space, care about her wishes and want to please her. If I stopped doing these things, or kept "forgetting", or kept putting them off or kept doing them half-assed, I would be sending a different message to her, a message I don't want to send – that I don't respect her wishes or care about our living space. It would also send a larger message. "What you want doesn't matter," and an even more encompassing message, "I don't care about your feelings." I do what needs to be done. I want my message to be, "I am dependable, I care. You can count on me, I love you."

Aside from taking care of necessary business, the result of my being dependable is that Alice knows that she's in good hands. She knows she is safe and taken care of. She knows she can trust me and that her wishes are being taken seriously. This is comforting to her and feels right and good to me. Alice trusts me. Her trust in me didn't appear out of thin air. I earned it. I earned it by demonstrating trustworthiness.

LOVING PROMISES

When I act responsibly, I feel potent, I feel strong, I feel productive, I feel good about myself. When I act in an undependable manner, I lose potency. Every time I tell Alice I will do something and then don't do it, or do it half assed, or put it off till the last moment, I lose credibility in her eyes. What's worse, if I tell myself I will do something and then don't do it, I lose credibility in my own eyes. My integrity is at stake as well as my sense of potency.

Of course, there will be times where there are extenuating circumstances that make it impossible for you to achieve your stated goal, no matter what effort you apply. When you are late because you were stuck in traffic caused by an accident that closed the road, when a coworker you depended on drops the ball at the last minute, or when the dog ate your homework, there's not much else to do but throw up your hands in exasperation. However, these kinds of circumstances are rare. More often though, when something that needs doing doesn't get done, it's a choice, a choice to neglect.

In prior relationships, I was able to avoid domestic chores by claiming that I had a disability. I was afflicted with CD, (Cleaning Disabled), meaning I would purposely do such an incompetent job that my mate would give up on me and do it herself. Alice would have none of it. She understood that my CD was just a ploy to get out of doing what I didn't want to do. My "disability" has cleared up quite a bit now. When I do a competent job, I still have a bit of the "Look mommy, see what a good boy I am" mindset with Alice.

I've noticed that when I'm confronted with something that needs doing that I don't want to do, I sometimes hear my father's voice in my head, "You must do this, you cannot do that." Sometimes I hear dad's voice in Alice's demands, especially if she is abrupt or pushes hard as she is sometimes known to do. My Peter Pan persona rebels because I feel I am losing my freedom, "I don't want to be responsible. I don't want to be told what to do. I want to play, be creative, spontaneous. I don't want to grow up." And that is just the point. To be a mature adult requires that when something needs to be done, I take responsibility, confront what needs doing, suck up my feelings . . . and simply do it.

The Promise asks of you more than to just "simply do it." It asks you to do your tasks with care. When I was living in an ashram, one of my jobs was the kitchen cleanup detail. This was quite an intense task as we were sometimes feeding hundreds of people daily. We were told, "when you clean, clean with consciousness, thoroughness and love, as if the pots and pans you are scrubbing are for the personal use of our beloved teacher." With that in mind, I would scour each pot shiny clean, each plate spotless. In the same way, my intention is to do what chores need to be done as if I am serving the Queen. Alice is my queen.

I am dependable because I love and respect Alice and I love our home and our life together. I love myself and I love my life. My dependability is an expression of that love. I do what needs to be done as an offering to love.

18. I WILL BE TRUTHFUL WITH YOU. *I will not tell you anything I know to be false, nor will I omit telling you what I know to be true. I will not bend the truth in order to gain advantage, protect myself, or keep peace.*

As children, we learned that lying can be useful. We learned that if we did something that our caretaker didn't like, they would react with anger and punish us. So if we denied guilt, we might be able to escape the rod. Dishonesty may have saved our skin when we were kids, but it is destructive in adult relationships.

Here, in a nutshell, is what I know to be true about lying or withholding truth in relationship.

- Trust is the cornerstone of a relationship. A lie is an attempt to deceive. It is a severe breach of trust.
- Call it a fib, a yarn, a white lie, exaggeration, rationalization, stretching the truth – all are an effort to deceive and a breach of trust.
- Lying is habit forming. Each lie requires additional lies in order to cover it up.
- Lies always take their toll on the liar, the person lied to, and the relationship. Big lies take a big toll, little white lies take a lesser toll, but all lies, large or small, have their effect.
- If a partner is caught in a lie, it could take years for the relationship to heal.
- Healing is never complete because a lie which is exposed is never completely forgotten by the person lied to.
- A lie, unexposed, even if the partner never finds out, creates a festering separation within the couple.
- The only way to heal the fallout from a lie is to tell the truth and accept the consequences

People lie mainly for two reasons: fear or greed. They lie because they are afraid that someone will find out about who they really are or about something they have done that is harmful and of which they are ashamed. Or, they lie in order to obtain something – some gain, or some advantage. When you make a commitment to not lie, you are making a commitment to confront your fear and/or your greed. This is not a minor thing. By pledging truthfulness, you touch the very foundation of your integrity.

Honesty is the simple, direct path. It leads to calm and inner purity. Honesty is standing up and speaking your truth, even when you are vulnerable and afraid. It takes real courage and inner power to choose the truth when lying would be so much easier and seemingly less messy. The result of that courageous, honest choice is a sense of inner strength. The result of choosing dishonesty is that you propagate suspicion, disharmony and complication. When you lie, you must be ever vigilant to make sure the lie remains undiscovered. If others sense your lie, you must now cover up with additional lies. You can easily lose track and be caught in the complicated web of your dishonesty. Lying to your partner makes you feel dirty and leads to a furtive sense of inner weakness.

Dishonesty builds upon itself as lies, withheld feelings, and unexpressed grievances accumulate. It becomes more and more difficult to be truthful the longer the truth is withheld. Like water accumulating behind a dam, pressure builds and there is fear that the dam will break and the lies will pour out and be revealed. Even the revelation of only one lie brings on the suspicion that there are more lies which remain unrevealed...maybe a lot more. So we reinforce the dam with more lies. Your partner can sense that things are not right, and this creates distance and a whole raft of negative consequences such as distrust, withdrawal, arguments, loss of sexual passion. The way out of this dilemma Is simple – tell the truth.

The truth is potent. When we speak our deepest truth, something very powerful happens – our hearts crack open and two people who were conversing in superficialities suddenly drop into the depths of honest feelings. Truth is electric. Truth telling is contagious.

There is a major prerequisite for honesty in relationship--the ability and intention to be honest with yourself. This requires that you be able to look directly into your heart and mind without judgment or defensiveness and be willing to receive authentic truth. What is true, what is right is not a mystery. It is there for you to hear. It exists in your mind as a voice. If you listen with awareness you will hear that voice, even if you do not like what it is saying. Only when you hear that inner voice can you begin to see clearly and be mindful about what is true and what is false. And then, with that clarity, you will be more able to take in the truth about yourself from others and communicate your truth to them.

I remember a moment, years ago, when hearing the naked truth was transformative for me. I was with my friend Lisa in a rowboat in the middle of a

UNDERSTANDING THE LOVING PROMISES

lake. In the course of our conversation, she made the observation that I was a fearful person. She said it in passing, without judgment, just stating it as fact. Her words slammed me in the belly. Of course that was true. All my life I had been fearful of many people and situations, but I had hidden it from others and from myself. I had never defined it as fear. Fortunately, at that moment, I was ripe to hear it. From that point on, I was able to see my responses to what I perceived as threatening people and situations for what they were – fear. Simply by understanding and naming my responses as fear, my anxiety in those situations began to dissipate. I am grateful to Lisa for her willingness to be so honest and straightforward with me.

The injunction to always be honest, to be real, to not hold things back, is an ideal. The reality is that sometimes telling the raw truth is hurtful, or premature, or unkind. Truth spoken at the wrong time or delivered in the wrong way is not truth. It is aggression. Therefore, it is important to use discrimination and avoid blurting out what you believe to be true, or else your honesty will cause unnecessary pain or shut down communication. I am not advocating lying. I am suggesting you modify your truth in ways your partner can hear. Postpone speaking until your partner is receptive. Delay hard truths until you are feeling clear and harmless. Withhold truth if it would cause needless suffering. If I was forced to make a choice between being honest and being loving, I wouldn't hesitate. I would choose loving.

While it is important to be sensitive to those with whom you are speaking, it is possible to be too careful, too "nice," so much so that, in the guise of protecting the other person, you avoid telling the real truth or the whole truth. That "carefulness" may be an avoidance of mutual authenticity. It can be an excuse for sidestepping an uncomfortable confrontation or avoiding depth by keeping the relationship on a superficial level. That's not being nice. That's being fearful.

Don't confuse honesty with reality. It is important to keep in mind that being honest doesn't necessarily mean that you are correct. You can tell your truth and still be totally mistaken. Your truth is simply that – *your* truth--what you think, perceive or believe. I would add, your truth is what you believe *at the time*. It should be remembered that "truth" may be fleeting, and what we considered absolute truth one minute may be replaced by a different truth a half hour later. If you understand that, you can be more open to discover other people's truths. And you might be less inclined to spread your "truth" to others, especially those who might be hurt by your perceived honesty.

An essential element in truth telling is confidentiality. In order to feel safe, partners must know that what they reveal about themselves will be kept in strict confidence if that is their wish. Only then will they feel free to speak truths that might expose vulnerabilities that could be used against them or that could prove embarrassing if known by others. The issue of confidentiality is covered in Promise #22.

19. I WILL BE TRANSPARENT WITH YOU. *I will allow you to know the real me. I will not attempt to protect myself by maintaining a false facade and by withholding my true feelings, thoughts and motives from you – especially when I feel vulnerable.*

I am moved by the image of the sculpture of Jesus in our garden. He stands, one hand drawing back the edge of his garment, the other pointing to the exposed heart beating in his chest --the picture of love, the picture vulnerability, the picture of transparency. It was Christ who spoke about entering the Kingdom of Heaven as little children. I believe that in order to dwell into the kingdom of Love, we must also enter as innocent children--open, defenseless and transparent.

Transparency means you are being "seen through," nothing hidden. To be truthful, transparent and non-manipulative (Loving Promises numbers 18, 19, 21) with your partner requires that you reveal yourself to them. You stand vulnerable before them without trying to control the image you project in order to look good. You show up simply and honestly as you are. You don't have to speak or act sweet, you don't need to fulfill the other person's expectation of you, and you don't need to expend the energy to constantly maintain a false image.

Without being "seen through" there is no real connection. A true criterion that is a measure of the depth of your relationship is how open you are, how transparent, how undefended, how willing to *feel* and share yourself by giving voice to your feelings.

It is normal and proper at the onset of a relationship to withhold parts of yourself until you feel comfortable and trusting of your new partner. But to keep withholding is asking for trouble. Over time, as your relationship deepens and becomes more important to you, superficiality is unsatisfying. You want more depth.

Self-revelation is a growth process, a willingness to be known that takes place over a lifetime. When two people first meet, they are blank tablets, two unknowns. Gradually, stories are told, memories recounted, thoughts revealed. A picture of the other is constructed in each person's mind. Transparency is about the accuracy and completeness of that picture – what is included, what is held back. When a person is willing to let their partner see the whole unedited picture, the fears, desires, failures, innocence, only then is it possible for them to fully relax and be themselves. Few people are willing to go so far. Most reach a point where fear takes over and they shut the door.

It's a paradox. Being known is both terrifying and a relief. We yearn to be known and loved for who we really are, yet we are petrified by the thought that people would know us. Deep down, many of us have the fear, "If you really knew me you wouldn't love me, you might even leave me." "If I showed you who I truly am, you would hurt me or take advantage of me." So we hide our true selves, either by creating a false mask, or avoiding revealing ourselves by speaking about ourselves in terms of impersonal facts and cliché. In so doing, we can never truly be loved. If someone loves us, they can only love the superficial mask we have shown them, never the real person behind the mask. This effort to seduce others with a false presentation of self is a prescription for isolation and loneliness.

Transparency requires courage, trust and strength. *Courage* to be yourself, reveal your secrets and open yourself despite the possibility that you might be judged, or hurt, or that someone may take unfair advantage of you. *Trust* that your partner would be kind, and fair, and trustworthy, and will appreciate you for who you are. *Strength* in knowing that you have the ability to handle yourself if you are judged, not appreciated, or hurt, or if someone attempts to take advantage of you.

In many people's minds transparency is equated with vulnerability. Vulnerability is seen as being weak and helpless. Vulnerability is not weakness. Vulnerability can be strength. It takes strength to open yourself, take down your guard, remove your mask and be exposed to your partner. It takes strength to drop the carefully crafted persona and reveal painful and humiliating feelings of helplessness, guilt and low self-esteem. It is weakness to maintain your mask and hide your vulnerability. And it's sad and lonely to pass through life without ever being really known by anybody.

When you appreciate and accept yourself, it is easy to be transparent. You have little preventing you from opening up to others and sharing who you are. It becomes a lot more difficult if you judge yourself and reject parts of yourself. In order to become more transparent, you must consciously feel those parts of yourself you don't accept, the parts you would be horrified if others knew, the parts you don't even want to know. With all our insecurities, pettiness, kinky sexual fantasies, letting others into our unedited inner world is not an easy thing to do. Shame can hold us in a powerful grip. At all costs, we hide those things we are ashamed of from others, especially our partner, and sometimes even from ourselves.

LOVING PROMISES

It has been one of my difficulties to feel comfortable enough to fully reveal my neediness and vulnerability in my relationship with Alice. It is as if I expect that I should be strong, smart and invulnerable at all times, in every situation. These are traces of old habits of mind that have been with me since adolescence. Those times that I need help and comfort are the times when I find it most difficult to ask. I know Alice will respond to my need. She always has and always will, but my old mental habits are persistent. Fear of being weak, ridiculed, taken advantage of, put down, keeps me reluctant to speak out. These fears keep me isolated and erect a self-created barrier in our relationship. It is self-created because these are my thoughts, not Alice's. I know it is true that these thoughts originate in my own mind, but it is difficult for me to break away from the "If you knew the underlying *real me,* you wouldn't like me" mentality. I believe Alice has an inflated picture of who I am, and I like that. I like looking good in her eyes and I am reluctant to deflate that image. So, at times, I still hide my mistakes, weaknesses and stupidities from her. (In reviewing this last paragraph, Alice commented, "I already knew you are "stupid" so forget about the mental bullshit. I know the underlying person that you are is a magnificent human specimen and there's nothing you can say or do that will make me change my mind.")

My fears keep me from being completely transparent; yet, despite my efforts to play down my defects, Alice knows me. She knows me better than anyone else, sometimes more than I know myself. She sees the good, the bad and the ugly and still she loves me. It is mind boggling for me to be seen so clearly by someone and still be loved and admired. I cannot describe how much safer that makes me feel. This is the power of transparency.

When it comes to showing loving enthusiasm for Alice, I have absolutely no reticence. I'm as transparent as a piece of glass with my adoration of her and couldn't hide it if I wanted to. I feel like a puppy greeting its master when we see each other after even a few hours of absence. The great blues legend, John Lee Hooker, described the feeling beautifully in his song "Puppy Dog."

I want to be your puppy dog, babe.
When you pop your fingers, I'll come runnin'.
If you whistle, I'll come to you.

No manipulating, no maintaining a macho, "cool" image – just pure, transparent enthusiasm. What makes it easier to be an enthusiastic puppy with Alice is that she is a puppy with me.

UNDERSTANDING THE LOVING PROMISES

To be transparent doesn't mean that you have to blab anything and everything that pops into your mind. Imagine if the entirety of your interior life, your innermost embarrassing petty thoughts, judgments, narcissism, lies and schemes, were to be broadcast to everyone you meet. People at the office, at the bus stop, in the elevator, would be treated to the crazy, disordered but totally honest movie of your mind. In order to function, we must have private space. Parts of us must remain unknown to the world.

Some people are naturally more open and expressive about themselves; others are more reserved and refrain from revealing their thoughts and feelings. There is no fault in this. It's just a difference in style. Where a person can run into problems is when they consistently withhold expressing their thoughts and feelings of shame, weakness, fear and confusion to their partner out of fear of being harshly judged by them, put down, or of losing them. Withholding yourself out of fear sets up a secret life where part of you is in hiding from your partner. Enough of these secret lives, and only a fraction of your real self will be available in your relationship.

There are times though, when transparency is not called for and it is beneficial to exercise caution. When there has been harm or threat of harm, such as a partner's breach of trust, it is probably good to retreat for a bit and gather a protective shell around yourself in order to marshal your resources and heal. Once the threat has passed, that shell, originally worthwhile, can become hard and impermeable. Though it is true that while the shell insulates you from further hurt, it can also numb you and rob you of vitality and spontaneity. It keeps you encapsulated. Maintained too long, the shell becomes hard and thick and you are not free to be yourself. You cannot allow others to know you. You cannot be transparent.

The shell is created and sustained by fear. To crack the shell requires you to address that fear. The vow to be transparent (and honest and non-manipulative) is a commitment to confront fear and be undefended. Your non-defensiveness is a catalyst, an invitation that can bring out the same in your partner. When you lay down your defenses, there is no need for your partner to maintain theirs against you. Your self-disclosure makes you safe with your partner. When you are safe, they can feel freer to trust you with their secret life. That feeling of safety cannot be rushed. They feel safe when they feel safe, as do you. It is frightening to let go. For you both to lay down your defenses requires an act of trust. If done prematurely, you can be overwhelmed by anxiety.

Transparency is a gateway to love. I have seen this countless times in group therapy sessions. A participant would open up and expose a vulnerable, real part of themselves. Invariably, that opening to truth would induce other members hearts to open and they would feel a connection with that person they had never experienced before. The intimate connection would not dissipate. It would grow stronger and diffuse to the entire group, leading to a whole new level of shared intimacy. It is the same with a couple as with the group. As you open up and share your true self with your partner, there's more of you available to love. Your partner is touched, their own defenses melt and they can more freely open up to you.

The truth is that we are all human. No matter how strong we appear on the surface, we are all dealing with essentially the same issues of fear, weakness and vulnerability. When we take the risk and share our struggles, we share our humanity. We are most lovable when we reveal our raw, naked humanity, not when we pretend to be someone we are not.

Transparency with others begins by being transparent with yourself. The following questions will help you examine some of the things you might withhold from your partner. Read each question and answer honestly to yourself. It would be helpful to list your answers and write them down. You might be surprised at some of your responses.

- What feelings do I have that I don't want you to know?
- What fantasies do I have that I don't want you to know?
- What thoughts do I have that I don't want you to know?
- What desires do I have that I don't want you to know?
- What failures do I have that I don't want you to know?
- What fears do I have that I don't want you to know?
- What weaknesses do I have that I don't want you to know?
- What things have I done that I should not have done?
- What things have I not done that I should have done?
- Take it farther. For each of your responses, ask, "What do I fear about expressing this to my partner?"

Becoming aware of what you are withholding from your partner is an important step toward being transparent, a first step. As long as you keep your fear and shame a secret, there is little chance for healing. Take the next step and share the things you are afraid to share. Even if you take an initial step and do this with a neutral third party, a witness whose only function is to listen with compassion and non-judgment, your edifice of secrets and lies will begin to dissolve. If there comes a time when you are feeling close and courageous, show what you've written to your loved one. When you are able to share the secrets you are withholding with your beloved one, a fresh ease, quality and simplicity will enter your relationship.

You are in relationship to share your true self with your partner. Being transparent is a gift you give to them. The gift is you.

20. I WILL SPEAK TO YOU WITH CARE. *My words have power for you, so I will take care to honor your feelings and your dignity, not only with what I say to you, but also how and when I say it. I will be especially aware when we are in conflict.*

When we were kids, if someone said an insulting or hurtful thing to us we would retort with the maxim, "Sticks and stones can break my bones but words can never harm me." Well, it's not true. Though they don't leave a visible bruise, uncaring, harsh and belittling words can hurt much more than a slap, and the pain can last far longer. Having lived together for so many years, Alice and I are fairly certain of the effect of our words on each other. I am still surprised, though, at how quickly and intensely the wrong choice of a word or an abrasive tone of voice can rouse us to anger or hurt. Therefore, we are always mindful of how we speak with each other.

Our #1 rule in communicating is to speak to each other with kind intention – respecting each other's feelings, respecting each other's dignity. Clear and effective communication is important, but that is secondary to kindness. You can use all sorts of effective communication techniques, but if your ulterior intention is to hurt, control, put down or subtly manipulate, those potent communication techniques will be used in a negative way and effectively achieve detrimental ends. If your intention is to be kind and respectful, kindness and respect will be communicated. Even harsh or murky communication will be forgiven if there is underlying kindness.

Alice and I are able to break the rules of civil speech and exaggerate, humorously mock or lovingly criticize each other. We can get away with saying things like, "That was a stupid thing you did," or "I hate you. I want a divorce," or "Change your clothes, you dress like a clown." It's just our style of communicating. We are OK with being mocked and criticized because we know that, even if there is a kernel of truth in the criticism, the flow of our love is always there. I wouldn't recommend this communication style to all other couples though. Sometimes we'll play at being angry with each other and jokingly give rude responses to the other's questions. It's kind of fun to occasionally break the monotony of sweetness with a bogus argument. I'm not sure I would recommend that to other couples either.

LOVING PROMISES

Alice can be a bit more sensitive to harsh speech than I, so I have to sometimes monitor what I say. One of the most difficult, yet necessary, things I have had to learn is when to "hold my tongue." At those times when Alice is not in the right mood, or is focused on something else, or not receptive in the moment, I may need to restrain my impulse to speak. It can be hard for me to do this sometimes. I feel cut off, powerless and unassertive if I have to quash my speech around her, but I've learned it is better for both of us if I do. If there are discussions we need to have where Alice might feel sensitive about the subject, I will use special care in my choice of words. To smooth the way, I might preface the conversation by saying things that will let Alice know she is loved and appreciated.

Over the years, I engaged in sarcastic humor that I felt was harmless, but Alice thought was demeaning and did not appreciate it. I picked up this kind of humor from my father, who was an expert. Alice worked to extinguish that behavior by commenting, "Hello Jack" (my father's name) every time I would let go with a sarcastic remark. This served to bring my attention to how often I was sarcastic. She rarely has to remind me now.

There is a rule of thumb I can suggest that has been helpful for me. If you have even the slightest inkling that your verbal response will cause needless upset or hurt, stop and ask yourself, "Will this create distance?" Using this rule has helped avoid unneeded aggravation and countless arguments.

Most people assume that arguments are inherently bad and are the sign of a troubled relationship. This is not necessarily true. An argument is a form of communication. There are destructive fights and productive fights. Destructive fights lack goodwill. The intent is to hurt, control or get even. They often involve blame, sarcasm, name-calling and put-downs. The result is that both partners come away feeling defensive and angry, with the sense that nothing has been resolved.

Arguments can be productive and have a positive outcome. Sometimes an emotional storm is exactly what is needs to happen if feelings are bottled up or you are being too careful, too "nice." An uncontrolled outburst can reveal your true, unvarnished feeling and get to the center of truth long before hours of cool and cautious "processing." Lose your cool, fume and yell and argue if you must, but one caution – keep love in your heart. Don't dam the flow of love, even for a second. Remember, the harsh words of an intense argument can lose their sting if infused with love.

I will never forget an argument Alice and I had years ago. We were in our parked car, nose-to-nose, furious and screaming at each other at the top of our lungs. In the middle of the ruckus, we both looked down and at the same time became aware that we were holding hands. Even in the midst of an argument, we instinctively maintained our connection. The realization of the importance of our loving connection trumped our disagreement. We broke into laughter. That was the end of the argument and the beginning of a productive discussion.

Even the best communication at the wrong time can be bad communication. There are times to push, times to remain at rest, and times to retreat. Knowing what to do requires sensitivity to yourself and to your partner. It is especially important for me to monitor my state of mind before Alice and I are to speak about emotionally touchy subjects, or if I am emotionally wrought. At those times it is best for me to look inside, "Am I feeling angry, hostile, fearful, upset?" It's not that we should always wait until we are calm and centered before we speak, but if we are not conscious of our mental state, we can sometimes muddle into an emotional storm and wonder why our ship has foundered and sunk.

One common trap a couple can fall into that can precipitate an argument or lead to a misunderstanding is to assume telepathic communication. Most people are not mind readers. Don't assume you know how your partner feels or take for granted that they know how you feel. It is important to check things out. Ask. Clarify. Sometimes a simple question or two can avoid a big mess.

Our familiarity with each other doesn't exclude Alice and I from the use of proper etiquette. The words, "Please," "May I," "Thank you," "You're welcome" are still an important part of our vocabulary. Using them is a way we demonstrate how much we value and respect each other. Making a request without a "please" before or after it will sound bossy. "Clean up the mess you made and take out the garbage," sounds parental, controlling and demeaning. Receiving a gift or help from your partner without a "Thank you," sends a message that you do not appreciate what they have done for you.

The Golden Rule of "couple-speak" is "Speak to each other in the manner in which we would like to have others speak to us." Most of the world's communication problems would be solved if everyone would implement this simple rule.

Care-filled speech requires that we receive the other and are sensitive to them. This incorporates the third Promise, to be awake – to be awake to them. When you intently receive the other person and can also share yourself honestly, directly and respectfully, you open the possibility for deep conversation. This is a communion that goes way beyond the words that are spoken. Connecting on this level is heart-to-heart connection, an offering of self and receiving of other. It is healing and uplifting for both of you.

This promise can be shortened to read, "I WILL SPEAK TO YOU" and still be relevant. Alice and I were dining at a restaurant recently. The dominant sounds were the clink of utensils against plates and the low drone of dinner music. The murmur of conversation was absent. At least half of the patrons were on their phones, reading or texting, leaving their dinner companions to stare at the ceiling. And at home it is the same. Few meaningful conversations can be expected to take place by the light of the television screen. There was a recent study that showed couples with kids on average spoke together 35 minutes per week. Per week! That's five minutes a day. How much of that conversation is meaningful and how much consists of, "Please pass the TV channel changer?" Another frightening statistic--It has been estimated that the average child of five years old will spend 40% their waking hours in front of a screen. This will probably increase. Think of the effect this will have on the communication abilities of future generations.

The yoga tradition has a very useful way of evaluating communication between one person and another. These are four tests of right communication called "The Four Gates of Speech". They are posed as questions.

Is it true? – If not, don't say it.
Is it necessary? Is it beneficial? Does it improve on silence? – If not, don't say it.
Is it timely? Can the receiver take it in? – If not, don't say it.
Is it kind? – If it's harmful, don't say it.

If what you have to communicate can pass through these four gates, then it is worth saying. I guess that eliminates idle chatter, gossip and about 90% of everyday conversation. These are strict tests, maybe a bit too "yogic." Chatter and gossip have their place as social connection. What would pass through the four gates though would be guaranteed to be meaningful and kind.

A general practice that would incorporate this Loving Promise is, *"Pay close attention to the words that issue from your mouth. Listen before you speak to make sure that your words are consistent with your highest values."*

21. I WILL NOT MANIPULATE YOU.

I will not exploit your vulnerabilities in order to control you. I will not belittle you, blame you, threaten you, deliberately hurt you with words, or intentionally withhold money, favors, information or affection from you in order to get my way.

The person who loves you most is the one who can be hurt most deeply by you. When someone opens their heart to you, they become vulnerable. They want to please you. They want you to appreciate and approve of them. They are afraid of losing you. Because they are in this vulnerable position, what you say and do can bruise them emotionally. A harsh word, a physical "pulling away," a slight criticism or an angry glance by you can be very painful. This gives you power over them. Manipulation is the abuse of that power. Manipulation is using another's vulnerabilities to your advantage. It is exploiting their weakness, fears, ignorance and insecurity in order to get your way.

I know Alice's weaknesses and vulnerabilities. I know what buttons to press and she knows mine. With a few key words we have the power to induce emotional uproar in each other. We have chosen to lay down our weapons. If either of us begins to manipulate, we just say "no" to ourselves, "no" to the other in order to stop it in its tracks. We have made the choice to meet and connect with our hearts and work out our differences on an even playing field. It cannot work for us any other way.

Manipulation can range from the extreme – physical violence and intimidation, to subtle – things like turning on tears in order to get your partner to feel guilty or sorry for you, or ignoring and withholding affection to punish them or make them want to please you. The list goes on – acting helpless, putting on the charm, inducing jealousy, bartering gifts or sex in order to bribe for something in return or using the "silent treatment" to punish. Even something as subtle as changing a tone of voice or giving "the look" can be a signal to your partner that you disapprove of what they are saying or doing, and they better stop or else there will be uncomfortable consequences.

Manipulation is destructive. It poisons love and leaves a partner feeling unsafe. Love cannot survive in an environment of dishonesty and fear, competition, or tactical maneuvers that are used in order to gain advantage. It poisons love by creating an "I win, you lose" mindset that encourages a selfish atmosphere. It poisons love because it is dehumanizing, it is treating the one you love as if they are an object or an obstacle that stands in your way. It poisons love because it is dishonest, and thus it introduces a lapse of integrity into the relationship.

Manipulating is effective because the manipulator is aware of the subterfuge while the other person is unsuspecting. Because it is an effective technique, manipulation can be addictive. It can grow into a habitual pattern that is self-perpetuating and can eventually become the predominant way a couple relates with each other.

An essential initial step in being able to reduce or eliminate manipulation is to become aware of how and when you manipulate. This could be difficult because manipulation is an accepted aspect of our culture and not necessarily looked down upon. It is probably learned through a lifetime of observation and practice, most likely originating in the family of origin. Because much of manipulation takes place below awareness, you must devote some time and attention to focused self-observation. Then, when you become aware in the moment that you are manipulating, make a committed effort to stop. It all pivots on your awareness of when you are manipulating and your willingness to relinquish the advantage manipulation provides you. A good place to start is to become aware of which manipulations you use most often. (We all use some manipulations to one degree or another.) Below I have compiled a list of common ones.

WITHHOLDING – *Holding back from giving what your partner wants or needs until you exact punishment or get what you want.* Becoming emotionally cold, ignoring, cutting off sex or physical contact, refusing to discuss (silent treatment) or minimizing ("I'm fine; nothing's wrong.")

BRIBERY – *Giving to your partner, but with the unstated expectation on your part that you will be given something you want in return.* Trying to make the other feel guilty or feel as if they owe you something. Giving sex in exchange for favors, or favors in exchange for sex. Giving gifts when you want something from them or when you've done something wrong.

THEATRICS – *Acting, taking on a false persona or attitude in order to get your way.* Turning on the tears to get your partner to feel sorry. Acting helpless to get them to assist you. Acting angry to scare them. Pouring on the charm, inducing jealousy, playing "hard-to-get."

ENLISTING AN ALLY – *Bringing in a third party in order to bolster your position or pressure your partner.* In a conflict, involving another, a "neutral" person, or person in authority (who you know supports you) so your partner will believe that they are wrong and outnumbered.

REASONING – *Justifying your position or actions using intellectual argument to overwhelm and belittle your partner.* Debating, teaching, preaching, disputing, acting like a lawyer. The game is not to seek a fair or honest solution but rather to persuade and pressure your partner with what seems like reasonable arguments.

GUILT OR SHAME INDUCTION – *Doing and saying things that make your partner feel that they are wrong or bad.* When they feel down about themselves, they can be more easily manipulated. Attacking their self-esteem with cutting criticism, calling them demeaning names, continually bringing up their shortcomings, comparing them to someone "better."

HARASSMENT – *Continually doing and saying things that bother your partner so that they eventually will give in to what you want.* Constant pleading, incessant demands, nagging, name-calling, "joking" (not for humor, but to bother), relentless arguing, spite attacks.

THREATS – *Trying to gain leverage by warning your partner about what you will do if you don't get your way.* Threatening to leave, threatening to have an affair or get a divorce, threatening suicide, threatening to withhold money or favors.

Recognizing your favorite manipulations and understanding how poisonous they are to your relationship will help bring you to the point where you can consider giving them up.

The source of manipulation is anxiety, stemming from the feeling of powerlessness, of not being able to control or get what we want. We are aware of some behavior of our partner's that is harmful to them, or more likely, harmful and uncomfortable to ourselves, so we push them in order to conform to our wishes. But the more we push our partner, the more they resist us and the more they resent us. When we use force, they feel judged, coerced, confined. Their freedom is threatened. So we attempt to control surreptitiously in order to circumvent their resistance. By attempting to control our mate, we ourselves are controlled by our fears. When we take responsibility for ourselves and work to fulfill our own needs, while wanting what is best for our partner, offering what we can, and allowing them the freedom to choose what best serves them – only then will they, and you, be free.

True power is not about control and manipulation. It is about the ability to build, restore and maintain love.

22. I WILL PROTECT OUR CONFIDENTIALITY. *I will not share anything about you, me or us that you would not want others to know.*

Confidentiality is refraining from sharing personal or impersonal information with outsiders that might compromise or embarrass your partner or yourself. This is a very important Promise. If you did not respect your partner's need for confidentiality, they would not feel safe to reveal sensitive personal information to you. They would be wary of telling their truth. People have different levels of comfort in revealing to outsiders their personal information and their inner thoughts and feelings. It is important that you become aware of these differences and that they be honored. Respecting a persons need for confidentiality is an essential foundation of trust.

Confidentiality is a vitally important issue with Alice. While she is more protective of what she considers personal information, and is more restrictive about what she tells to whom, my tendency is to be more loose-lipped about my private life and our private lives. Alice is especially sensitive to public criticism. If we are in public and there is a hint of a belittling remark, even jokingly, she feels she has been demeaned. This embarrasses her and drives her crazy. (She also thinks this type of humor is thoughtless and unnecessary.) Since this is so important to her, I must abide by her wishes no matter how I feel. (I have checked out the foregoing paragraph with Alice to make sure it is okay to include.)

In spite of this promise of confidentiality, there are times when it is unavoidable or advantageous to divulge personal information to others regarding your partner and your relationship. You may need to receive support, either in consultation with professionals, or with people with whom you trust who can provide insight. This is not gossip. Gossip is sharing with an outsider and having the intention of tearing someone down, creating an alliance or proving you are right. There is an aroma of enjoyment when gossiping. When sharing personal information, the focus should be about solving problems, not making the other into the bad guy, or portray yourself as the innocent. It is tempting to play the righteous one. Do not tell "family secrets" to others to gain support in the guise of seeking advice from a "neutral source." Probably you are conferring with other people who you know in advance will agree with you and will give you advice which will confirm your bias. (Just what you wanted.).

People's attraction to gossip is almost universal. The desire to give and receive juicy tidbits about what someone said or did is hard to resist. A couple of Rules of Thumb regarding sharing information that your partner may feel is confidential are: *Don't share with others any information about your partner that you would be unwilling to tell them to their face,* and further, *If you have any intuition that your partner would not want this information about them shared, don't do it.*

If you ignore those rules and reveal private information to others about your partner without their knowledge or criticize them in public, it is not innocent, it is an effort to put down, humiliate and control.

Anytime you divulge information that will touch on issues of confidentiality, it should be with the full knowledge and permission of your partner. With that in mind, if someone shares with you issues they have with your mate — complaints, criticisms, etc., it would be best to direct them to speak face-to-face with your partner rather than get involved in a three-way conversation that doesn't involve you and could lead to suspicion of breach of confidentiality

If you truly want to obtain help and support from friends and family regarding a problem you are having with your mate, make this request of them. "Please help me see my part in causing the problem." Be warned though. You may get the answer you need rather than the one you want.

23. I WILL RESPECT OUR INDEPENDENCE. *You are not my possession. I will honor your freedom to think, say and do what seems right to you – even if I do not agree or understand. I trust you can take care of yourself. I will foster my own independence so I can be free and autonomous when necessary.*

We must start with the premise that all individuals are free. Even though we yoke ourselves to another person through our commitment to them, ultimately, we are all independent individuals, free (within society's legal boundaries,) to choose to live our lives as we see fit. The rights our partners have to disagree with us, to come and go as they please, to speak their minds and to act in ways that they perceive as in their best interest are sacred. It is their prerogative to live in accordance with their strongly held values and deepest wishes. This is true, even if it is painful and confusing to us, and even if it is harmful to us.

Though these freedoms are our birthright, they are in effect only if we choose to pursue them. A partner who always agrees and will not stand up and voice their likes and dislikes, who cannot confront when necessary, who reflexively adopts the opinions and lifestyles of their significant other, is not really present in relationship. In a sense, they voluntarily forfeit their claim to independence. They may be easy to get along with, have few demands and present little resistance, but relating to them is like relating to a ghost.

The journey to a magnificent relationship is not only about developing intimacy. While developing a healthy relationship involves learning to overcome separateness, it also involves striving to develop individuality and cultivating the ability to be separate. When you are comfortable in yourself and have established your separate identity, you are then free to lose yourself in another. You can experience that joy of melding in oneness without fear that you will permanently disappear in your partner. And you can easily flow between intimacy and separateness.

LOVING PROMISES

Ideally, a couple should be in balance – not too dependent, not too independent, but interdependent. Too much dependence is when you are fused, you cling to the other person and need them to complete you – two half people trying to become whole. You can lose your sense of self and become absorbed in your partner if you are over dependent. On the other hand, too much independence and you are isolated, you live a separate life with little shared connection. You may allow each other freedom, but that freedom may border on indifference. You are unfettered because you don't really care and you don't want to go deep. You avoid intimacy like the plague because you know how dangerous an open heart—yours and theirs—can be.

Between the extremes of fusion and isolation are the positive qualities of interdependence and autonomy. Healthy, interdependent and autonomous couples are each individual, whole and complete within themselves. They have come together because they want to, not because they need to. They can be comfortable in being apart when they want to be. They have joined because they enjoy each other's company and derive benefit from each other's presence. They can handle their own needs, goals and emotional life. When needed, they can ask for, and accept support. If one partner has needs that are not being fulfilled in the relationship (no partner can fulfill all your needs) the other partner has, within limits, permission to seek fulfillment elsewhere. They can travel alone or with friends if their partner is a stay-at-home type. If they are more social, they have the freedom to go alone to parties, meetings etc.

A couple's relationship is only one aspect of a well-rounded, fulfilling life and it is a mistake to make it their whole life. Social needs are satisfied by family, friends and co-workers. Productive work provides both income and a sense of accomplishment. A gratifying hobby or endeavor that arouses passion, uplifting spiritual pursuits, engaging entertainment – these are all elements that contribute to a full and independent life, yet don't necessitate the involvement an intimate partner. When these elements are in balance in each partner's life, participation with each other is a choice rather than a necessity.

Alice and I have a powerful connection, an inseparable union. We feel we are an integral part of each other, yet we also feel we are separate individuals. Alice has a strong independent streak. While it can be uncomfortable for me at times, I value and admire Alice's capacity to follow her own inner guides. Her willingness to doggedly pursue what she thinks is right, press for what she strongly desires and to confront me when I frustrate her, although distressing for me at times, has provided me a model of positive assertive behavior and has helped train me to be a more humane and considerate companion.

UNDERSTANDING THE LOVING PROMISES

Any discussion of independence must include the topic of possession – seeing your partner as belonging to you. To some people who consider their independence to be a paramount value, freedom from all sense of ownership between partners is considered a virtue. I cannot accept that for myself. While I value Alice's independence, and my own, *we belong to each other*. I cannot help but consider her mine, and I consider myself hers. There is something human and comforting, in a sweet way, about "owning" Alice, and being "owned" by her in turn. We have, in a sense, used our freedom to yoke ourselves to each other, and it feels good. While I don't really own Alice, I have borrowed her for a while. I want Alice to be happy, but if she ran off with the mailman and was blissfully happy, that would not please me. I want her to be happy with *me*. If that means I am possessive, so be it.

There are exceptions to the premise that all people are and should be treated as free and independent. It is an essential precondition that in order to honor a person's independence, it is necessary to trust that they can take care of themselves. In some instances and with some people, that is not possible and, therefore, we have justification in curtailing their independence. Children and some young adults do not have the knowledge and experience to be independent yet and still require our guidance and protection. The mistakes they may make can be injurious to themselves and to others. The same holds for adults who are mentally unstable or temporarily debilitated. They require guidance and control.

This issue is not clear-cut, especially with adults. People learn and grow from their mistakes and we could be overprotective if we attempt to prevent them from making errors. If we are overprotective, we send the message "you are incapable." Conversely, when we allow independence, we send the message "you are capable." To do this requires your trust. You must trust your judgment that the person is capable and *is* deserving of independence. Since outcomes are never known for sure in advance, there is always the element of the unknown, and allowing independence can be a leap of faith.

Allowing your partner the freedom to say and do what they consider right is one aspect of independence. Another aspect, which is very much related, is your own ability to be free and independent from them. If you have strong dependency ties to your partner and have exclusive needs for sustenance, affection and emotional support from them, you will feel panicked by the thought of losing them. It would be exceedingly difficult for you to freely allow them their independence. When they exercise their freedom, you will feel threatened. That panic will drive you to try to control them. In my work with men who batter their spouses and girlfriends, I found many of these men to be extremely emotionally dependent on their partners. They were also dependent on them for daily functions like cooking and cleaning. Their dependency made them vulnerable and they tried to control their anxiety by dominating their partner through threats, intimidation and physical abuse.

In order to allow your partner to be independent, YOU must be independent. An important aspect of your work, then, is to accomplish your own independence. The most durable relationships are those where each individual doesn't *need* to be with the other . . . but *wants* to be with them.

In past relationships, I felt threatened by my partner's power. If they were strong and independent of me, I felt insecure. If they were weak and needy, it made me feel stronger. Subconsciously, I chose partners who had some fatal flaws of which I could take advantage. I subtly tried to undermine their strength and independence. As I became more secure within myself, I was able to be comfortable with their power and had more willingness and ability to empower them.

When you nurture your physical, mental, social and spiritual selves, you are strong, you are not a needy individual, and you are self-sufficient. You stand on your own two feet. You are not dependent on your partner's strength to hold you up, but can be their support if they need you. You are trusted by your partner, loved and admired. You can feel pleased with yourself.

With all this talk of the necessity of being independent, I may have overstated its importance and made dependency out to be a villain. It is not. In fact, being able to be dependent on our partner and thus being vulnerable to them is an important and valuable part of a relationship. Biologically, we are herd animals whose natural inclination is to live collectively and cooperate communally. Without depending on each other, the human race would have perished long ago. Couples need each other and depend on each other, and this is good. One of the great benefits of being in a relationship is that you don't have to carry your load all by yourself. In a sense, it takes strength and fearlessness to allow yourself to be vulnerable. If you are compelled to be too independent, too self-sufficient, especially if that is motivated by fear of vulnerability, your drive for independence will be instigated by fear.

Alice and my days are filled with mutual dependencies. It feels good for us to know that individually, we don't have to do everything ourselves. In all honesty, I don't understand the extent of our dependence on each other, but I intuit that it is much more than either of us is aware of. Our daily living tasks are apportioned out according to each of our interests and skills. Things get done, bills get paid, food prepared, social arrangements made, the car and house maintained. Those are obvious dependencies and are apparent. What confounds me and scares me are the hidden emotional dependencies. These are so complex and unconscious that I am afraid they will only be revealed when one of us dies.

24. I WILL BE CONSIDERATE OF YOUR DESIRE FOR PRIVACY AND SOLITUDE. *Periods of interior time are necessary and healing. I recognize your occasional need for privacy, silence and alone time, and I will abide by your wishes.*

Solitude is a sanctuary, a place of healing, a quiet forest pool where we can go to be by ourselves and rest and refresh. Yet, many of us fear being alone. We don't know what to do when we are in our own company. When there is a lull, we immediately need to fill it. We make our way to the computer, turn on the television or radio, talk on the phone, go to the refrigerator and nibble on a snack – anything to avoid the panic of loneliness.

This anxiety when we are alone is usually a symptom of insecurity. The less secure we feel within ourselves, the less self-reliant we are, the less complete we feel, the more we tend to fear being alone and the more we compulsively seek the companionship of others. This fear of being alone often drives the need for relationship. If the relief from the panic of being alone is the basis for a relationship, we are bound to be disappointed, because loneliness is a bottomless hunger that can only be temporarily satisfied by being around others. As soon as we are by ourselves again, the emptiness and the anxiety begin anew. People think that having a relationship is a cure for loneliness. It is not. The only cure for loneliness is to become friends with aloneness.

Aloneness is a hunger also, but a hunger for solitude, a desire to rest in inner peace. It is ease and comfort in being with ourselves. Aloneness is noble, it is powerful. To be comfortable in solitude is freedom. When aloneness is the ground of our being and the ground of our relationship, we are centered in ourselves and we are free of the unending hunger for companionship. Aloneness is being able to choose and relish the spaciousness of being alone.

It is through aloneness and silence that we can learn most about ourselves. Being in the crucible of silence, our true thoughts and feelings are free to arise, unimpeded by the noisy pull of the conflicting needs of the outer world. That silence and aloneness, be it in meditation, or contemplation, or in just ambling down a country road, allows us to hear the quiet voice within, the most subtle urgings of our heart.

All of us have a quiet inner core, a place of serenity. Our busy activities, our manic mind and the sights, sounds, touch and tastes we experience can draw us away from our center. A healthy balance between the inner world and the outer world is needed, as is the ability to float easily between the two worlds. Sometimes just a few moments are all we need to bring us back to balance – a walk in the woods, reading a book, a short meditation. But at other times a protracted withdrawal is called for – a retreat or vacation alone. There is a distinction between a retreat and a vacation. A vacation is for relaxation and enjoyment and for blowing off steam. The purpose of a retreat is to enter seclusion in order to delve within, contemplate, meditate, and when the period of isolation ends, return to everyday life with fresh insights and deeper understanding.

In a couple relationship, the ebb and flow between aloneness and togetherness is healthy and natural. In the past, I never realized this. If my partner wanted time alone, I took it as an attempt to reject me. Since I was being rejected, I assumed I had done something wrong or that there was something wrong with me. What I didn't realize at the time is that the separation is as important as the togetherness. Without the ability to disconnect when needed, a couple can too easily become enmeshed and lose themselves in the other. When a couple finds their right balance between togetherness and solitude, the times of solitude allows for the greater enjoyment of togetherness, and the togetherness makes solitude more meaningful.

Balance between togetherness and solitude is a dynamic balance, always changing with the circumstances and the couple's feelings. If they have been separate for a while, they may long for closeness. If they have been continuously in each other's company, they may desire solitude.

It is not always easy to find balance. It is in some people's nature to have a strong need for privacy and space, just as it is in others' nature to be gregarious and seek frequent companionship. One may desire lots of alone time, with occasional periods of closeness, Others may desire lots of closeness, with occasional periods of alone time. Neither is right or wrong. However, if the one who wants closeness pressures and pursues the one who needs distance, that person who needs distance will probably instinctively respond by pulling away. This is a recipe for frustration. While both parties are just trying to get comfortable in accordance with their own nature, they only succeed in making themselves and the other uncomfortable.

Compromise helps. I am a more private person than Alice and require more alone time. Our life is a lot more social than I am comfortable with, but I don't want to deny Alice's pleasure in others' company. We do lots of visiting and have lots of guests. If I have the need to be alone, it is not unusual for me to retire to our bedroom or my workshop. Though we might be mismatched on the gregarious scale, our difference has been beneficial for both of us. Without Alice,

UNDERSTANDING THE LOVING PROMISES

I could easily become a hermit. She pulls me out into the world. I believe I have influenced Alice to be more inward, and this has been beneficial for her.

Solitary time in relationship doesn't necessarily mean being alone. It can also mean time spent away from your partner in the presence of others. Most likely this would be for women among their women friends, and for men among male companions. This can be very important. Time spent among "your own kind" can be restorative. For a woman to bask in feminine energy and a man to savor masculine energy is healing medicine. There was a period when I devoted a lot of time, both as a leader and as a participant, in the men's movement of the 80s and 90s. We talked straight, camped in the woods, challenged each other with playful competition. I was able to be with other men in new ways that helped me understand myself as a man among men. Sharing our common experience as brothers, sons, fathers and lovers created a healing bond for me that I had never experienced before. The meetings, celebrations, retreats away from Alice amplified my masculine energy and gave me invaluable gifts I was able to bring back into our relationship.

Allowing each other solitary time doesn't always mean you are physically separate from your partner. You can be together and also be in solitude. It is more like allowing silence to be, resting in the easy, natural stillness between you. *The evening meal finished and the kids put to bed or planted in front of the TV, wordlessly, you and your beloved put the leftovers away and wash and dry the dished together. Quiet time. Alone, together.*

Alice and I spend a lot of quiet time together. We could be reading or working quietly on separate projects or simply involved in our own thoughts. We are in our own separate worlds, but also together. There is a feeling of peaceful sweetness and an unspoken, felt connection.

The deepest expression of love is not found in words, but in stillness. Many times we feel exquisite communion when we are silent in each other's company. As the poet Kahlil Gibran wrote, "Even as the strings of the lute are alone, though they quiver with the same music."

We have friends who make silence and solitude a regular practice in their lives together. They take one entire 24hour period in the month when they enjoy complete silence and contemplation. They are following an age-old tradition. The ancients knew the value of this practice when they created the Sabbath to end their active week of work – Sunday for Christians, Friday for Muslims, Friday sundown to Saturday sundown for Jews. This 24-hour period is intended to be spent in quiet time with loved ones and in prayer and contemplation. In America we seem to have lost the meaning of this very important practice. Our day of rest is usually spent in the bustle of shopping, running errands, socializing and entertainment.

When the Sabbath is honored collectively, the effect is amazing. Years ago we spent two months in the Orthodox Jewish section within the walls of the old city of Jerusalem. Every Friday at sunset, sirens would go off throughout the whole area to mark the beginning of the Sabbath. Within a minute or two, that entire part of the old city would gradually become enveloped in silence as the residents stopped driving, turned off their phones, ceased use of any machines and began a 24-hour period of internal life. As life moved quietly at a snail's pace, time outside of time, the effect was amazing. The experience of peace was palpable.

25. I WILL TOUCH YOU AND WELCOME YOUR TOUCH. *I understand that touch is a gift and a healing. I will welcome physical expression of our love for each other through loving caress, in ways that are reciprocally appreciated and at times that are mutually desired.*

We express the love we feel for our partner through our actions. We help our beloved, we listen, we give gifts, we speak loving words. The most concrete way of expressing love is through touch. For most people, touch is essential for health and happiness. Infants who are touch-deprived in impersonal institutions such as orphanages are almost always emotionally handicapped to some degree when they grow up. Older people living alone often express that they are hungry to be touched and held.

Touch acts to lower the level of the stress hormone cortisol, while it increases the so-called "love hormone," oxytocin. Oxytocin has been shown to be related to mother and child bonding and also is secreted when couples cuddle and stroke one another.

Touch plays an important role in Alice's and my life. We spend lots of time together nuzzling, holding hands, embracing, massaging and cuddling. Our day starts out in bed in the morning with kisses and hugs. It feels so good for us to wake up, reach out and squeeze that warm, familiar hand, smooth the hair, massage the shoulders of this person we love. Our day ends at night with kisses and caresses. What a pleasure and honor it is to curl up in the same bed with this familiar warm body and drift off to sleep together.

As time has passed and we have grown older, we take even greater pleasure in each other's touch. I feel the incredible preciousness of the moment as I massage Alice's hand or run my fingers through her hair. Even simply holding hands is a source of great joy for us. That childlike gesture carries a lot of meaning. It says, "I love you. I am here. We are connected."

UNDERSTANDING THE LOVING PROMISES

Often I become aware that when I extend my hand to touch Alice, I have the subliminal intention that my hand radiate love to her. The experience is very different from touching just any object, where the dominant feeling is of receiving sensation. Touching with loving intention is sending love. It is as if I request the love from my heart to radiate down through my arm into my hand, then, onto her skin. I know that Alice feels my love more acutely when I do this. And I do too. It is well worth that you try this with your partner. It amplifies the experience of love.

Though touch is wordless, it speaks volumes. The simple act of physical contact can convey many messages, both for the one touching, and the one being touched. Reaching out, caressing, holding, embracing another person amplifies and clarifies the feelings we have towards that person. Receiving touch – being caressed and held also amplifies the feelings we have toward the person touching us. With the right person, under the right circumstances, being touched can evoke pleasure, security, passion, encouragement, comfort, and healing. With the wrong person, it can evoke fear and disgust. Even with the right person, but at the wrong time, or approached in the wrong manner, touch can be an unpleasant experience.

Sexual touch amplifies feelings even more. There is a clear line of demarcation between the comforting touch of a friend and the sensuous caress of a lover, and you are instinctively attuned to the intention of the person who touches. When you take off your clothes and make skin-to-skin contact, you instantly remove layers of defense. You become vulnerable. No other human experience reaches such depth of vulnerability. When Alice holds my penis in her hand, I feel that she is holding me, all of me. I love the feeling because it opens me to the experience of sweet surrender. There is no other way than physical touch that I can surrender to her so concretely. And there is no other way I can feel Alice's surrender more concretely than through my loving touch.

Sexual touch is not simply the contact of skin on skin. It carries the weight of personal history and meaning. Included in the mix are idealized notions of romance, parental prohibitions from childhood, religious injunctions, struggles for power and remnants of past sexual abuse. None of this is on display. Because of these unknowns, a person entering a relationship with a new partner has no idea of what they are getting into. Becoming involved in such a complex brew requires the utmost sensitivity and tact.

Through our sexuality we can come to know our partner and be known by them. It is no accident that in the Bible, "knowing" is used euphemistically as having carnal knowledge, (sexual intercourse.) The experience of physically opening to our partner is potentially exposing ourself to being seen, to having our raw, needy hunger revealed, being judged and rejected, being "entered," "taking" and being "taken." This emotionally powerful stuff.

Because of this power, sexuality can be one of the most confusing and emotionally highly-charged terrains of human experience. A person's sexuality could be tied in with satisfying needs that are way beyond the simple function of the rubbing of two bodies together – releasing stress and tension, overcoming feelings of inadequacy and insecurity, gaining conquest, being accepted, welding power and control, exacting revenge or assuaging loneliness – basically, using sexual touch as a way to distract oneself, achieve a goal or feel better. To expect sex to accomplish all these things is a tremendous burden placed (or rather misplaced) on sexuality. This is a job that would be better achieved through internal psychological therapeutic work rather than a workout in the bedroom.

Being such a "hot button" issue, it is important to be able to place limits on others and on yourself in regards to touching and being touched. I would suggest the following as ironclad rules.

> *"I am in charge of my body. I will not allow myself to be coerced by anyone into doing anything sexual I do not want to do."*
> *"You are in charge of your body. I will not coerce you into doing anything sexual you do not want to do."*

The heat of the moment may make these rules more difficult to implement, but if you are able to clearly define, assert and maintain your limits, you can feel safe and avoid regrets later.

It is important to be able to take responsibility for your own pleasure, I.e., ask for what you want. Giving your partner direction can be awkward, but how else will they know unless you show them. Being able to communicate to your lover what you want and what you don't want can really boost sexual satisfaction. Indicating with words or pleasure sounds, "Higher, lower, faster, slower, harder, softer, here, there," can guide your partner and teach them to be an expert lover.

While letting a partner know what pleases you can add to your mutual enjoyment, it is not always easy to talk about. Growing up, sex was often treated as a secret, a source of hidden shame. People commonly have "secret pleasures," odd fantasies, masturbation, obsessions and fetishes that they would feel ashamed of if their partner knew about. If these can be shared, a new level of intimacy, physical and psychological, can be achieved. Sexual pleasure can manifest in many forms. There's no right way to "do it," no fixed standard as to what constitutes good sex. Sexual response is unique to each individual, to each couple and to each encounter.

UNDERSTANDING THE LOVING PROMISES

The state of a couple's sexuality is often a bellwether that exposes things in the relationship that might be in need of improvement. Not being turned on to each other, obsessive masturbation, compulsively viewing pornography, unsatisfactory intercourse, rare or non-existent sexual contact are often indications that something may be lacking in the relationship. This is not always true. Perfectly happy couples may choose temporary or permanent celibacy. Viewing pornography can serve as a sexual stimulant for some couples, as can playing out sexual fantasies. Whatever pleases both partners is good sex.

The complaint of sexual boredom is not uncommon with long-term, monogamous couples. Monogamous is not a synonym for monotonous. Avoiding sexual boredom doesn't require novelty – changing partners or learning new techniques, although these can temporarily pique interest and excitement. Novelty is more about what you reveal about yourself rather than some new position. There will be novelty if you are present for your partner moment-by-moment and willing to focus on their delight, and be present for your own delight. Being in the moment can ramp up satisfaction for both of you. Who would reject a partner who is fully focused and present with them? Who would reject a partner who takes great pleasure in giving them pleasure? And who would reject a partner who takes great pleasure in receiving the pleasure you give?

Another common issue that arises is that couples are rarely perfectly matched in their sexual preferences. One partner desires sex more frequently than the other or at a time when the other is turned off. One prefers a certain kind of touching that the other finds unappealing. How to handle the disparity? With a large portion of patience, sensitivity, flexibility and generosity – all qualities of the Loving Promises. Sexuality holds so much vulnerability that, without these qualities, it is easy to wound or be wounded, frustrate or be frustrated. The sexually frustrated partner faces sometimes monumental challenges. Their mate is in the driver's seat and has the power to control the nature of the sexual connection simply by their willingness to "do it" or not. To deal with their frustration, the more sexually-motivated partner will need to call up all the patience, understanding and loving qualities they can muster in order to avoid falling into lazy, harmful responses like anger, blame, coercion and guilt induction. It is important for both partners to understand that, whether high or low desire, both partners suffer frustration.

The partner with lower sexual motivation can be a force for healing, both for their mate and for themselves. If they are able to understand touching, caressing and sex as the gift that it is, a gift of letting their partner know that they are desired and desirable, appreciated and loved, in addition to sensual pleasure, then both will be healed. This may mean engaging in erotic play even if the desire is not initially there. Common belief is that first comes interest, then stimulation, then intercourse. But it doesn't have to be that way. Stimulation can often lead to interest. Bestowing the gift of generously saying "yes" when not turned on can quickly change, and can result in some very pleasant interludes for both.

What happens in the bedroom is not separate from what is happening in the rest of life. Desire is very sensitive to what is currently occurring in a couple's relationship and daily life. Your state of mind – stress, worries, busy schedules, sense of distance – these all play a role. How you treat each other outside the bedroom very much influences what happens inside. You can't expect that if you ignore your partner, antagonize them, act indifferent or belittle them, they will be excited to jump into bed with you. While being good to each other won't guarantee good sex, treating each other unkindly will likely result in unsatisfying sex or no sex at all.

Lack of technique is not the primary issue that cools the fires of sexual desire. Near the top of the list of passion killers is if there is a backlog of unexpressed negative feelings. Unresolved conflicts and withheld anger and frustration make it difficult to feel generous toward your partner. You are not anxious to pleasure that jerk, even at the expense of your own pleasure. The famous "after argument sex" is a demonstration of the power in communication. After a flight, garbage has been aired and the exhilaration of clear communication is a strong sexual stimulant.

Withholding sex from a partner is a common form of punishment as revenge for some transgression or as a way to manipulate them. It is a very effective and very hurtful, destructive manipulation. Other forms of sexual manipulation are selfish sex, where the other person's desires are disregarded, mechanical sex, just going through the motions, bored sex, where the partner lies there and is obviously disinterested, where the partner wants their mate to "just hurry up and finish." Denying sex or manipulative sex with your partner is a two-way street. It denies you closeness, warmth and pleasure. You both end up punished. But you get to be right, obtain "payback" and be in control. Not very rewarding.

Years ago I did a series of sculptures titled *Old Lovers*. These were nude elder couples in sensuous embrace. The sculpture in the opening pages of this book is part of the series. Viewers, especially younger people, are shocked by the bare wrinkled flesh, as if nudity and sensuality are to be reserved only for the young. Not so. Desire for intimacy and pleasure has no time limit. Alice's body has begun to morph into the forms of my sculptures, but I still very much enjoy looking at her naked form. (Call me a dirty old man). We sleep nude and I love to stare at her when she gets out of bed in the morning to put her clothes on. Age has made her skin soft to the touch, like a baby's bottom, and it gives me great pleasure to stroke her. Her hair has turned grey, her face has wrinkled, but it's the hair and face of the one I love, and it fills me with great joy just to look at her. No kidding.

There are seasons in life for sexuality. Spring and summer, where interest and hormones are most active, give way to fall and winter. We are in winter. Our erotic episodes are rarer now that we are older. I sometimes miss the frequency of the early days, but the present sweetness and intensity of our sexual interludes more than make up for it. Having less sex makes each encounter so much more special. I'll take quality over quantity any day.

I believe that the decline of our sexual energies has allowed space for a special, more engrossing intimacy to arise between us. As sexuality decreased, sensuality has increased, closeness has increased. In the past I used sex as a way to soothe loneliness and overcome separateness. Now it is a celebration of our togetherness. Also, the ebbing of the fixation on the physical aspects of love has made room for the spiritual aspects to take its place. Alice and I have a sense of our bodies as holy temples. With this understanding, our sexual act can be a celebration of love and a worship of the body and of the beautiful spirit that dwells within the body.

The human body is such an incredibly sensitive instrument. Our senses allow us to experience the world. Sexual encounter encompasses all our senses. If we avoid speeding through to the finish line, we can have a delicious feast of the senses. Our enjoyment can be enhanced if we slow way down, focus on the pleasurable sensations that arise and surrender to them. You wouldn't quickly gobble down a gourmet meal, would you? It is so much more enjoyable to take your sweet time and savor the tastes and textures. Like enjoying a good meal, savoring the erotic experience means to be awake and sensitive to the moment-by-moment experience. It means to take time and be present with your partner, and present with yourself.

You don't rush through a fine meal in order to get to dessert. Why then would you rush through a sexual encounter in order to get to orgasm? For many couples, orgasm is the payoff, the be-all and end-all of sex. Foreplay is considered merely a warm-up, a job that gets you to the Big Moment. Not for Alice and me. Foreplay is our playground. What better way of demonstrating our love than by giving and giving and giving sensual pleasure to our beloved (and what a fine practice of sharing generosity). The act of giving physical pleasure to our partner is a concrete act of generosity. Patient, generous foreplay enhances closeness, enhances love.

I notice a subtle difference in the way I feel about Alice the day after we've made love. There's kind of special relaxed closeness and familiarity, a knowing smile. Is this glow the effect of the remnants of hormones remaining in our bodies? I think not. The previous evening we have adored and been adored, opened ourselves and been opened. We have shared a deep experience and the subtle fragrance of that experience remains with us.

The sexual revolution of the 60s overturned many stiff, repressive taboos of previous generations. But it seems that the pendulum has swung too far. For many people, sex became the thing to do when you first met and felt attracted. It became a purely physical exercise and lost its depth and sweetness. Sex didn't require love, or even "like". Divorced from love, sex can become a matter of technique – placement of hands, fingers, tongue, organs, and variations of postures. Sex becomes a performance, with finely honed and practiced moves, but without any real self-revelation or soul. When united with love, sex becomes the expression of that love and deepens love. That is the difference between "having sex" and "making love." To make something is to create, construct. Having sex can satisfy the body. Making love can deepen love and can satisfy the heart and soul as well as the body.

I don't mean to imply that sex united with love is the only acceptable form of erotic expression. There are many paths to sensual enjoyment, among them – tender fuck, wild fuck, sensual fuck, playful fuck, polite fuck. Each variation is another color in the sexual palette. Different arrangements, like multiple partners and "friends with benefits" can bring excitement and adventure to the erotic experience. Whatever turns you on. But a word of caution – these forms of sexual activities may have increased potential for heartbreak for one or both. The sexual act can make us vulnerable. Over time, with feelings of compatibility, sex has the tendency of bringing on the desire for deeper emotional connection. This is especially true for a woman, whose need for intimacy is greater than a man.

The difference between satisfying bodily needs and needs for intimacy and connection can be an area of confusion and frustration for couples. Both partners will be frustrated following a sexual encounter if one is primarily driven to satisfy bodily need and the other craves intimacy and emotional closeness. This could lead to the person wanting connection, (more often ascribed to the woman), feeling used, and the one wanting carnal experience, (more often the male), feeling deserted. In the long run, for a long-term committed relationship, fulfilling both emotional connection and lust is essential for a full sexual experience. Both men and women will benefit by expanding their comfort zone and exploring the areas they are less familiar and comfortable with.

Ideally, a full sexual experience, then, involves the alignment of heart and body. When your heart – your tender feelings, generosity and openness, is fully present with your body – your senses, lustful excitement and physical arousal, the sexual encounter can be ecstatic. This joining of heart and body is, for most of us, the closest we come to the spiritual experience of creating oneness with our partner.

The highest form of sexual generosity is when my pleasure is yours and yours is mine. Your pleasuring me increases your pleasure, and my pleasuring you increases mine. No one is in control, yet no one is out of control. I ravish you with powerful lust, yet am ravished by your lust.

Soon there is no you or me, no separation. Our separate egos are lost in the experience. This is union.

At the first stirrings of desire, you may be pleasantly surprised if, instead of pursuing lust and rushing to make physical connection, you initially attend to emotional connection. Make it your intention to first connect with each other heart-to-heart. Focus on the love you feel for this person who will soon share their body with you. Feel your desire to give them joy. Send each other loving energy, make extended eye contact, hold hands, embrace one another with loving tenderness, reach out and touch each other's hearts with your fingertips. Make these moments a special, conscious ritual. When you delve deeply into the vibration of love in your hearts, your love will find expression through your bodies.

Since the Loving Promises are love in action, the most potent aphrodisiac is bringing the Loving Promises to bed with you. There is no sexual technique more fulfilling than being embraced with love.

26. I WILL REMAIN FAITHFUL TO YOU. *Sexual fidelity is a bulwark of our relationship. I consider you my exclusive sexual partner and reserve intimate caress for you alone.*

Alice gives her body as a gift to me. Mine is a gift I give to her. For us, these are special exclusive gifts, sacred gifts. No one has access to our bodies; no one can touch us as we can touch each other. We have vowed sexual exclusivity – a commitment to contain our sexual experiences within our relationship. This vow has not imprisoned us, but has freed us.

Every choice entails a loss, every road taken entails a road not taken. This pledge to forgo the excitement of physical intimacy with other partners is seen by some as a sacrifice. Resisting the temptation for immediate pleasure *is* a sacrifice. The reward for this sacrifice is that we experience far greater depth and fulfillment with each other. Without the Promise of sexual exclusivity, there is a tendency to fall into a predatory mindset, ever on the lookout for new, potential erotic partners. We would tend to place people we meet in one of two categories.

Category 1: Would I want to take this person to bed? Category 2: Or not? And it's impossible to avoid time and energy being pulled away from the primary relationship when involved in intimate relationships with one or more additional partners.

These are minor consequences compared to the devastating effects on your partner and relationship caused by a rupture in trust from having an affair. When you, the person they trust the most, the one they are most intimate with, choose to be intimate with another, and do this secretly, how can they ever trust you again. How can they ever trust anyone again. They picture you and your paramour together and question, "Am I lovable? Are they better in bed than I? You lied; you cheated. Can I ever again place my faith in your word?" The road back to trust from such a severe rupture is long and difficult. Some couples never make it. And once broken, trust can rarely or never return to the level it was before the affair.

Sexual exclusively with Alice doesn't mean I am not able to be attracted to other women or even admire a handsome man. A beautiful face and body and a buoyant spirit are a joy to behold and there is no reason why I cannot appreciate them. Many a time I have fallen in love (or lust) for a minute or two with a cute waitress or salesperson. The world is filled with many wonderful people. Why not have permission to admire them. Alice gives me permission. I'm very clear about my limits within myself and with others. I don't send mixed messages. I freely acknowledge my momentary infatuations to Alice and she indulges me. Even a rare innocent playful flirting is okay with her. She doesn't feel threatened. She knows "she's got her man." And I know I am hers . . . all hers.

The commitment to monogamy we have made makes us "safe" with the opposite sex. Since we are no longer in search of other sexual partners, we are "sexually neutral" and give off an air of chastity that is palpable. It clearly signals, "We are available only for friendship." People, especially those with a history of sexual abuse, instinctively trust us as celibate friends because they can intuit we want nothing more from them than innocent friendship.

The thought of sharing intimate relations with another person can be an enticing fantasy. How exciting to begin a sexual dance with someone new. For me, as for most people, over time, sexual passion wanes with familiarity. It's just a fact of life. There is no way a long-term sexual partner can compete with the excitement of a new liaison. The adventure of a different person, a new, unfamiliar body, the absence of the old daily routines, the uncertainty, the danger and especially the ego satisfaction of sweeping someone off their feet, can reignite dormant passion. However, the intoxication can often be like a mirage and, over time, with familiarity, begin to settle down. Then what? Seek another partner and begin another cycle with hopeful expectation.

For us, an affair is not an interest, nor an option or even a remote possibility. I love the relationship I have with Alice and would do nothing to compromise it. Monogamy is our choice and is the choice of the preponderance of couples in long term relationships (despite the numbers of married couples who have affairs).

Some couples, though, have chosen to have ongoing open relationships with one or more additional partners. They see monogamy as confining and limiting to individual and personal growth and freedom. Societies' knee-jerk reaction against polyamory may not be deeply considered. What if a couple's sexual relations are barren and unsatisfying? What if they feel emotionally or intellectually unfulfilled with their partner in some areas of their life together, but actualized in others? What if they genuinely believe that an additional relationship will be a positive growth experience for all involved? Might having an affair or bringing another person into the relationship be constructive rather than destructive? Maybe. However, it's a self-evident fact—the more partners you try to share yourself with, the less you have available to give each. In nearly every instance we are aware of, adding another person into the emotional and sexual mix has eventually proven destabilizing, so much so that the primary relationship ended or was so severely tested that the negative effects persisted for years afterward.

Open, multiple relationships that include emotional attachment can, willingly or unwillingly, lead participants to an exploration of topics that normally don't arise in committed, monogamous partnerships – safety, ownership, jealousy. When one or both partners experience the green-eyed monster of jealousy or the fear of loss of the partner, this can sometimes indicate the existence of feelings of lack of self-worth. The people I know who have become involved in polyamorous relationships tend have a willingness to confront these difficult feelings. I find this admirable.

I admit, the specter of jealousy and loss would be overwhelming for me. I enjoy the safety and durability of our partnership. The thought of Alice leaving me to be with someone else would be too much to bear. Not just someone else, someone "better." The lack of her presence would be horrible, but the ego crush would drive me up the wall.

Is a sexual liaison with another person outside of the relationship the only act that determines adultery? There can be lesser degrees of infidelity. What if one had obsessive sexual fantasies about their neighbor? What if one routinely viewed pornography? Compulsively masturbated? Got a massage with a "happy ending?"

Played flirtatious games with people at the office? Some would say that whatever draws sexual energy away from your partner is a form of being unfaithful. In a sense, this is true, but it is important to remember that we humans are just a higher order primate. Our behavioral and mental activity is strongly influenced by hormones. That fact however doesn't give us permission to act on all our impulses irrespective of the consequences.

The issue of infidelity is rich in meaning. If we explore it more deeply, it can reveal valuable truths about long-term committed relationship. The usual assumption is that people have affairs for deeper reasons than just a momentary lapse, too many drinks or a chance opportunity. If things are OK at home, why would you stray? There must be something wrong with you, or your partner, or the relationship. However, it's not as simple as it seems.

I believe that not all affairs occur because things are bad with the couple. The relationship may be fine, but possibly one partner is longing for some personal need the relationship is not satisfying. It can be less about the sex and more about passion, a search for vitality lost, an effort to recapture youth, a need to feel special, desired, a yearning for exploring an unlived life. Time is passing. The question keeps recurring, "Is this all there is? Is this all there will be with us?"

These are real needs, real questions. An affair can bring these issues to the light. It's a heart-rending way to learn and I surely don't recommend it, but if handled with respect and with heart, this breach of trust can redefine the relationship, lead the couple to further growth and self-awareness and, if it survives, renew the partnership on a deeper, more honest level. While this greater understanding can be beneficial for the relationship, it's best to do your soul-searching before starting an affair.

It seems that monogamy would be a moral issue. For Alice and me, it is a spiritual issue. For us, taking the Promise of sexual fidelity seals our commitment to each other and raises our relationship to a consecrated realm. We firmly believe that without the commitment to monogamy, most couple's level of spiritual evolution would be severely curtailed.

27. **I WILL PLAY WITH YOU.** *An essential purpose of our connection is to create mutual joy. I will do what I can to make humor, entertainment, curiosity, surprise, creativity, imagination, romance, excitement and childlike playfulness vital elements in our relationship. I will make sure to schedule playtime in our calendar.*

The opposite of play is not work. The opposite of play is deadness, heaviness, depression. Play brings us alive. When we are into the experience of play, we are fully engaged. Our senses are more acute, our mind becomes more alert, our body more alive, our spirit buoyed. Unless you are a pro, when you play a game, the real goal is not to put the golf ball in the hole or smack the baseball out of the park. The real goal is to play for the joy of it. If you play only to win, that is work.

Over the years, it seems that almost all the happy couples we've known have had a playful streak. They are lighthearted with each other and don't take the other or themselves too seriously, even when they are at odds. Conversely, most of the unhappy couples we've known cannot laugh together. As Wavy Gravy said, "If you lose your sense of humor, it's not funny." Humor is not just the punchline at the end of a joke, it's the way you view the world.

When we first met, there were lots of things that drew me to Alice. I loved her looks, the sound of her voice, her quick mind. But the thing that grabbed me the strongest was her playfulness and sense of humor. She could find the humor in anything. And she knew how to make me howl with laughter. (She still does after over three decades of marriage.) That sense of levity is one trait that for me is indispensable.

Looking at all the Loving Promises might leave the impression that maintaining a magnificent relationship is a lot of hard work. Yes, it's no easy task to always be honest, accepting, generous, awake, grateful, forgiving, dependable, etc. It sometimes takes difficult work. However, we don't enter into a relationship in order to do hard labor. We want to find happiness. Why else would we pursue our life's partner other than with the expectation that our union would bring us joy? The glue that holds a couple together is their enjoyment of each other's company.

Having the leisure of being retired, Alice and I are blessed to be able to spend a lot of free time together. Even what would be boring activities become excursions for us. It is a pleasure to do our shopping together. Waiting in line the other day at the Motor Vehicles Department was a painless opportunity to hang out together. Though we are in our 70s, Alice and I still play a lot with each other. We often tease and wrestle. (I like to try to bite her knees; she likes to smack my butt). We play goofy jokes on each other, act silly and generally carry on like a couple of pre-teens. Love brings out the child in us.

Finding joy together is an essential part of any relationship. It's too easy, though, to sink into the "serious" business of living, taking on the burdensome adult responsibilities for support and maintenance of self and family. Nothing can kill joy faster than having to be a grown-up all the time and in the process, neglect to leave time for play. The Bible, in Corinthians says, "When I grew older, I put away childish things." As adults, it is necessary to take on mature roles. Unfortunately, some of the childish things we put away are precious –

silliness, boisterous laughter, wonder, innocence, openness, creative imagination. Instead, we become polite adults, go about the serious business of making a living, being a parent, connecting with the "right" people, saving for retirement. The playful child in us becomes abandoned. It's not that we're looking to go back in time and be a child. The goal is to engender childlike qualities, the freshness and innocence of a human being not yet jaded by years of having to act like a responsible adult.

I love the quote by George Bernard Shaw. "We don't stop playing because we grow old. We grow old because we stop playing." If we could only take a hint from our children – watch them play, see how totally involved they are. That's the thing about play – it takes us out of our mind and immediately puts us into the moment. There is no yesterday or tomorrow – only the present. Joyfulness resides in the present moment, nowhere else. No matter what we are doing, if we are present, we feel more alive. If we are not present, we are numb.

Alice and I used to facilitate a college playshop, (not a workshop) called Creative Expression. The goal was to help people let go of mental inhibitions, embarrassment and self-judgment by providing them the opportunity to jump into the moment and engage in uninhibited play. Participants danced to lively music as they twirled long pieces of colored fabric, held serious conversations while wearing "beagle beaks," (Groucho Marx eyeglasses with a big nose and fuzzy eyebrows and mustache), created spontaneous drawings and tried their hand at improvised acting. There was a lot of laughter and people pushed through many of their inhibitions. They all left with smiles on their faces. They had come in touch with the child part in themselves.

Often a couple's main shared leisure activity is watching television. Zoning out by staring at the moving images from a lighted rectangle in a darkened room is not conducive for joyous connection – or any connection. Rather than connect, TV watching separates. Alice and I haven't had a television for over 30 years, and we are none the worse for it. As an experiment, try turning off the tube for a while. Instead, create a romantic evening with a candlelight dinner, share leisure activities like sports, playing board games or exercising together. Take trips and excursions. These are not just enjoyable shared activities, they are essential to the health of the relationship. Even a short change of scenery, any escape from the responsibilities of everyday life – a walk in the park, an hour in a day spa, a visit to a museum or art gallery, can reinvigorate, recharge and provide a fresh perspective.

You don't need entertaining electronic gadgets or expensive toys – you have each other. Skip, dance, tumble, make noise and yell at the top of your lungs. Hold hands while you stare at the moon. Celebrate holidays and special occasions. If there are no special occasions, create them. Celebrations remind us how blessed we are. They draw us together and give us a sense of continuity. Alice and I have things we do and places we go year after year that have become like ritualized ceremonies with us. The stop we make at the same restaurant in Pismo Beach for clam chowder when we head north, the shop we always go to in Santa Barbara and the walk along the sandy beach in Ventura are some of our special occasions.

Be spontaneous; be creative. Surprise him, surprise her. Do something special that the other person doesn't know about. The element of surprise is exciting. There have been times when I told Alice "Get dressed up. We're going out," or I would pack an overnight suitcase. She would have no idea where we were going or what we were doing until we reached our destination.

It is impossible to create and maintain a magnificent relationship without spending quality playtime together. Even if partners are each holding down two jobs, struggling to find time for the kids and for household duties, it is essential to create time to be able to relax and enjoy each other's company. What free time that is available is taken up with the essential tasks of daily living – do the laundry, take care of the kids, change oil in the car. These are our priorities. We do these things first, save play for "later," but then there is little time left over for being together, talking, relaxing, playing. Later never comes. Let's be honest, obligations, limited time and shortage of money are excuses. If you really wanted to make time for play, you would. If you had regularly scheduled playtime written into the calendar, in ink--maybe a weekly dinner date or a movie, that might make it easier. Creating room for quality time in a busy schedule may take some strategy and planning, but the health and stability of the relationship depends on it.

We all need to eat. Alone or together, it still takes the same amount of time. Taking meals together sustains love as well as body. Alice and I always make it a point, whenever possible, to prepare and eat our meals together. We take in sustenance from the food as well as from relaxing in each other's company. And before every meal, as we had for 33 years, we close our eyes for a moment, hold hands, and feel thankfulness for the blessing of the food and for each other's company.

A common complaint from long-term couples, (and maybe not so long-term) is "The feeling of romance has gone out of our relationship." Romance is a feeling, but more important, *romance is action*. If the romantic feeling has gone from your relationship, most likely you no longer take romantic action. You know how to have a good time with your partner. You know how to romance your partner. You've done it before. Remember when you first met and fell in love? You acted differently towards him or her. You did what you could to impress them and make them feel appreciated. You flirted with them, went out to fun places, made sure you were clean, smelled nice and were well dressed. You listened to them, made clever conversation, laughed at their jokes. You surprised them with little gifts, cooked their favorite meal or took them out to a nice restaurant. But then, after a while, when things cooled off and settled down, you took on the "I got my man," "I got my woman" mindset, took them for granted and let things go. If you treated your partner now the same way you did when you first dated, the relationship would still sizzle. So do it! Date your mate. Get out of the rut and invite some fun and romance into your relationship. Play! Delight together in the joy of being alive.

28. **I WILL VITALIZE OUR RELATIONSHIP**. *A partnership that does not continually grow can stagnate. I will instigate and participate in uplifting activities, learnings and adventures which inspire us to evolve physically, intellectually, emotionally and spiritually.*

We humans have an inborn hunger for new and diverse stimulation. We are oriented toward growth and expansion. We are energized by passion and creativity. If the impulse to grow is thwarted or lies dormant, some part of us is switched off, deadened. That deadness cannot help but impact a relationship. Yet, at the same time that we are enlivened by novelty and excitement, most of us also have the tendency to want things to remain the same. We are disturbed by the unfamiliar. We resist change and value safety and stability. These two opposing tendencies--expansion and stability, can be at war with each other in the psyche.

Do we use our relationship as a "safe harbor" for security and comfort, as a protection to buffer us against fear and the unpredictability of life? Do we use it as a challenging ocean voyage of adventure on the high seas, where we dive into wakefulness and encounter danger and the unknown? Or do we find a dynamic balance between the two extremes, retreating to security and comfort when stressed and overwhelmed, and reaching out to confront what we find fearful and challenging when we feel emboldened?

I think we all have the inclination to fall into repetitive patterns after a while – wake up, get out of bed, wash, get dressed, have breakfast, go to work, come home, have dinner, watch television, wash, go to sleep – repeat. It is easy to fall into a rut, become lazy and too comfortable. Rather than venture out into the big wide world, we stay home and polish the bars of our cage. We trudge through our days and become bored and boring. This will dampen a relationship and drains the life out of it.

Vitality and aliveness are the most prominent characteristics of a magnificent relationship. A vital and alive partnership avoids those boring ruts. It energizes each partner and brings energy to, and receives energy from, everyone they come in contact with. Partners who desire to grow are curious. They will reach out to meet new friends to bring into their dyad who will enliven and stimulate them. They will search for new and challenging shared activities – hobbies, entertainments and intellectual pursuits that stretch mind and body and bring aliveness back into a relationship.

Not just any activity will do. This Promise specifies that it should be more than a pastime or a mindless activity. It should be a challenge. It should stretch you, stimulate you and push you to grow. It should encourage communication and spark interest and foster discovery. Take a yoga class together or engage in a challenging sport, share your love of art and theatre, attend classes and lectures, travel. Do something you haven't done before, go places you've never been. Push beyond your comfort zone. When you become engaged in activities that are new and stimulating, you feel more awake and alive.

Alice and I were in middle-age when we first met. After several years we had a call to adventure. We quit our jobs, rented out our house, bought backpacks and sturdy shoes, and took off on a trip around the world. During the thirteen and a half months we were gone, we stayed in an ashram in India, walked along the Great Wall of China, rode camels over the dunes to the Pyramids in Egypt, sailed in a sloop off the coast of Greece, got lost in the souk in Marrakesh, Morocco, hung out with traditional musicians on the island of Crete, got drunk with flamenco dancers in Seville, Spain, were hosted by the Sheik of a Whirling Dervish temple in Istanbul, Turkey and climbed Mount Sinai early in the morning and reached the summit in time to see the sunrise. It was the trip of a lifetime that gave us memories we will forever cherish.

You could do things by yourself, but there is something special about participating with your partner. Shared experiences are fun and cross-pollinating ideas make joint activities even more significant. But it's not only shared activities that can energize. When one partner is energized, both will benefit. Encourage each other to take up individual pursuits that can be brought back into the relationship. The stimulating new energy will spark both of you. A person who is turned on to life is very, very attractive.

Invest yourself. The word "invest" is meaningful. When you invest, you give something valuable in order to receive value back. Invest your time, interest and passion in order to grow and uplift yourself. When I look back at our history together, it is clear that many of the high points of Alice's and my life were times when we invested ourselves and collaborated on challenging projects and adventures – developing and instituting programs for a psychiatric hospital, teaching college workshops, creating and promoting our art, traveling around the world, writing our book. We were challenged, we were learning, we were growing, and the excitement and stimulation of these activities expanded our being, cemented our relationship and added immensely to our lives.

Alice and I are still growing, still enjoying, still learning. We don't intend to stop till the sand in our hourglass runs out.

29. I WILL HONOR YOUR FAMILY. *Familial ties are complex and binding. I will treat your family with respect and graciousness, ever mindful that my first loyalty is to you.*

Parodies about mothers-in-law used to be a part of every comedian's staple of jokes. It was taken for granted that married couples would invariably be having issues with in-laws. There is reason for this perception that our partner's relatives can be a source of problems.

When you and your mate form a committed partnership, it is more than the coming together of two people. It is the melding of both of your families and both your social networks. Outside of the couple bond, for most people, their relationship with family is of greatest importance. Your partner's family now becomes your family and your family becomes your partner's family. This means that whatever issues you and your partner are having with your families now become part of your relationship.

Especially in long-term, committed relationships, family ties differ from friendships, which can come and go. Families are connected for the long haul. Over time, you and your partner become witness to and participate in the lives of members of your respective families: births and coming of age, decline and death. Your own growth and decline are also witnessed.

The family's influences on an individual are pervasive. Much of that influence is unconscious. Growing up within the family crucible, the adult caretaker's ways of perceiving, communicating and behaving become part of you, not subject to questioning or even awareness. It is only when you begin to leave the nest that you discover other ways of being. Entering into another's family takes you into uncharted territory. It is like crossing the border into a foreign country that you have never visited before. New personalities, new relationships, new history, new traditions become part of your life and can expand you and offer rich and rewarding experiences.

UNDERSTANDING THE LOVING PROMISES

Being a participant in your partner's family puts you in an interesting position. You are at once both an insider and an outsider, and there are advantages and disadvantages to each. Not being a "blood relative," you may be treated differently, somewhat as an invited guest. The family may be reluctant to share secrets or reveal things that would show family members in a bad light. You may be able to remain aloof from family conflicts and infighting, but if you are not careful, you can be drawn into a web of family intrigue.

The following are some suggestions that may help prevent you from being caught in that confusing, entangling web.

Follow the wishes of your partner in regards to their family. Your partner's family is theirs, not yours. They are the ones that have intimate ties with their parents, siblings and other relatives. They are the ones that have access to information and experiences that you do not. They know their own feelings. And they are the ones that will bear the blame and feel the greatest pain if they are alienated from their clan. Even if you are right about the way to behave in a situation involving your partner's family, it is not your decision to make. Exert influence if you must. Be a pillar of strength and support for your partner when needed.

Educate yourself about your partner's family. It is valuable to know your partner's background. Ask about his or her family history. What were the defining events that had important impact? What are the ongoing family dramas and traumas? Who's in, who's out and why? Are there alliances that divide the family? What are family rules about what is talked about and what is not, what is okay to do and what is forbidden? These things will help you better understand your partner. They will also help you avoid getting entangled in the web of family intrigue.

Use discrimination concerning what you share with the family about your relationship, your partner and yourself. During a particularly difficult period in our relationship, an ex-partner spoke badly of me to her parents and family members. Naturally, they supported her. That communication poisoned the relationship I had with them and I never again felt a close part of the family. Word gets around quickly in a close family unit. Sometimes it is necessary to take family members into confidence; however, if there is information that doesn't have to be shared and that might cause harm or discontent, assume it will be spread and think twice before disseminating it. Always be sensitive to your partner's feelings about confidentiality.

Avoid unnecessary negative conversation with your partner about their family. One of my ex-partners was very judgmental about my parents and never tired of telling me in detail how odd they were. She was psychologically sophisticated and knew exactly what diagnostic category to place them in. I knew my folks were a bit odd, but they were well-meaning, loved me and their oddness never really bothered me. Over time, though, I started to adopt her judgmental attitude, and that began to create an uncomfortable rift between my parents and me. Negative input has power to create negative feelings and should be used sparingly. Your mate may have intense loyalties with close relatives. You may be unaware of these. It can cause unwanted consequences if you meddle with those loyalties.

Be cautious about taking sides in family conflicts. Entering into your partner's family dispute can be like stepping into a minefield... blindfolded. There was a time years ago when a couple of close relatives were embroiled in an intense dispute where each had strong emotions attached. Thinking I was "the voice of reason," I offered my thoughts, which happened to coincide a bit more with one relative than with another. I was attacked with a fury I had never seen before and I retreated to a corner to lick my wounds. This is not to say that you should always remain neutral. Just be aware of the minefield.

Remember that the bond with your partner is the most important one you have. Loyalty to your partner and concern for his or her wellbeing takes precedence over any other connection. No other relationship is more important.

Cautions about potential problems aside, being included in your partner's family can be a wonderful experience. Coming into Alice's family more than doubled the number of relatives I had. I became like an adopted son, brother, nephew, father and cousin. I felt love for, and felt loved by every member of her family. The experience expanded my ability to love. The simplest and best advice I can offer for becoming a loving and beloved member of your partner's family is this – honor your partner's parents and family elders as your own elders. Honor your partner's brothers and sisters as your own siblings. If in a blended family, honor your partner's children as your own children. As with every relationship, when you give the best of yourself, you receive the best of others.

I have not touched on a very important component of many families--ex-partners. If you are divorced or separated, there is a good chance your ex or your partner's ex is still in your life. Shouldn't you honor them too? My ex-wife,

Tiana, is a beloved friend to both of us, more like a sister. We have vacationed together and she spends a few weeks every year staying at our house. Dennis, Alice's ex-husband comes to all of our family events. We maintain contact with her ex-boyfriends and my ex-girlfriends. At one time these people were an important part of our lives. We value their love and continuing connection. It would be a loss if we cut off love.

To augment what I've written about dealing with your partner's family, there could be an additional Promise – I WILL HONOR MY FAMILY. I cannot stress how important it is to come to peace with your own family, especially parents, and be able to connect with love. You have inherited their genes as well as their worldview. Their imprint has influenced all your relationships. The state of your connection with them cannot help but have an effect on your primary relationship.

I know that it is not always possible to come to completion with parents. What your parents did to you or didn't do for you is in the past. It cannot be changed. What has importance in the present is what you are doing now. Are you extending love to them, forgiving them? Or are you withholding and blaming?

Sometimes, the history of hurt and abuse on both sides may be too painful to transcend. But if any possibility exists for love and reconciliation, it is worth it to make the effort. If you don't settle accounts before they pass away, it will be much more difficult after.

30. I WILL BE ALERT TO NEGATIVITY IN OUR RELATIONSHIP. *I will not allow harmful feelings and destructive situations to persist and fester. I will attend to the first indications of disharmony between us so that minor problems never have a chance to become major.*

A fire in a wastebasket is easier to extinguish than if it is neglected and allowed to spread to the bedroom. The fire in the bedroom is easier to extinguish than if left to spread to the whole house. So, why not put out fires as soon as they appear. Better yet, don't play with matches.

Many couples tolerate negativity. They allow adverse situations and detrimental feelings to persist far too long in the hope that things will get better if just left alone. Neglect won't solve problems. What often happens is if problems go unaddressed, the situation at best remains the same, and by not improving, gets worse and turns into a festering wound. Feelings are hurt, the hurt held inside. Anger heats up and boils over. In order to maintain equilibrium, the person tamps down and deadens emotions to avoid a blowup, or alternatively, releases them and explodes. Neither of these is healthy or productive.

It is a common human tendency to ignore an uncomfortable situation. A proactive approach – to face down your fear and do it anyway, or to confront your laziness, gear up, and do what needs doing, is really the only viable option. By withdrawing from challenges, you feed your fear and lethargy. Avoiding uncomfortable situations only makes them more uncomfortable. You end up feeling weakened and ineffectual. Facing uncomfortable situations empowers you.

Fight or flight may function well for an organism in stress situations, but not well for couples who are having problems. It is unskillful to pick fights, (attack) or take flight, (withdraw) as your usual way of dealing with conflict with your partner. These are emotional responses to issues rather than an attempt to get to the source of the problem. They take you farther away from the solution. So much can be accomplished by simply sitting down together and talking about what is causing the distance between you. The sooner, the better. By doing nothing, things will get worse.

Alice and I are highly sensitized to negativity. Harmony is our normal state – the only condition that is acceptable for us. So, even a slight twinge of irritation or hurt by one or the other immediately gets our attention. We respond quickly with earnest discussion of our feelings and exploration of what might be the cause of the disharmony and make a sincere effort to set things right. Because of our zero tolerance for discord, we can honestly say that we have no backlog of emotional baggage – no unexpressed blame, guilt, anger, hurt. This is not to say that we have never done things that have hurt or upset each other. But, if one of us is feeling hurt or upset, they will let the other know. We will then both immediately address it. It is too painful not to.

Negative feelings and situations do not occur spontaneously. They are caused by one or both partners acting in unloving ways toward each other. Thought is precursor to action. Unloving thoughts lead to unloving actions. This is why it is important to monitor your mind and be aware of thoughts that could lead to selfish grasping, hurtful words and unkind actions. The sooner you are aware of those thoughts, the easier it is to abandon them so you won't act on them.

There is a well-known saying, "Couples should never go to bed angry with each other." This is sage advice. How painful it is to climb into bed at night and lie next to someone we are furious with and who is furious with us. If you make up your mind to never go to bed with your partner while holding on to unresolved issues, your disharmony can never last for more than one day.

31. I WILL ASSUME RESPONSIBILITY FOR MY DETRIMENTAL BEHAVIOR. *When there is discord, I will curb my tendency to act in ways that create more problems. I will take impartial account of my part and do what is necessary to make things right. I welcome feedback that shows where I can be more loving.*

The reason we need the Loving Promises is because we are not perfect. Every one of us has personality quirks and habits that make it difficult for us to live with others, others to live with us, . . . and for us to live with ourselves. We may be uncommunicative, defensive, emotionally reactive, unreasonable, quick to anger, afraid to assert ourselves, judgmental and blaming of others. We may have to be right, have to be in control, or need assurances that we are lovable. Each of these things causes problems and creates suffering for ourselves and for those close to us. They become especially problematic when there is conflict. This Promise asks us to look for and identify these qualities in ourselves, remain aware of them, and if not change them, at least prevent them from interfering with the free flow of love – especially during times of duress. And it asks that if we have made a mess, to clean it up. In short, this Promise asks us to be accountable for our actions.

Identifying our defects and failures is difficult. First of all, nobody wants to look at how they fall short. And we don't want to hear about it, especially from our partner. Second, nobody is eager to admit their faults to others, especially under duress. Thirdly, and most important, we all tend to be blind to our defects – maybe even see them as normal or even positive. It is almost automatic to look for fault outside ourselves and think that it's the other guy that screwed up when things go wrong. When we are unaware of these problematic tendencies, it makes it easier for us to become reactive and defensive.

If you believe you may have caused a problem by your behavior but are uncertain as to what you have done, one way to clarify your responsibility is to view it in your imagination from another person's perspective. What would you feel if others had witnessed your behavior? Would you be ashamed? What would they think? What if children had witnessed your behavior? Would this be an example you would want to set for them?

What can make things confusing is that you are usually not the sole villain. In most cases, your partner shares at least some responsibility. This can provide you with an easy avenue to attempt to defend yourself and blame them. However, as long as you defend and blame, you and your partner will be locked in a grappling match, unable to release, unable to hear the other. Once you are able to let go of defensiveness and look at your part, hear the truth in what your partner is saying and admit your responsibility, then your partner can more easily release their defensiveness and admit their part.

So, that's the first thing. When there is discord, look for your responsibility. If you are unable to find your part, ask your mate. They will probably be happy to tell you. The question, "What have I done to hurt you?" asked in a sincere and non-defensive way, can demonstrate to your partner your genuine intent to take responsibility and make things right. If you are open to hearing, their response can be enlightening.

The source of much defensiveness is simple. WE TAKE THINGS PERSONALLY. If your partner criticizes you for staying up late every night watching television, they are giving information about themselves, not you. Maybe they are a morning person, or maybe when they were growing up, their parents turned the television off and went to bed at nine o'clock. Often, your partner's judgments about you are their genes talking, their family history talking, their own preferences talking. If you can see that and understand that you are not bad or wrong (i.e. it is not a personal attack), it will be easier for you to not react defensively.

What if your partner is providing accurate information about you? Your staying up late truly is affecting your health and job performance. Again, try to see it as them providing information rather than attacking you. You can more easily do this if you are able to observe the movements of your mind as if you were an impartial witness. Without judging, observe as the defensiveness begins to arise. Feel the defensiveness as it forms in your body, as tightness in your belly or clenching of your jaw. Listen to your mind as it creates one defensive thought after another. Then, having some distance from the sensations, thoughts and feelings of defensiveness, you will be able to listen and absorb information. Rather than reacting emotionally, you can more easily evaluate and, if appropriate, choose to change your behavior.

It's not always easy to get distance from your defensiveness. If you've hurt your partner, often the consequence for yourself is guilt and self-recrimination. This can result in greater defensiveness. A way to modify self-blame is modify the way you conceive of your detrimental actions. Rather than seeing your behavior and yourself as bad and stupid, redefine it as "unskillful." This change in perspective takes the focus off of you and tones down the judgment, while moving the focus on to behavior. It becomes about what you could do to be more "skillful" i.e., act in a more loving way.

On a scale of weighted values, an act of kindness and an act of hurtfulness are not evenly calibrated. Just one hurtful action is so powerful that it can cause your partner pain and distrust which will undo a hundred acts of kindness. And that

UNDERSTANDING THE LOVING PROMISES

pain and distrust can last a long time. What can you do to make things right if you have genuinely screwed up, and your words and actions have hurt your partner? You told a lie and got caught. You failed to show up when you were needed. You hurt your partner with unkind words when they were in a vulnerable place.

The bad news is that once you have broken trust, you can never make things the same as they were. Once you have torn a fabric, even if you sew it or put a patch on, the tear is still there. Your transgression is always somewhere in your partner's mind. It may be buried below their conscious awareness, but it will never be completely forgotten. A memory trace remains. The good news is that your subsequent behavior can weaken your partner's memory trace so that it is so faint that it will recede into their subconscious. How? By making things right. Don't be defensive, don't ignore your mistake and hope your partner will forget about it. Don't try to minimize it or explain it away. Be accountable. Own up to your error. Mean it. Do what is necessary to make things right and do it immediately. The longer you wait, the greater the damage to your partner's feelings and to the relationship.

If I haven't already done so, I want to make it clear, ALICE AND I ARE NOT PERFECT. Like everyone else, at times we goof up, say and do dumb things that hurt each other. But we don't sweep our mistakes under the rug. We make repairs, we talk, take responsibility, try to understand where we went wrong.

These are the steps that I try to take in order to be accountable after I have goofed up with Alice by doing something stupid and unfeeling.

- ✓ *I recognize that Alice feels hurt and I acknowledge those hurt feelings.* First off, I need to know, either by Alice communicating to me or by my surmising, that I have hurt Alice, and I must let her know that I am aware of what she is feeling.

- ✓ *I contemplate the situation and try to understand where I have erred.* I need to think about and be clear in my mind what I have done to hurt her.

- ✓ *I admit my culpability to myself and then to Alice.* I need to acknowledge my responsibility, first to myself, and then speak with Alice about it.

- ✓ *I ask Alice for forgiveness.* Apologizing is a way of admitting that I screwed up and at the same time letting her know that I am unhappy about my actions. I speak with Alice, express my genuine remorse and ask for forgiveness.

- ✓ *I attempt to make amends if possible.* If there is something I can do to repair or make amends for my behavior, I do it.

- ✓ *I resolve to never again repeat the offense.* I give my full intention to not repeating my actions if a similar situation comes up in the future.

If any chance of clearing the air exists, all these steps must be taken in an earnest and heartfelt way.

Acknowledging hurt, understanding error, admitting responsibility, asking for forgiveness, making amends, resolving not to repeat offense – how rational, how reasonable. But, we humans are not always reasonable, especially when it comes to admitting when we are wrong. At these times the quality of humility is a necessity. Humility makes it easier for us to admit when we are wrong. It also makes it easier to not boast when we are right.

The truth of the matter, though, is that assigning percentages of blame is foolish and trying to figure out who is the source of problems is of secondary importance. If Alice is hurting for whatever reason, whether I am at fault or not, the most important thing is to assist her to get to the cause and help her to resolve her pain.

Alice tells a story about the power of making amends. It began during her time as a single mother when she had very little money. There was a gardener who took care of her lawn. When he knocked on her door for his pay, Alice didn't have money to give, so she hid from him until he went away. Over the next few weeks he returned several times, Alice didn't answer the door, and he finally gave up. Since that time, Alice would avoid him when she saw him around the neighborhood. When Alice and I got together, we decided, in order to get a fresh start, we would complete any unfinished business in our lives. This unpaid debt came up for her. The next time she saw the gardener, she paid off what she owed. He didn't even remember, but when Alice returned home, she broke down in deep sobs of relief. Apparently, the guilt she held weighed upon her even though she wasn't conscious of it. Paying the debt freed her and released her feelings.

There is a Talmudic tale told about Rabbi Eliezer, who taught that we should repent our wrongs the day before we die. When his disciples reminded him that no one knows for sure the day of their death, the Reb replied that we should repent today, lest we die tomorrow. If we do that, we will be conscious of and atone for our hurtful actions every day for the rest of our lives.

32. I WILL INVOKE THE LOVING PROMISES WHEN WE ARE IN CRISIS. *During stressful circumstances our relationship requires greater loving from me. At those trying times, I will attempt to apply the Loving Promises to the best of my ability.*

Just as there are peaks in life, there are also valleys. We live with triumph as well as defeat, joy as well as sorrow. When enmeshed in crisis, we are caught in life's valleys.

Some dictionary definitions of crisis:
1. An emotionally stressful event or traumatic change in a person's life condition.
2. A situation that has reached critical phase.
3. An unstable condition involving abrupt, decisive change, especially one with distinct possibility of a highly undesirable outcome.

Crisis in relationship can be caused by stressful circumstances external to the relationship dynamic, such as physical illness, intrusive relatives or financial setback. It can also be caused by internal conditions such as a couple's conflict, incompatible goals or a partner's dishonesty. No matter what the source, crisis is stressful and is a test of a couple's bond. The tension from a crisis can rend a couple apart, or it can draw them together in order to preserve the integrity of the bond.

Every crisis, if we engage with it and don't run away, contains within it the opportunity for growth and resolution. Crisis grabs our attention and demands we garner our resources in order to overcome the challenge. The imminent German bombardment of England during WWII drew the populace together and would produce what Prime Minister Churchill called, England's "finest hour." The 9/11 World Trade Center disaster generated a feeling of unity worldwide, and gave rise to story after story of bravery, generosity and compassion as people reached into their heart in response to the crisis. This rise to challenge can occur when relationships are in crisis.

The way I suggest to deal with crisis is simple, but not easy. I can think of no better way of approaching and overcoming the effects of a crisis in relationship than by invoking the Loving Promises. During perilous times, the supportive atmosphere created by the Loving Promises is ideally suited for resolving conflict, reducing stress and inducing mutual support. How better to work through difficult problems than with a large dose of honesty, respect, generosity and loving kindness.

Unfortunately, during times of crisis we tend to find it more challenging to work with the Loving Promises. Our stress, anxiety, exhaustion, resentment or agitated emotional state depletes our resources and makes it necessary for us to put out that extra bit of effort to utilize the truth and power of the Loving Promises. It is at these times that we must garner our energy in order to take the lead and do the loving thing, say the loving words and act in a kind and generous manner. When we reach into our heart and act from our most loving space in times of crisis, we and our partner both can reap the greatest rewards.

It is not only your partner who is in need of greater love during crisis. It is imperative that you treat yourself with loving kindness. Give your body, mind and soul needed nourishment. If you are running on empty, it is difficult to garner the resources to provide loving care to your partner.

Alice and I experienced a devastating crisis several years ago, Jason, my stepson, had heart problems for over a decade, which grew steadily worse until the only thing that could save his life was a heart transplant. For months, we stayed at the hospital from sun-up to sun-down, until the heart was found, the operation performed, and Jason recovered enough to go home. Alice was a mother lion throughout our family's ordeal. She was also understandably emotionally wrought and out of balance. For me, the process of letting go, maintaining emotional stability and coming back again and again to the Loving Promises, allowed me to be of service and a pillar of support for Alice without being drawn into an emotional maelstrom. I have no doubt that Jason's crisis and the Loving Promises brought all of us together even closer. It has been several years since the transplant and Jason is thriving.

Sometimes the route to heaven takes us through hell. Our time in hell, however, gives us a greater appreciation of heaven. The suffering we endure during crisis can open us, deepen us, expand us and give us a greater appreciation of each moment of our life.

33. I WILL HONOR MY OWN NEEDS AND MY OWN FEELINGS.
When trying to uphold these Loving Promises, I will attend to the way I feel. I will not disregard my needs and desires, compromise my values or allow others to overstep my boundaries. I will ask for what I want. I will be who I am.

Almost all of the Loving Promises look at the way you are with your partner. This Promise approaches from a different angle. It asks that you look at yourself

UNDERSTANDING THE LOVING PROMISES

and question: "What is right for me? How will I protect myself? How will I get *my* needs met?" These are very important questions, but also very tricky. This Promise could be used as a protective safety valve, or as weapon, or as a cop-out.

The Loving Promises is a document that sets out ideals of behavior. The Promises serve as guidelines. Even the most diligent person will fall short. This Loving Promise takes into consideration our humanness and imperfection. It gives us permission to accept ourselves with our limitations and not beat ourselves up if we have pushed too far, too fast, exceeded our present limitations or need to beat a hasty retreat. If we didn't include this Promise, we could force ourselves into situations where we are unready. When we say to ourselves, "Ouch! I cannot go there. It asks too much of me at this time. I am too scared, too rushed, too uncomfortable," we are not giving up or running away, we are acknowledging our present reality. With this Promise, we are able to take on all the others with self-care and self-acceptance, rather than self-accusation. This is the key to success of the Loving Promises – do it with loving consciousness. Do it when you are ready – or not quite ready, but don't take on any Promise that will cause you to suffer more than you are able to endure at present. As the Burmese meditation master, Ajahn Chah, has said, "You have to know the strength of your ox cart. You can't load it up too much or it will break down."

If you are on overwhelm and have reached the end of your tether, it is probably time to take stock and see if you have overreached and exceeded your limit – overloaded your oxcart. If you have, it is important to take a stand, even if it is at variance with what your partner wants. Just as it is important for children to know and abide within limits, it is important to define the limits of your own and of other's behavior. "What is acceptable behavior on my own part? What is acceptable behavior by my partner? What is unacceptable? At what point should I take a stand? Am I being too easy on myself . . . or, too hard? Am I being too easy on them . . . or, too hard?" These are questions we must ask ourselves at times. There are no stock answers.

As with most things, the key is moderation. Avoid extremes. Avoid inflexibility. Pursuing the Promises too far, too fast or being too rigid can prove destructive. Without limits, you can overdo it. The Loving Promises are not meant to be followed mindlessly. If you place no limitations on how far you will go to fulfill the Promises, you might be too steadfast and commit to stay together with your partner when it would be harmful to both you and them (Promise #1). You might serve your partner's best interests, making it your life's mission to care for them – and lose yourself in the process (Promise #4). You might be too unselfish with your partner to the point where you neglect your own needs (Promise #5). You might be ruthlessly truthful with your partner to the extent that it causes them needless pain (Promise #18). You might be accepting of your partner's selfish and demanding behavior when that behavior is totally unacceptable and inappropriate (Promise #8). This is why it is necessary to use discrimination when applying the Promises.

In order to work with this Promise it is important to stay in touch with your feelings. Feelings guide you and provide insight into your inner state. This Promise asks you to attend to those feelings and honor the messages they are sending. A question to ask yourself, "Is this course of action beneficial to my body, my mind, my psychological and spiritual growth and well-being?" Listen closely to the feeling texture of your answer.

Attending to and honoring your feelings does not mean always expressing them or acting on them. It does not mean repressing them either. Just allow feelings to arise as they will and try to avoid getting caught up in them and being carried away. An Eastern scripture describes the mind and emotions as represented by a team of horses that pulls a chariot. You are the driver. You hold the reins in your hands. If you do not exercise discipline, the horses will go where they want, dragging you along for the ride. The object of practicing disciplines such as meditation and yoga is to put your unruly mind, body and emotions at the service of your intellect.

A necessary key to implementing this Promise is making your wishes known – being willing and able to ask for what you want and expressing what you don't want. Your partner is not a mind reader. Clearly setting your own boundaries helps your partner by letting them know what your limits are and when and how they might be overstepping those limits. The clearer the boundaries, the easier it will be for your partner to honor those boundaries. And it won't be necessary for you to have to continually negotiate to re-establish them.

Occasionally, Alice will bitch at me, which is not a good thing, even if I need to be "motivated." Or she will push me to do something that she wants done right away, but is inconvenient for me. If I don't handle it well, I will acquiesce to her wishes and then later feel a bit put off, a bit weakened. That's because I didn't honestly address issues that were bothering me during our interaction. I don't deserve bitchiness. It's demeaning. I deserve to do things in my own time, unless it is truly necessary to do them in hers. But Alice deserves a clear, timely and civil response from me. When I address my feelings with her clearly, directly, at the time they are occurring, it serves both of us.

Expressing what you want is difficult because it makes you vulnerable to being rejected or having your request denied, or, if your partner does not want to comply, risking their anger and resentment. So, instead of stating directly what we want, we take an indirect approach. We put off asking or simply make do

UNDERSTANDING THE LOVING PROMISES

with not having our needs met. Or we nag and complain, or try to reason and make a case like a lawyer, or try to manipulate or put out hints. Then we wait and hope for a positive response.

It is more forthright to be direct, but tactful. Ask without demanding. Ask with sensitivity to timing and to the receptivity of the other person. Ask with the understanding that you may be refused. But, if you are not being respected, treated honorably or spoken to in an appropriate manner, do not stand for it. Being loving doesn't mean that you allow yourself to be abused, neglected or your needs ignored.

Saying "no" is usually not enough. Behind your "no" is usually a demand for what you *do* want. Fail to voice that demand and you waive your right to vote. Be sure to state your demand clearly, so the other can understand. Possibly even give consequences if that demand is not met. Not as a threat, but as a likely eventuality. Do not allow for opening a discussion. Opening a discussion will take you off track into arguing pros and cons. Simply state your position and give consequences if appropriate. Example: "I cannot be late for this event. If you are not ready, I will have to leave without you." If you state consequences, follow through. If you don't follow through, you won't be taken seriously next time.

Some people are unwilling or unable to stand up for what they want. Their fear of conflict is so pervasive that they are willing to pay any price for peace. However, when they run from conflict, often the price is too steep and the peace too fragile.

By remaining silent, not taking a stand, not setting boundaries, not expressing disagreement, you are actually sending a message. What you are conveying without words is passive agreement. Most likely, not disagreeing is seen by the other person as actual agreement. You have effectively relinquished your ability to choose in the matter. Failing to state your wants allows the problem to continue. And you feel bad about yourself for being weak and ineffective.

Safeguarding your needs usually doesn't involve taking an inflexible stand and insisting your partner bow to your demands. It usually involves a process of negotiation and compromise. With compromise, I get some, but not all of what of I want, and you get some, but not all of what you want. Negotiating is not about gaining advantage. The aim of fair negotiation is to try to give what your partner needs without denying your own needs. The truth is that you cannot be of service to others by denying your own needs. Ultimately, betraying your genuine needs will harm you and the relationship.

The one thing that should not be negotiable is your integrity. To be at peace with yourself, you must not compromise your moral principles. The way you treat yourself and others must harmonize with your conscience.

Here is the stance Alice and I take with each other in regards to this Loving Promise:

- We do not compromise our deepest needs and values in order to accommodate one another or avoid conflict.
- We do not shy away from telling each other what we think and how we feel, even if our viewpoints conflict.
- While we will hear and respect what each other has to say, we do not let the other's demands and opinions force us into decisions which make us uncomfortable.
- We are prepared to persuade, influence and negotiate with each other when we have conflicting goals.
- We directly ask for what we want.
- We can say "no" and disagree with each other without having to qualify, apologize or make excuses.
- We can demand of each other the right to speak and be heard and have our voices respected.
- We reserve the option to change our mind.

These are the ways Alice and I assertively state what we want and stand up for who we are. Without excuses and justifications, we can say "This is me. This is what I want and need. This is what my limits are. This is what I deserve." By taking a stand for ourselves like this, we affirm that we each are a separate, valuable individual, whose voices and needs deserve to be heard and respected.

All the other Promises focus on helping your partner meet their needs. In the process, an atmosphere of mutual reciprocation is generated that will influence your partner to help you meet yours. Ultimately, a magnificent relationship requires that we are able to strike a balance between satisfying both our own needs and the needs of our partner. If we give too much, we will feel depleted and come in touch with our sense of unfairness. If we take too much, the imbalance fosters guilt and creates tension. The balance we seek is not static; it is a fluid balance. At times, circumstances require that we give more. But other times we are in need of receiving more. What we strive for is a dynamic equilibrium based on the circumstances and requirements of the moment, which supports the other person while supporting ourselves.

UNDERSTANDING THE LOVING PROMISES

This Promise affirms your right to be as you are – without shame, without apology, irrespective of pressure from others. This is a sacred birthright. It deserves to be honored, not only by others, but also by yourself. Especially by yourself, because if you don't fully accept yourself as you are, you won't assert your right that others accept you, and you won't feel worthy of receiving the things you rightfully deserve.

34. I WILL NURTURE MYSELF FOR BOTH OF US. *My well-being affects you as well as myself. I will strive to choose wholesome alternatives in my life that keep my body healthy, my mind positive and my spirit uplifted. I will look after my own needs so I am not overly dependent on you.*

Once you are in a committed relationship, you are no longer a lone individual. You are involved in an interdependent complex of shared responsibilities and shared consequences. Because you are so closely bound, the way you manage your life intimately affects your partner. This Promise acknowledges this fact, and asks that you take exquisite care of your whole being, not only for your own sake, but also for the sake of the ones you love and love you.

The clearest example of the shared effects of attending to your self-nurturance or lack thereof, is how you care for your body. If you neglect your body through faulty health practices, your beloved suffers with you. They have to watch you with helpless anguish as your health declines. They must expend their time and energy, and both of your financial resources, taking care of you when you fall ill. And they will mourn their unlived life with you after your early demise. Conversely, they can also share in the benefits of your healthy, vital life if you eat nutritious foods, exercise, attend to your body when something goes wrong and avoid things that weaken it. Your partner will also share in the effects of the choices you make in nurturing your mental and spiritual health-- the loving attention and care you give to your mind and your soul.

This Loving Promise affirms that we have choice. It remains for us to stay conscious of the choices before us and keep in mind the consequences of those choices. . . then responsibly choose to cultivate behaviors based on self-love, the love of our partner and others we share our lives with. For the most part, wholesome alternatives are self-evident. It is obvious that if my diet consists of sweets and junk food, my health will be impacted. Or, if I fail to address the stresses in my life, my mental stability will be affected. Or, if I lie, cheat and steal and fail to address the hunger in my soul, my spiritual growth will be stunted.

One area that has the potential to cause tremendous suffering and great harm to self and relationship is the misuse of intoxicants. Addictive substances such as alcohol and drugs have been the cause of the downfall of many individuals and the destruction of many relationships. It's not that drugs and alcohol are bad per se, but when they are misused, they have the tendency to incrementally bring on greater and more extensive misuse. Consciousness and carefulness go out the window. Eventually intoxicants distort a person's values and make it their primary goal to get high and stay high. The body, mind, heart and soul are neglected, as is their partner and the relationship.

Beyond the obvious, a wide range of choices before us contributes to our well-being:

Our family: Are we able to commit enough time and attention to our family unit and family of origin?

Our finances: Are we bringing in enough money so that we and our loved ones are living comfortably?

Our career: Are we doing work that provides us a sense of fulfillment and is in alignment with our life's calling?

Our leisure: Do we take pleasure in our free time, and do we have enough?

Our environment: Does our living and workspace suit our needs. Is it clean, neat and attractive?

Our community: Do the people we associate with stimulate, enliven and uplift us?

Our spirit: Do we allow ourselves time and space to be alone and in the company of like-minded seekers in order to replenish our inner reserves?

Our endowment: Are we able to contribute to society to make the world a better place for present and ensuing generations?

All these areas of our life are conducive to living happily or unhappily. How we choose to engage has an impact on our loved ones as well as ourselves.

To nurture yourself requires that you take full responsibility for your physical, mental, social and spiritual well-being. Whether or not your partner participates is not the issue. The issue is whether you assume responsibility. Promise #23 covers the issue of independence in more detail.

Take care of your body. Take care of your mind. Take care of your friendships. Take care of your soul. Master yourself. Confront your issues that drag you down. The greatest gift you can give the ones you love is your own happiness. As you work toward your own fulfillment, you are also working toward your loved one's fulfillment. Taking care of yourself in this way is not being selfish. It is being kind. It is being generous with those you love.

35. I WILL MAINTAIN THE AWARENESS OF THE SPIRITUAL ESSENCE OF OUR RELATIONSHIP. *You, our love, and the bond we share is a sacred gift. It is an essential aspect of my spiritual path. That understanding will inform all the choices I make.*

Previously, I wrote about the evolution of love as a process of moving from a self-serving, "What can I get?" to a generous, "What can I give?" This Promise prompts us to ask, "What can I become?"

The traditional view of the span of a human life is an arc. You are born, grow, peak at early adulthood, begin your decline in middle age, and it's a downward trajectory from then on. That may describe the body, but not the soul. More often, the trajectory of the Spirit is an upward evolution, increasing with age. Conscious effort can affect the angle of that trajectory and this in turn will have a profound effect on your relationship.

What is spiritual? What is the spiritual nature of relationship? The word "spiritual" can conjure images of dimly lit rooms, burning incense, new age music and pictures of foreign looking people in white robes on the walls. These are all merely trappings. That which is spiritual is concerned with a reality greater than oneself. It can be most easily understood in contrast to that which is "unspiritual" – the material, carnal world of the flesh and senses, versus the unseen, intangible world of the Spirit. The temporal versus the eternal. The small self-concerned world of the ego (that which identifies itself with body, gender, profession, social status, etc.) versus an expanded Self that seeks connection with all creation and taps into an elevated consciousness and/or a connection with a Divine Being. The experiential aspect of the the ego-bound self includes feelings of tension, greed, competition, separation. The experiential aspect of this larger Self include feelings of serenity, joy, reverence, awe, a dropping away of boundaries and a sense of kinship with all sentient beings. These states have been likened to intoxication.

Our contemporary culture encompasses material values that are at odds with spiritual values. We are immersed in these values that are passed down through the powerful propaganda of the popular media and by parents, teachers and friends. They tell us that our material world – our cars, clothes, bank accounts and influential friends, is more important than who we are. They tell us that those possessions are the source of happiness. They tell us that we have value only if we are young and beautiful and "with it," and if not, are to be relegated to the junk heap of anonymity. They tell us that there are not enough "goodies" to go around and we must fight others in order to get our fair share . . . and our fair share is never enough. And we are told that we can satisfy any deep spiritual yearnings we have by spending an hour or two in a house of worship every once in a while. These are values of the contracted self. . . not the unbound Self.

When, through spiritual practice, you aim to bring the energies of the Self into your consciousness, you are not trying to add or develop something that is not there. The Self already fully exists within you. The work of spiritual practice is to make manifest the radiant being that you are.

As you identify more with the expanded Self and relinquish identity with the small, ego-dominated self, tendencies toward grasping, ambition, jealousy, need for control and power – all begin to evaporate. In their place flow feelings of serenity, unity and joy that result from identifying with a source of infinite power, infinite consciousness. In the realm of relationship, those same characteristics of serenity, unity and joy are descriptive of the feelings loving couples in magnificent relationship have toward each other. In this sense, *the love couples share is a spiritual experience.*

The farther you progress along the spiritual path and the more closely you identify with the expanded Self, the more deeply you enter into love. This is because *the fullest expression of spirituality is love.* Whether Hindu, Buddhist, Muslim, Jewish or Christian, whatever religion or type of spiritual practice, the single characteristic shared by advanced spiritual practitioners is love. This is not the kind of love reserved only for the near and dear, but unlimited love, love that is extended to all beings. Since love is the essence of spirituality, a person can enter into greater love through engaging in spiritual practices, or they can enter spirituality through the practice of greater, more expansive love.

All religions and spiritual traditions have practices which can help us tap into the Self and transport us to spiritual realms – among them prayer, meditation, chanting, contemplation, study of scripture etc. The purpose of these practices is to help us turn inward in order to become familiar with the Divine energy that permeates the universe and also resides within. This serene, timeless, boundless essence is cloaked and hidden from us by our everyday mind that jumps, like a crazy monkey, from thought to thought, sensation to sensation, desire to desire. By quieting the mind and tapping into that essence, it is possible for us to enter a pool of peace and serenity.

Discovering even a taste of this inner essence and the resulting tranquility and harmony will have a tremendous impact on your relationship. Any change in one partner will invariably affect the other, whether or not they join you on a spiritual path. Your inner harmony will lead to harmony with your partner; your tranquil mind will help calm your partner's mind. As the experience of the Self grows within you, that evokes your partner's Self, and visa-versa. This mutual growth is the purpose of your shared spiritual practice. The ultimate effect on your relationship of your practice is that you will be more able to connect from the Self in you, to the Self in your partner.

This connection with Self is one of the paramount reasons you are in this relationship game. You can have the most magnificent of magnificent relationships, but it's still just a relationship. You'll be deliriously happy and you'll enjoy each other and have an easy life together. But the quest for spirit is more than the pursuit of a happy life. If you want more than a happy life, you will seek out *oneness* with your partner. That search for oneness is a hunger in your soul that cannot be fully satisfied in relationship because that hunger is for connection beyond relationship with your partner. Your ultimate desire is union with the cosmic One. We begin as part of the One. We take form as separate body and mind, yet yearn to return to union with the One. A way to that union is through the relationship, using the relationship as a springboard to catapult you beyond relationship to an ongoing experience of Self.

Although the spiritual quest must be taken by each individual alone, it doesn't have to be taken unaccompanied. In fact, if couples are so inclined, they can be a great support for each other on the path. The power of the intention of two intimate partners working together to elevate self and other is so much more potent than one alone. Even more potent is three spiritual partners. Though I don't have extensive experience of the Judaeo/Christian tradition, I know of many couples who have brought God or Christ into their relationship. What a blessing to have the guidance of a Holy Spirit, the power of prayer, instruction from sacred texts, counsel from a compassionate cleric, inspiration from uplifting religious services and support from a flock of like-minded friends. For many loving couples, their belief in God, acceptance of His love and willingness to listen to His voice and follow His instruction is the very foundation of their magnificent relationship. Their love of God is the glue that bonds them together.

LOVING PROMISES

If you are open to the search for the sacred together, you and your partner can be spiritual teachers for one another. You can lift each other up. When your partner is your co-teacher and shares a life and a home with you, your relationship can become like your church and your home like an ashram, a place of spiritual practice. Actually, spiritual practice in the controlled and rarefied air of a monastery or ashram is easy compared with a practice within the worldly grind of a marriage or intimate partnership. The stresses you must undergo in worldly life makes those that arise in monastic life pale by comparison.

Living in close proximity with your teacher/mate is like living with a spiritual mentor. You are seen and have few places where you can hide. Every day, 24/7, he or she is a witness to you. It is as if they hold up a mirror for you to see clearly when you are being loving, when you are being honest, when you are being respectful, when you are being generous . . . and when you are not. The honest feedback from your partner when you stray from being your best and highest self can be enlightening, as well as humbling. It cuts your ego down to size. Letting go of pride and ego is an uncomfortable but necessary step on the path. I have had my ego shaved by Alice a time or two

Years ago I asked my teacher, Swami Muktananda, the question, "What is a spiritual marriage?" His answer was simple and profound. "Treat each other as gods and goddesses." To see the divinity of the other and treat them with reverence is honoring and serving God. In a similar vein, Mother Teresa, who spent years ministering to the poorest of the poor in India, described the people she helped as *"Christ in His many disguises."* This attitude of honoring your partner as a manifestation of the Divine is a foundation of a spiritual marriage and is the very essence of the Loving Promises. It is also a sure path to a magnificent relationship.

The rub comes when our "god" or "goddess" partner frustrates us by behaving like a selfish, lazy or stubborn, not so godly god. When they act in this ungodly manner, it is easy for our reverent attitude to disappear as we are forced to deal with our own anger, disappointment, annoyance and resentment. This is our test and our burden. But it is also a path to our higher Self. If we use our frustration with our partner as our practice to work with and overcome that frustration, the manure from our vexation can be used to fertilize and grow a magnificent relationship and work to elevate us from self to Self. In simple, practical terms, when your partner is always late, practice patience. When your partner is agitated, practice serenity. When your partner is selfish, practice generosity. When your partner is moody, practice equanimity.

There are many ways Alice and I maintain and expand the spiritual portion of our life together. We read spiritually uplifting books, participate in retreats, attend lectures and services. Alone and together, we engage in meditation and prayer. These have all played a part in helping us cultivate spiritual awareness. People we associate with have a powerful influence on us. Therefore, we make an effort to be in the presence of people who are enlivening and uplifting, while avoiding those who might bring us down. Often we invoke wishes for each other's well-being through prayer and affirmation. Prayers for Alice's health, peace and happiness are part of my (almost) daily meditation sessions.

You create outside what is inside. A person's home environment is a reflection of their heart and soul. The place where Alice and I live is an important aspect of our spiritual life. Our house is an expression of our love and an extension of our spirit. Just as we wish to make our love beautiful, we have aimed to create a beautiful home. We consider our home as our temple, as sacred ground. There is much we have done to maintain it as if it were a place of worship.

We have a small room in our home where we meditate. There is an altar against the wall and behind the altar are pictures of our spiritual teachers. Among the pictures hangs a photograph of ourselves. This is the way we honor each other as spiritual beings and acknowledge that we are teachers for each other. While a separate room for prayer and meditation is helpful, it is not necessary. Even a quiet corner where you can set up an altar, a candle and a comfortable cushion or seat will do. This corner becomes sacred space, imbued with the energy of the spiritual practices performed there.

In most every room and in our garden we have pictures and sculptures of exalted beings – Christ, Buddha, gods and goddesses, saints and various spiritual teachers. These serve as reminders for what we aspire to.

It's good to have reminders. They help us remember to bring to our awareness the holiness that surrounds and infuses us. There is a "bell" that hangs in our garden. I cut off the bottom of a large metal oxygen canister and hung it in a tree. When struck, it has a prolonged, melodious ring. Sometimes, when I pass by, I will sound the bell. I silently intone the mantra, "This moment is sacred," and try to hold on to those words and that sense of the holiness of the moment as the sound vibrations become softer, till they completely die away. Just another way of bringing me into the present and reminding myself, this moment *is* sacred.

There is a lovely poem we came across by author/poet/artist Ingrid Goff-Maidoff, which hangs by our front door and characterizes the spirit in which we wish to inhabit our home.

HOUSE BLESSING

This house is Love's house.
It is a sanctuary, a garden,
a safe haven.
May it be delightful.
May it be a home that encourages
creativity and peace,
togetherness and private time.
May it be an environment
that celebrates life, untidy and ever flowing.
May simplicity be honored in this house,
valuing love above all else.
May daily chores and small moments
all be approached with reverence and with love.
Mistakes may be be seen as lessons learned.
Kindness, forgiveness, laughter, joy
and calm enthusiasm
will nourish all who enter through its doors.
May all who visit leave refreshed.
May all who live in this house
live in contentment and harmony,
dreaming many beautiful dreams,
rejoicing in the way things are.

It is Alice and my desire to make the intentions expressed in this poem always remain alive and well in our home.

A word of caution about the tendency to "spiritualize" with this Promise. We want to be good and kind and spiritual, so we may sometimes deny our anger because we think anger is not "spiritual"; we put up with our partner's hurtful behavior because we want to be "compassionate;" we fail to assert ourselves because we must be "humble"; we withhold judgments because we believe it is "unspiritual" to judge others. As much as we try to live up to the image in our mind of what it is to be a spiritual person, our reality is that we are not saints; we are human. If we deny our humanness in an effort to take on an aura of piety, we deny our aliveness. Our spirit resides in the "juiciness" of who we are. Our holiness is in our shortcomings as well as in our brilliance. If we don't embrace those darker, rejected aspects of ourselves, we become estranged from our power and our true spirit.

UNDERSTANDING THE LOVING PROMISES

We also become estranged from the person we are. When we overreach and attempt to prematurely wrap ourselves in the cloak of spirituality, we can use it to avoid rather than encounter. We try to do this by attempting to rise above real problems by meditating them away or short circuiting our feelings. For example, if our partner has done something to hurt us, we can, in the name of forgiveness, smile, offer our hand and pardon them before we have gone through the necessary process for genuine forgiveness – feeling our hurt, experiencing our anger, expressing that hurt and anger to our partner and demanding accountability from them. Without undertaking these steps, what we have done is simply smooth over the situation, let them off the hook, denied our feelings and avoided a potentially uncomfortable confrontation. This is not spiritual. Unfortunately, by doing this, we have given away our power and missed the opportunity for honest encounter, authentic forgiveness and real growth of the relationship.

The path of spirituality has many twists, turns and dead ends. As you progress farther down the road, the passage becomes narrower, steeper and more tortuous. This is good reason to follow the instructions of a guide, one who has traveled the road and knows the terrain from actual personal experience. Legitimate spiritual teachers are often part of a continuing lineage that carries on the tradition of ancient wisdom. Teachers receive spiritual knowledge from *their* teachers, who received it from *their* teachers, sometimes going back for millennia. Becoming a student, you enter into and are supported by that lineage. In the company of a wise being, you are able to experience firsthand what is possible for a human to attain.

Near the beginning of this Promise, in defining spirit, I describe the opposition of the mundane and the spiritual. That opposition is artificial. Many people believe that to enter into our spiritual nature we must deny our animal nature, as if our physical body, with its passions, grittiness and weaknesses, is of a lesser order that our spirit. But in truth, we are spiritual beings as well as animals. We inhabit our belly as well as our heart and soul. Our body is the vehicle through which our spirit expresses itself. We are one. Our spirit and body are each different sides of the same coin. If we attempt to deny the juiciness of the world and of our bodies, our experience is dry and lifeless. If we deny our holiness and attempt to live only in the world and in our bodies, our experience is also dry and lifeless.

To be fully human we need to embrace it all, exclude nothing. Yes, life is messy, our bodies frail and in process of disintegration. But even with its difficulties and frustrations, the material world is sweet and exciting, entertaining and full of the unexpected. God doesn't make mistakes. He created this world and these bodies as a playground for our enjoyment and edification. We should play, learn and be thankful.

Without a doubt, what has played the largest role in enhancing our spirit in relationship has been maintaining the Loving Promises. The Promises are spiritual practices in themselves. The qualities of awareness, unselfishness, patience, acceptance, kindness, forgiveness and gratefulness that are inherent in the Loving Promises are spiritual attributes. By following the Loving Promises, we expand our spirit. If, as has been said, "God is love," you bring godliness into your life and relationships as you practice and perfect the Promises. That godliness permeates your partnership and makes it holy. Bringing a spiritual sensibility into your relationship is not a luxury. It is a necessity.

36. I WILL REMIND MYSELF OF THE FLEETING NATURE OF OUR TIME TOGETHER. *At some point one of us will be alone. I will endeavor to keep this in my mind and savor the preciousness of each moment I have with you.*

The second hand of the clock ticks away the seconds; the tides flow in and flow out; the earth circumnavigates the sun, marking the passage of another year; a child is born, grows old and passes away; time keeps moving forward. It is a certainty – death will end your relationship. One of you will die first. You won't know when, or how . . . or who. The surviving spouse will live out their remaining years, possibly alone.

Two opposing processes are at play in our life, *attachment*--holding on, and *surrender*--letting go. Attachment is more prominent at the beginning of our life. We acquire physical strength, knowledge, friendships, accumulate material goods and struggle to hold on to what we have acquired. At the end of life, one by one, these things are taken from us. We are forced to surrender our strength, our friends, our possessions. Our final surrender is death.

Every loss is a "little death." If we aspire to "hold on tightly, but let go lightly," we can release the people and things we love to the universe as they pass through our life. And we can be grateful that we have been blessed to be able to share our moments with them.

When your relationship is good it is natural for you to want it to go on forever. As Alice exclaims, "Freeze time! Freeze time!" But time marches on. The price you pay for a magnificent relationship is the excruciating pain you will experience at the death of your beloved partner. That's the downside of a great relationship – you have so much more to lose. When your partner is taken from you, it is as if an essential organ is ripped from your body. No wonder that it is

UNDERSTANDING THE LOVING PROMISES

not an uncommon occurrence for elder couples who are close, that when one partner dies, the other follows a short time later.

Nothing is a more powerful motivator than the remembrance of our mortality. It serves to remind us of the fragility of life and the sweetness of the relationship with the one we love. Being in our 70s, Alice and I have done the math. We know our time is limited. And so, each morning, as we awaken, we smile at each other thankfully and say, "Well, we made it another day." And each evening and at times when we take leave of each other, one of us will often say, "If I don't see you again Babe, it's been a great run."

In the past, Alice and I would have marriage vow renewal ceremonies from time to time. It was good to celebrate our magnificent relationship and a great opportunity for a party. Several years ago we decided to have our last ceremony. We had been living our vows and felt we didn't need to repeat them. We decided on one vow that, as we grow older has greater meaning for us. "May we always remember that this day could be the last day we might be together." The meaning behind that vow continues to reverberate within us and has added to the sweetness of our life together. It left us with the feeling of being "privileged." Even simple acts like doing the dishes, listening to each other's complaints, having a meal together, are a privilege. In fact, simply being human and being alive is a great privilege.

No matter what our age, we are all engaged in the process of dying. Our dying started the moment we were born. Each day we live brings us a day closer to death. If we could love our beloved with the understanding that this year, this month, this week, or this day, could be the last time we see them, speak with them, touch them, how beautiful that love would be and how deeply felt our gratitude that we are able to share this day and to have had all those yesterdays together.

Unfortunately, no amount of sitting at the feet of wise teachers and listening to profound discourses on impermanence, reading elevated spiritual tracts, or deep contemplation on the transitory nature of life, will put you in touch with the truth of your ephemeral existence. Oblivious to the ticking clock, you go about living your busy life, working, doing the laundry, complaining about the lousy weather, traffic, rising prices. Yet, to really wake up to the reality of the fragility of your life, you need an actual experience – a life-threatening illness, the death of someone close to you.

Several years ago I had a serious health issue – a heart attack in a remote village in Sicily. This abruptly brought on fears of my imminent demise and thoughts of the possibility that I would never again be with Alice. Fortunately, I came through better than before. Afterwards, tastes became sweeter, colors brighter and the delight and comfort of holding Alice my arms was amplified a hundredfold. Much of that loving feeling and deep thankfulness has remained with me to this day. Every moment after that fateful day I consider gift. For the rest of my life, I will celebrate June 21st, the day of my attack, as a second birthday, a re-birthday.

How easy it is to forget though. It is difficult to conceive of your own death and even more difficult to maintain that awareness. It takes a conscious effort to bring your mind around to the impermanence of your existence. Most people's tendency is the opposite – they want to obliterate the thought. On the contrary, Alice and I want to keep the idea of impermanence in our awareness. We find it helpful to place reminders of our impermanence right in front of our nose. Together we read the obituary section when we get a hold of a newspaper, knowing that one day we too will be listed. For years I have worn a ring with a skull on it, the skull facing towards me. The plastic patient identification bracelet from the hospital where I was treated for my heart attack hangs on the wall near the door, where I will see it every time I pass. Right below the light switch in our office is a copy of the digital x-ray of the whole of Alice's skull, with her name printed on the bottom. At some point this is what she will look like.

Actually, we can easily do away with obituary notices, rings and x-rays. We have reminders of impermanence right in front of our faces. All we have to do is gaze into the mirror or look at each other and we will see ample evidence that the sand in the hourglass of our life is running out. We watch the physical effects of our aging with a mixture of amusement and regret, fascinated by what time is wreaking on our face and body, but saddened by the drawing down of our life.

This contemplation of aging, death and impermanence is important work. It is far too important to save it till death is close at hand. Don't assume you can do the work on your deathbed. It is too late then. You have no idea of what your mental state will be at that time, So start now, start a dialog with impermanence at whatever age you are. When you have incorporated the wisdom from impermanence into your life, you will be able to draw on it when the time comes.

Alice and I have had discussions, as I am sure many other couples have, of the question, "If we had a choice, which one of us would go first?" Our answer, "I'd go first, I can't stand the thought of living without you." Or, "Maybe you should go first so you don't have to experience the pain of being without each other." It's not up to us. Life will make that decision. Either way, the pain of separation is almost unbearable. I say "almost" because the years of love and joy we have given each other is a gift that can make even the pain of loss worthwhile. And that love will give us the strength to go on.

UNDERSTANDING THE LOVING PROMISES

Several years ago we had a conversation with the spiritual teacher Ram Dass about our fears of separation from each other by death. For many years Ram Dass had worked with the dying in hospice settings. He told us his belief that love is eternal, that there is no separation between souls and that our higher Self is one with each other. He shared that even years after the death of his guru, Neem Karoli Baba, the experience of his presence is even stronger than it had been when he was alive. The thought that we might one day reunite after death gives us solace. We shall see.

Contemplating our end of life is not a morbid thing that we do. It is simply an unvarnished recognition of reality. The cycle of birth and death is the nature of the universe. All are subject to impermanence, from a tiny bacterium to the largest star. All you see and know will arise, maintain for a while, and pass away. The reward for bringing this to your awareness from time to time is a deeper appreciation of your relationship, thankfulness for the presence of your beloved partner and greater enjoyment of each precious moment of your life together.

That appreciation can translate to action. Since you don't know when your life will end and when will be the last time you will see your beloved, seize the moment. With the knowledge that in the end you will inevitably lose, love with all your heart. Don't hold back! Give love! Give the best of yourself! Express your love! Love not expressed will cause you pain later on. Don't hold on to anger. Don't judge. Don't delay. Feel your love, speak your love, act your love. The most precious gift you can give is your loving heart.

37. I WILL DEEPEN MY LOVE FOR MYSELF. *If I do not love me, I cannot give love to you, nor can I be available to receive your love. I will aspire to acknowledge myself as unconditionally lovable. I will adapt the Loving Promises so that they apply to myself.*

This Promise is a quintessential one. Self-love is the prototype for all love. Without self-love you cannot give and receive love. Though the Promise is about giving love to yourself, the effect of loving yourself is that you become better able to receive love from others. This is crucial. If you don't believe you are deserving of love, you will not be open to receive love. You will be running on empty and therefore be unable to replenish your reserve. Without a cachet of love in your tank, you will hoard and have little available for others. You will be miserly in your giving and constricted in your receiving. However, when you overflow with love and acceptance for yourself, giving love to others and taking in their love for you happens easily. So, self-love is the key to both receiving and giving love.

Though we think we are able to hide the way we feel about ourselves from others, we cannot. If we do not love and respect ourselves, that message is broadcast in myriad ways, mostly unconscious. The words we use, our tone of voice, our posture, eye contact etc. reveals our true feelings of worthiness or unworthiness. Others pick up these signals and tend to respect and treat us to the same degree we respect and treat ourselves. And the way others treat us provides us feedback as to whether we are deserving or undeserving of love.

Self-love is not about the future, and it's not about deserving. If you think you can't love yourself until you live up to all the ideals you have set for yourself, right all the wrongs you have done, erase all the imperfections you believe you have, self-love will never happen. You will be engaged in working on your self-improvement for the rest of your life. To be self-loving you need to accept yourself and love yourself as you are now, not as you wish to be.

To see ourselves clearly for who we are, to know that we are capable of great kindness toward others (as well as great harm), great wisdom (as well as great stupidity) gives us the right to join the human race. Yes, under the right conditions, we can be cowardly, mean, lazy, or selfish. As much as we want to separate ourselves from owning these qualities, they are within us. Recognizing, accepting and befriending these disowned qualities opens the way for us to love ourselves. And that opens the way for us to love others.

Metta, the loving kindness meditation, traditionally begins with an affirmation of self-love, initially sending wishes for happiness, peace, health and kindness first to our self. Pouring loving thoughts and feelings upon ourselves is like spreading healing salve on a wound. The salve of self-love marks a ceasefire in the internal war and begins the process of softening the obstinate grip of self-loathing, self-judgment, self-condemnation and self-flagellation.

I believe that more than anything else, an increase in my openness to love myself was the factor that made it possible for Alice and I to come together as a couple. By the time I had met her, something had ripened within me that allowed me to know and accept that I was being genuinely loved by her and to understand that I was deserving of that love. This ripening was brought about by several factors. The immediate one was that I was in the presence of a person who was so obviously right for me that there was no question in my mind. Also, she was so steadfastly generous in her expression of love for me that I couldn't avoid taking it in.

This feeling that I was worthy of love was long in coming. For years I had a progressively awakening sense that I was a person who was deserving of love. I came to realize that I was intrinsically deserving. This was not based on my expansive knowledge, my limitless wealth, my fabulous possessions, my diverse talents, my fascinating history or anything else that I had tried to use in order to seduce others into admiring me. That bottomless well of unworthiness, inadequacy, of feeling not good enough to be loved (with which I had lived since I was a child) had gradually evaporated. I had little need to prove to others, and to myself, that I was deserving of love. I just was. And because I was, and I knew it, I reached out with open arms and accepted Alice's love.

Love of self is difficult to achieve in our society. Self-love is often disparaged and equated with selfishness and self-centeredness, though, in fact, they are opposites. The self-centered person is incapable of self-love, but supremely suited for self-seeking. Because they feel empty of love for themselves, they desperately struggle to grab what satisfactions they can in a futile attempt to fill the void in their heart. In contrast, individuals who love themselves have surplus love, love that can easily overflow to others.

This difficulty achieving self-love often originates early in life. Most of us are born into families where we are raised by people who love us conditionally – love is extended when we are good and withheld when we are bad. From childhood on, we are graded, evaluated and assessed. We are judged better or worse, good or bad, and are rewarded or punished based on comparison with our peers. Only if we are considered smart, beautiful, obedient, rich, glib or talented do we get the goodies. If we are not, we end up with the wrong end of the lollipop. Fearing being left out or "less than," we adopt and internalize these standards set by others. If we fail to measure up, we judge ourselves deficient and unworthy of love. This conditional self-appraisal poisons our soul and makes it difficult for us to give and receive love.

On the surface, the way out seems obvious – work harder at becoming smarter, more beautiful, richer, etc. – or at least fool others into believing you are. This rarely works. The truth is that you cannot earn the love of the person who wants and needs this love the most – yourself. You can earn others praise, approval, respect and admiration. But in your heart of hearts you want more. You yearn to be immersed in love, to be embraced and held by love. This can only come from you. For this to happen, your love for yourself must be unconditional. You must see clearly all your warts and scars, all your weaknesses and stupidities, all your past failings. You must acknowledge these and still be able to honestly say . . . "I am lovable. I am lovable just as I am."

This is so much easier said than done. All your life, you believed people would love you "Because" . . . because you did them favors, because you didn't create problems, because you had money, because you were beautiful, because you were interesting, because . . . All your life, you pushed away awareness of your shortcomings. All your life, you have presented this smooth and polished image to the world, while deep down knowing the "real" you was blemished and broken. It is risky to see all this. To openly acknowledge your imperfections might push you deeper into self-loathing.

One powerful antidote is to take a more spiritual perspective and grasp a larger understanding of who you really are. You are so much more than you have come to believe you are. You have a body, but you are not just that physical body. You have senses but you are not just those sensations. You have emotions, but you are not just your feelings. You have a mind but you are not just your thoughts. Who is this "you" that experiences the body, senses, emotions, and thoughts? Beyond the senses, thoughts and feelings is the original "I," conscious presence, the Self. This is the pure, serene awareness that watches and listens through the senses, thinks through the mind, is conscious of the passing thoughts, and witnesses the rising and falling away of the emotions. You are silent presence, timeless and without boundaries. Water cannot wet you, fire cannot burn you, no one can harm you. If you identify, even a little, with this expanded aspect of yourself, your perspective expands immeasurably. You are able to see yourself as both divine and mundane. This expanded perspective can lift you above conditional self-appraisal and allow you the possibility to love yourself and appreciate yourself as the imperfect, miraculous being that you are.

The Indian spiritual master, Swami Nityananda, said it beautifully and captured the breadth of this expanded vision of a human being when he would tell people, "You are a shit factory, a mere dog in my courtyard . . . and you are God."

The Loving Promises can help cultivate self-love. The Promises are guidelines for loving your partner. Why can they not be used as guides to loving yourself? They can! With a change in the wording of the Promises and elimination of those that cannot apply, the Loving Promises can be a useful guide for helping you to greater love for yourself. Below are some Promises that could apply to yourself.

SELF LOVING PROMISES

I will be awake to myself
I will be supportive of myself
I will be accepting of myself
I will regard myself as equal to others
I will emphasize my positive side
I will inspire myself to be my best
I will be grateful for the gifts I receive from myself

UNDERSTANDING THE LOVING PROMISES

I will appreciate myself
I will be forgiving of myself
I will be dependable for myself
I will be honest with myself
I will speak to myself with kindness
I will honor my independence
I will be considerate of my desire for privacy and solitude
I will bring joy and play into my life
I will seek to grow and evolve
I will be alert to my negativity when it occurs
I will assume responsibility for my self-detrimental behavior
I will honor my needs and my feelings
I will make a place in my life for the spiritual
I will remind myself of the fleeting nature of my life

Just as the Loving Promises are about coming to peace with our partner, these Self Loving Promises are about coming to peace within ourselves. Being awake, supportive, accepting of self, etc., brings about inner peace. This subject could easily be the basis for a whole book.

A recurring theme of this and other chapters has been, *accept yourself, be as you are*. But these Self Loving Promises and indeed, the Loving Promises themselves, seem to stand in contradiction to self-acceptance. Even the use of the word "will" (like "I *will* be unselfish," I *will* be flexible), implies that I am not generous and not flexible, and need to be. It seems to say, "I am not good enough as I am and I need to change." This is not self-loving and is not the intent of the Promises.

It is important to understand that the Promises are not about judging good or bad, but about becoming more skillful in utilizing your energies to more effectively reach goals that will bring yourself and your partner positive, life-affirming outcomes. By lacking the element of judgement, this concept of skillful/unskillful is very different from good/ bad. If you can incorporate the idea of skillful/unskillful into your life, it can be a powerful opening. Applied to your relationships, it can help resolve conflicts, avoid blame, and enhance your ability to love. Labeling the less than perfect parts of yourself as "unskillful" rather than judging yourself defective can also make it easier to love yourself.

38. I WILL EXPAND MY LOVE INTO THE WORLD. *My love will wither if it is reserved only for you. I will extend my love and care to family and friends, acquaintances and strangers, to nature and to all of creation.*

LOVING PROMISES

In order for love to be complete, it needs to reside in three domains – the domain of love between intimate partners, (which is the subject of most of this book), the domain of self-love, (the subject of the previous Loving Promise), and ultimately, the domain of love for the world, (which includes those people and things that extend beyond intimate partners and immediate family.) In a nutshell and oversimplifying, the process of the evolution of love is the movement from the focus on *me* (self), *to us* (intimate dyad), to *we* (the world).

Many people think that the true measure of love they have for their partner is that they love them exclusively. The refrain "I love you, only you, and nobody else but you," is considered a compliment. But is it? Can it be real love if your partner is the only person you care about and you remain indifferent to the rest of humanity? No. Love is the concern for the well-being of that which we love, and willingness to act on that concern. It is not a product of the partner or relationship, but rather is a quality of the person who is loving. It is the way they see the world, and is woven into the very fabric of who that person is.

Love has a natural tendency to enlarge and become more inclusive. The more love you have to give, the more you will automatically attract loving people into your life, and when they come, they will bring their love to you, and you will spread your love to them. Love will infuse your whole life. After I met and fell in love with Alice, my relationship with others transformed. The acceptance, generosity and compassion that were awakened in me spread out into my whole world. I took on Alice's family as my own as my love expanded to her two teenage children Jason and Angela, and her parents, aunts, uncles, cousins, nieces and nephews. My relationship with my own parents, whom I had kept at arm's length, vastly improved. We began to visit them regularly and I actually enjoyed and looked forward to the visits. Same with my brother Steve. Old friendships were rekindled. I reconnected with my ex-wives and we re-experienced the love that had been dormant for years, and took that love to a higher level. My work improved as I brought the love I shared with Alice into the workplace. Opening to love allowed me to bestow loving feelings on literally everyone in my life.

We can expand our love into the world through the process of inclusion. When the sphere of our love and concern is condensed and focused mainly on our self – in meeting our personal needs, we tend to fixate on others mainly as sources for the satisfaction of those needs. We also tend to see the rest of the world as being in competition with us for "goodies," for attention, for affection. If we are able to bring even one other person within that personal, self-focused sphere, and find joy and value in satisfying their needs, our world expands tremendously. However, the rest of the world is still left out and in competition.

UNDERSTANDING THE LOVING PROMISES

If we include family, friends, those in our religion, our ethnic group, our social class, our country, we still eliminate most of the world from our area of loving concern. Even if we include all of humanity, we have still left out other nonhuman living beings that we share our planet with. And what of our loving concern for our earth, its climate and resources. If we do this, include everyone and everything as if they are our beloved friends, relatives and intimate partners, we will be immersed in love. There will be no "me" vs "us" – only "we."

How wonderful it would be if the lines of separation we draw between each other were erased and we could include everyone as our beloved family. Even better, what if we could begin seeing all the others as manifestations of our own self, viewing them as our self, except dressed in a different body. That is the ultimate in togetherness.

The final *metta* affirmation is about expanding our love and good wishes to everyone, to the "we" in our consciousness. The affirmation reads:

May all beings be happy.
May all beings be peaceful.
May all beings be free of suffering.
May all beings love and be loved.

This form of *metta* could be an important practice to help us expand our love into the world and can be part of the *metta* practice that includes yourself and your loved ones.

The desire to love all humanity, love all living beings, love all of creation, is a noble purpose, but "humanity" is an abstraction. What is real and concrete is the person who stands before you "in the flesh." That is where your love of "all of creation" should start.

Mouthing the words of *metta* is easy. Practicing "in the flesh" is hard. As I walk down the street, I notice a disheveled man sitting on the sidewalk with a hand lettered sign, asking for money. He puts his palm out and tries to catch my eye so he can begin his well-practiced entreaty. Do I avoid his gaze and walk on as if I didn't notice him? Do I reach in my pocket to fish for a few coins to throw into his palm so I don't have to engage? Do I pause and place bills rather than change in his hand? Do I stop, look him in his eyes and see and connect with this human being who is obviously in need? Though I intone the lofty words of *metta* daily, more times than I wish to remember, I cast my eyes down and pass by such a person as if they didn't exist.

Expanded love has limits. I wouldn't want to invite that homeless man into my house to live with me. You cannot save the world. You have limited time, energy and resources and you must make decisions as to where you invest those resources. While you can try to offer love and care to all beings, it doesn't mean you need to be around them, especially those who will compromise your growth, safety and happiness. If a person in your life is an addict or has a debilitating mental illness, by all means, love them deeply, assist them in getting the help they need, but be discriminating as to how much you allow them into your life.

Loving in the expanded way described by this Promise is loving without limits. Loving without limits is very different from what we consider "normal love," which is based on our judgment of the attractive qualities of the object of our love or on their willingness to love us back. Limitless love does not involve judgments. It sees the lovability of everyone.

Like the sun, the light of our expanded love does not discriminate. It falls on everyone and everything. The warmth of that love is not reserved for people. We extend love and care to our pets, and further, to all animals. It is not reserved for living beings. We extend love and care to our home, and further, to our environment and to planet earth. As we grow into this limitless love, we approach the fulfillment of our life's purpose and the ultimate purpose of the Loving Promises– to imbibe love, to be love, to be a beacon of love whose beams radiate out to all of creation.

The 38 vows in this chapter encompass all the Loving Promises except the last one. The final Promise is an extension of Promise #38 and will be found in the concluding chapter.

The Loving Promises are true and powerful. And they are beautiful in their depth and comprehensiveness. You could design a fine poster, put it in a nice frame and hang it on your wall. Or you could read and reread the Promises until you have committed them to memory. But, in order to benefit, you must engage the Promises, work with them and integrate them into your everyday life. Use them as guidelines for the choices you make with your partner. Utilize them as a yardstick against which to measure your behavior. The Promises are meant to be translated to action and, until they are, they are essentially useless and not worth the paper on which they are written. You will never satisfy your appetite by reading recipe books. Get into the kitchen and start cooking.

UNDERSTANDING THE LOVING PROMISES

The following chapters contain some recipes, suggestions that might help in working with the Promises, and some thoughts about specific issues that may arise.

Part Three

Fulfilling the Promises

Chapter 6

ENCOUNTERING CONFLICT

A committed relationship can be compared to a rock tumbler. A tumbler is a device for polishing rocks. It is a tube closed at both ends that slowly rotates, powered by an electric motor. A number of rocks are placed in the tube, which then revolves for a long time. The rocks rub against each other and the constant friction causes their jagged edges to abrade away. After a while, the surfaces of the rocks are polished perfectly smooth and shiny, and the beautiful patterns and striations ingrained in each rock are revealed. The friction causes these rough, ordinary-looking stones to become magnificent. In relationships, the friction is the conflicts and disagreements that inevitably arise between partners through the process of everyday living. Rather than ignoring or wishing conflicts to go away, see them as opportunities to learn to be a more loving, beautifully-polished partner.

About Conflict

A long-term, loving relationship is an opportunity to open up your world by getting to intimately know another person. It's also an opportunity to open up your inner world by getting to know yourself. When you live alone, you are able to rest easily just being yourself and are free to see and do things your own way, unimpeded. There is no one around you to obstruct you, challenge you, or offer a contrasting perspective. When you are living with a partner and that person is sensitive to you, vocal with their opinions and not afraid to assert their boundaries, the inevitable conflicts you have with them will allow you to find out just how selfish you are, how inattentive you are, how sloppy you are, how intolerant you are. These are valuable insights

Conflicts can provide clarity. They can help you become more observant, more kind, more considerate . . . more human. In this sense, conflict is beneficial. It is the instrument that has the potential to wake you up, inform you, challenge you and help you grow. Often couples think that when they are having conflict there is something wrong with the relationship, that conflict is a bad thing and should be eliminated. Actually, the collision of desires and wills is an indication that the relationship is real and is on track. A relationship where conflict is ignored, avoided or covered up is in trouble. The absence of conflict is not an indication that the relationship is healthy, nor is the presence of conflict an indication that the relationship is in trouble. If you listen to your conflicts with an open mind, you can learn from them. With this understanding of conflict as teacher, we can ask the questions, "What can I learn from this conflict? How can I devise creative solutions?" This is much better than questioning "How can I avoid this conflict?" or worse, "How can I change my partner in order to get them to agree with me so that they will leave me alone?"

Early on in my marriage with Alice, I hit upon a perfect solution for resolving our most sticky conflicts. I suggested to Alice that if we were ever stuck in an impasse where we couldn't agree on a course of action, the final decision would rest with me. I would be the one, with my great wisdom and Solomon like fair-mindedness, to choose a just and equitable resolution to our disagreement. Alice, in her womanly wisdom agreed, knowing that a one-sided solution like that would never work. Needless to say, within a day or two, I told Alice to forget that stupid idea. Of course she agreed, and it was never mentioned again, except in jest.

Conflict originates between two people when their beliefs or needs or intentions do not match. When there is conflict, we are impelled to action. There are three broad actions we can take. We can move *toward* – placate, accommodate, give in, in order to avoid conflict. We can move *away* – withdraw, evade, ignore the conflict. Or we can move *against* – compete, argue and try to win.

Situations exist where passivity, evasion and assertion are appropriate, and situations where they are inappropriate and ill-advised. If you use an action in an inappropriate situation or use one action as your exclusive strategy for conflict resolution, you could inflame the conflict or sabotage yourself. The danger in moving *toward* is that you can frustrate your own needs and bruise your self-esteem. In moving *away*, you fail to address conflicts and therefore cannot resolve them. When moving *against*, you risk creating a nonproductive, combative situation.

Each action has its positive side. There are times when there is good reason to give in, times when withdrawing in order to avoid conflict is the best move, and times when setting limits, standing your ground and going after what you want is the right thing to do. A loose, eclectic approach, where you remain open and gauge your actions to the situation is the most workable.

Easier said than done. Each of us has personality characteristics that draw us to one or another method of conflict resolution. A person who tends to want to please and accommodate others might find it difficult to challenge and confront when needed. A person who thrives on engagement and competition might find it difficult to withdraw from conflict when that is the appropriate action. With an understanding of our personality tendencies, a clear appraisal of our partner's and our needs, and a genuine desire for a fair outcome, we have the basis for the resolution of all but the stickiest conflicts.

It would seem that two rational people can come to agreement on their differences. The problem is that though we have a rational brain, our nervous system is primitive. Prehistoric ancestors were faced with life or death challenges. There were saber tooth tigers roaming around that wanted to have them for lunch and roving bands of Neanderthals waiting to steal their lunch from them. Their bodies were primed for fight or flight. Our bodies retain those same primitive responses. In everyday life, conflict can be blown way out of proportion, experienced as a threat, as a catastrophic life or death situation when no such threat exists. Such events as being criticized by our boss, holding back anger, engaging in a heated argument with our partner, can cause powerful physiological responses. These give us a jolt of energy and can amplify strong fight or flight reactions. While our physical safety and survival might not be at risk, we see our beliefs, our sense of right and wrong and our ego being challenged. Our body automatically responds to the challenge by secreting chemicals that activate us and stimulate our emotions. Reason goes out the window and the dispute turns into war.

There are two divergent meanings for the word "conflict." There is conflict that is a fight, where partners are at war, competing with each other, each trying to win. I call this "combat conflict." Another kind of conflict is one that reflects a difference – different wants, different perceptions. These kinds of conflicts can be termed "disagreement conflicts." Disagreement conflicts are workable. With discussion and compromise, partners can come to an agreement if they are willing and able to put in the effort and compromise. Partners in combat conflict aren't interested in resolution. Their only interest is to engage in battle and emerge the victor. Disagreements are an inevitable result of living together. Two people cannot avoid having dissonant needs and differing perspectives at times, but **disagreements do not have to turn into combat.**

ENCOUNTERING CONFLICT

Tendencies toward Combat

Most people have immature and ineffective tendencies inherent in their personality makeup that in conflict situations can act to detonate disagreements and blow them up into combat. These *tendencies to combat* become energized in the heat of an argument. As the conflict progresses and heats up, these personality characteristics impel a person to take a rigid, polarizing position, one that evokes opposition in their partner. I believe all but the meekest among us have, at least to some degree, most of these tendencies listed below. I know I have.

While actively engaging in a heated conflict:

- We tend to be blind to others' needs and feelings.
- We tend to want to win and come out on top.
- We tend to need to be right and avoid being wrong.
- We tend to avoid disapproval by being defensive.
- We tend to blame others.
- We tend to take a rigid stance.
- We tend to be reluctant to reconcile.
- We tend to try to maintain control.
- We tend to take things personally.
- We tend to be impatient.
- We tend to take for granted that we know what is going on in another's mind.
- We tend to depend only on our own beliefs and perceptions.
- We tend to stir things up and provoke when challenged.
- We tend to become emotionally charged.

Each of these tendencies makes combat more likely. Fear, powered by underlying insecurity, is the motivation behind these tendencies. And fear is what makes them so potent – fear of being judged to be wrong or bad or incompetent, fear of being unable to control a person or situation, fear of not being able to get a fair share. Fear brings on defensiveness, rigidity, impatience, need to control and all the other combative tendencies on the list. What makes conflict so confusing sometimes is that the struggle in an argument is usually not about the issue being argued, but about the lurking fear and insecurity that lie behind the issue. Adding to the confusion, the *tendencies to combat* themselves ratchet up the conflict.

When these tendencies are active in an individual or couple, it is far more likely that the disagreement in which they are engaged will turn into combat, and when two people are locked in combat, they are stuck and there is little chance of problems getting resolved.

Though these tendencies are present in adults, they originate in our childish ego state. That's the part that believes and demands, "The world revolves around me, give to me – NOW! I know what's best, take care of me. I'm special, my needs come first." As adults, it is possible for us grow beyond these childish ego demands, espouse patience, awareness and generosity and thus moderate these combative tendencies. Approaching conflict in this mature way, we are able to create an atmosphere where conflicts can be resolved peaceably. That atmosphere is *goodwill*. In conflict, goodwill is the generous intention for the highest and best outcome for everyone involved. Goodwill feels safe because it helps to dissolve fear. Goodwill is a healing balm.

In conflict, goodwill creates safety and dissolves fear because you are:

—attentive and sensitive rather than unaware and indifferent
—fair rather than trying to win and take advantage
—flexible and open-minded rather than closed and unyielding
—aiming to be calm and rational rather than emotional and impulsive
—oriented toward problem-solving rather than blame

When you are attentive, fair, flexible, rational and solution oriented, you are actively demonstrating goodwill. You are evoking trust in your partner. With an atmosphere of goodwill, two people can feel safe enough to abandon their fears, lay down their defensive weapons and embark on the process of working things out.

It is not always mutually beneficial for both partners to be of goodwill in order to create an atmosphere of goodwill. Although it is faster, easier and less grueling when both partners work together harmoniously for a mutually-beneficial outcome, goodwill is such a powerful sentiment that it is possible for one person with goodwill in their heart to draw out the goodwill of the other. It takes two to tango and if one partner is gracious in their approach and unwilling to engage in the combat, there is no one available with whom the other can do the conflict tango. Even if your partner never comes to a place of peace with you, at least you can come to peace within yourself. That is the most important requisite for conflict resolution.

Goodwill can be cultivated. Basically, you create goodwill by acting as a mature, caring adult with your partner. Rather than turning your attention outward--grasping, blaming, attacking-- you focus inside yourself. You do this in order to uproot the habitual tendencies that reside in you which cause and perpetuate combat. You work with each of those child ego tendencies listed previously and attempt to transform them into loving adult intentions. Then you turn those intentions into action in the relationship. That is the process. The following are illustrative of ways I attempt to work with my tendencies to combat.

I intend to decrease my self-absorption – instead, I try to observe and listen for your thoughts and feelings. If we were involved in a conflict and my only concern was to push my point across, prove myself right or disparage your position, this would only serve to ratchet up the dissension. If, instead, I listen patiently to you, show genuine interest in what you say, take time for serious consideration of your thoughts and feelings, this would demonstrate to you that I have an earnest intention to reach a fair outcome to our disagreement. So the first and foremost activity in a conflict is to not promote, defend or explain your position, but to absorb your partner's point of view. That atmosphere of receptivity is the best opening gambit for resolving conflict.

I intend to curb my need to win or avoid losing – instead, I try for us to both win. "Winning isn't everything; it's the only thing." Coach Red Sanders' statement describes an attitude that will get you far in competition. However, relationship is not competition. It's about cooperation. I can compare it to playing music with a group of musicians. I play drums in a jazz combo. When we are playing, each of my fellow musicians supports each other. We all try our best to make the other members of the band sound good. When that happens, we all have a good time and make beautiful music together.

The *either/or* mindset incites fear, promotes competition and is fuel to the fire of conflict; *If my way is right, yours must be wrong. If I win, you must lose. My getting more, means you must get less.* Start off with the proposition that it is possible for both you and your partner to get your needs met. This counters the fear that one of us might end up the loser.

Alice and I work this way when we are in conflict. We are partners, not competitors. We try to avoid the win/ lose game completely – no trying to get our own way at the other's expense, no trying to defeat the other in an argument. Whether we compromise or give in or let go of caring about the outcome, it doesn't matter. What is important is that we are each in each other's corner. When that happens, there are no losers. However, if one of us wins and the other loses – we both lose. Conflicts don't end when one person has defeated the other. That's when they begin in earnest.

<u>I intend to eliminate my compulsion to be right and avoid disapproval – instead, I try to be fair with you and see the merits of your position rather than be blameless</u>. Being right – asserting, "I am the correct one, I am the fair one, I am the honest one, I am the mistreated one, I am the reasonable one" – gets you nothing more than the booby prize for righteousness. It doesn't solve problems, it derails solutions. It doesn't give you peace of mind, it makes you more agitated. It doesn't bring you closer, it distances you from your partner.

In our early days Alice and I would prolong a disagreement forever in order to prove our point. Being right was important to each of us. It was as if being proven wrong was an attack on our value as a human being. As we matured, we came to the conclusion that it is better to be loving than to be right. Now, unless it is an issue of real importance, we almost always let things pass, even if we know we are right. Alice's mom's oft-used non-combative phrase "You may be right," has been used by us to defuse many an argument that was not worth having. It is effective because it leaves very little on which to hook an argumentative response. (Care must be taken when using statements like this. It could be used to put someone off and avoid real encounter).

Asserting that you are right puts your partner in the position of being wrong. Nobody likes that, so they get defensive, angry, stubborn and argumentative. You are now in the difficult position of trying to provide evidence to convince them that they are wrong, and having to criticize, complain and nag them to change. Give up the right/wrong game when you are in conflict. Make goodwill your goal. Even if you are right, sometimes it is best to *keep it a secret.*

<u>I intend to counteract my tendency to become defensive – instead, I try to be open to hear your disapproval without needing to justify myself</u>. When someone, especially someone close to you, criticizes you, admonishes you, puts you down, says you are wrong, it is natural for you to become defensive. You might express your defensiveness by denying wrongdoing or trying to justify your actions, attacking your partner or distancing yourself by becoming silent and unresponsive. Defensiveness in any form escalates conflict because while you are busy defending yourself, your accuser doesn't feel that they have been heard. It's true, your defensiveness puts up a wall that prevents their message from getting through to you. Your preoccupation with defending yourself makes it impossible for any genuine connection to take place.

ENCOUNTERING CONFLICT

You have relatively little control over the feelings of defensiveness that overcome you. What you do have control over is your response. Rather than spontaneously react with justification or denial or with a counter-offense, you can respond in a way that the other person feels their message has been received.

If I sense my defensiveness coming on when Alice aims daggers (criticism) at me, I try to listen quietly, quash my immediate tendency to respond to her if I'm still having the dialogue going on in my head, "She's wrong. I'm not at fault. She shouldn't speak to me this way." Eventually this defensive self-talk will quiet down. Just giving myself a few seconds to go inside, collect my thoughts and calm my body allows me to suppress a defensive reaction. I can use that time to digest what Alice has to say, see the truth or falsity and either agree or dispute it. She may have a point and it would serve me well to listen, whether or not I like the way she makes her point. It's easier to do that if I can let go of being driven by my easily-hurt pride. Then I can be led by my intelligence.

<u>I intend to resist my seeking to blame – instead, I try to focus on solutions and on my responsibility, rather than condemning and finding fault.</u> Blaming others is an unproductive way to resolve conflicts. Rather than a genuine search for a solution, making accusations against your partner invites a fight, a defensive response or their self-recrimination. It brings up all sorts of emotional reactions in the person being blamed. "Am I guilty? Was I wrong? Am I stupid? Am I being unfairly accused?" When condemning others, the finger of guilt points away from yourself, so there is no examination of your own responsibility. Instead of finding fault, put all your attention on exploring the source of the conflict and on seeking a solution.

<u>I intend to moderate my rigid stance – instead, I try to be flexible, compromise and adopt and adapt to your needs and ideas.</u> Rigidity is seeing things only one way, as if everything is either black or white, right or wrong, good or bad – then tenaciously holding on to that opinion. "My mind's made up. Don't confuse me with facts."

When we hold this attitude in relation to others, we "should" on them. They should behave this way, think this way, or feel this way. This merely causes the person who is "should-ed upon" to perpetuate the conflict because they don't want to lose, be wrong and be dominated by you. Both sides stubbornly hold onto their position and unless someone is open to compromise, the conflict goes on forever.

Rigidity narrows vision and makes it more difficult to conceive of novel solutions. Flexibility, the opposite of rigidity, relaxes and opens space. Flexibility allows for creativity and creativity is an important key to resolving conflict.

<u>I intend to restrain my desire to dominate or be in control – instead, I try for us to feel equally empowered.</u> Only when we feel powerless do we seek power. Only when we feel lack of control do we seek to control. The need for control is caused by fear. Fear is a result of a sense of impotence and a lack of trust in our ability to handle ourselves and master our situation. When we trust, relinquishing control is not difficult. Each partner's desire to assume power and be in control is the source of many conflicts. When both partners want to be the captain of the ship, there is no crew or the crew mutinies and chaos ensues. The result is power struggle, where neither partner is willing to cede control. The true points of contention are lost, buried by the efforts of both sides to assert dominance. Each person is deeply into combat mode. The resulting stalemate prevents any progress. If one or both partners is able to let go of the struggle, the result is not a sense of powerlessness, but a sense of connection.

Some dyads are comfortable with unequal control. In those relationships, competition for who will be in the driver's seat is not an issue. If it is not important for the couple to resolve who is in the driver's seat, or if each partner is equally empowered, efforts to find solutions to the conflict can move forward.

<u>I intend to let go of my reluctance to reconcile – instead, I try to make the first move toward restoring harmony.</u> "They are wrong. It's their fault. They started it. They hurt my feelings. They should apologize. They should make amends." These are excuses we give ourselves for not making an effort to reconcile. So we wait for them to make the first move, and they wait for us to make the first move, and no one takes any action toward resolving the conflict. It can be difficult to overcome our ego's pride, come to our partner, offer our hand and ask that we let go of the past, make up and start anew. It can be difficult to take responsibility and say the words that are hard to say;

"I was wrong. You were right. I didn't know. I am sorry. Can you forgive me?" Sometimes though, saying those words is the only thing that will break a stalemate. It is being an adult and valuing finding solutions rather than soothing our fragile ego. As Indira Gandhi has said, "You can't shake hands with a clenched fist."

<u>I intend to avoid taking things personally – instead, I try to be clear with myself as to where my accountability lies.</u> We humans are egocentric. We tend to

think whatever happens is somehow related to us, even though there may be no causal connection. Just as people at their best can be saints and sages, people at their worst can be incredibly stupid, ungrateful, illogical, cruel, moody and neglectful. They often respond to us from their own vision, their own needs. They may see us as their worst enemy, their best friend, their judge, their competitor or their savior. Their view can flip-flop from one day to the next. It is helpful to remember that how others see us is their business. How we react is ours.

If we believe other's aggressive actions are personally directed at us, we become emotionally reactive. Our resulting feelings of hurt, insult, anger and indignation do not create the best environment for solving interpersonal problems. If we don't take a person's behavior as a personal affront, their actions become simply sources of information about what is going on inside their mind, rather than threats to our ego. More often than not, people are living out patterns from their history that have nothing to do with us. You personally are not the target. You just happen to be walking in front of the target as they released their arrows. Though their behavior may be impersonal, it can still affect you. Even if you realize "They know not what they do," it still hurts to be nailed to the cross.

<u>I intend to diminish my impatience – instead, I try to be tolerant and allow things to ripen in their own time.</u> Impatience is the experience of the discomfort of not having the world meet your expectations, or not doing it on your time schedule—and demanding it should. Sometimes that discomfort can be excruciating. Like a petulant child, we want to have our way NOW, need a decision NOW, want something to happen NOW. The more impatient we are, the more we suffer. If we could only sit back, relax and let go of our demand for immediate resolution, problems will often solve themselves in their own time. Sometimes the more appropriate action is inaction. Often, things need to be left alone to mature as their nature dictates. Our impatience won't allow that. You wouldn't keep on pulling carrots up from the soil in your garden in order to see if they are edible yet.

One of the benefits of the practice of meditation is that it can be used for developing patience. Just sitting, waiting, watching thoughts and impulses come and go, teaches you to patiently bear the discomfort of impatience.

<u>I intend to avoid thinking I am a mindreader. Instead, I try to use my powers of observation and question you if I am unclear about the meaning of your words and actions.</u> It is not so much the actions of others cause us grief. Our

interpretation of those actions play an important role. We make assumptions that have no basis in fact, then act on them, and this can cause conflict. One day our partner seems emotionally distant, therefore we assume, "She doesn't love me anymore" or "I must've done something wrong" or "He must be depressed." If we reign in our assumptions, base our conclusions more on what we observe rather than what we fantasize and directly ask for clarification when we are confused, we can avoid many conflicts.

<u>I intend to be aware when I am closed to appreciating viewpoints that differ from my own – instead, I try to listen to and welcome your divergent perspective.</u> Many conflicts could be avoided if, to paraphrase the Native American saying, "we could walk a mile in our opponent's moccasins." We can get so caught up in pushing forward or defending our own agenda that we are blind to the other person's viewpoint. If we could, even for a moment, put ourselves into another person's skin, we could open our mind and see the logic of their position. The way to do that is to place our agenda aside and listen to our partner from the viewpoint of a disinterested third-party. Better yet, listen as if we are our partner, and feel into their thoughts, reasoning and experience. That emptying of our mind and welcoming in the thoughts and experiences of another is the beginning of the process of resolving conflict.

<u>I intend to minimize provocation – instead, I try to pacify and use neutral, non-inflammatory language.</u> The words from Proverbs are appropriate. "A soft answer turns away wrath, but a harsh word stirs up anger." There have been occasions when Alice and I have been mired in a heated conflict and I am overcome by frustration, when I have an attitude of "the hell with it," and I deliberately, maliciously ratchet up the heat. I know exactly where Alice's emotional hot buttons are and I know when to push them at the opportune moment. Needless to say, this is counterproductive. It is also unkind. It is a control thing, sort of like a cat tormenting a rat. (I am sure Alice will appreciate the analogy.) Provoking a person can easily get out of hand, spark tempers to a boiling point and create full-out war. Not a good idea. When I recognize this tendency beginning to arise, I stop, breathe and make the effort to calm myself.

<u>I intend to curtail impulsiveness and emotionally charged outbursts – instead, I try to ensure that calm and reason predominate our disagreements.</u> Temper tantrums, angry threats and screaming matches are what children do when they don't get their way. Conflict is frustrating. Immediate response to frustration is impatience and anger. Young children have yet to learn to channel their

frustration so that they can communicate in productive ways. Without the ability to contain your feelings so they can become expressed in a way that could be received by your partner, you are liable to say and do things that can create more problems rather than resolve them. Your angry outbursts elicit anger, hurt, defensiveness and possibly payback, hardly an atmosphere for peaceful resolution.

This process of turning tendencies to combat into goodwill and goodwill into action is not instant, and it is not easy, but I can attest that it is effective. We use it and it works. And it generates love, not war.

As I stated in the introduction, the Loving Promises are not appropriate for everyone. Some people will not benefit or may even be harmed if they attempt to follow the Promises before they are ready. The same goes for working with overcoming the above tendencies to combat. Acting as a mature adult in high-conflict situations that beckon you back to immature responses is very labor-intensive work. Throughout the book, I have made several basic assumptions about human nature and about the psychological motivations of individuals who are reading this book. I assume that they value goodwill. I assume that they want to resolve their issues in order to have a peaceful and harmonious relationship. I assume that they are willing to and able to understand their own responsibility for the origins of their problems and conflicts. I assume that they are motivated to put in the hard work that it takes to resolve conflicts and create a magnificent relationship. With some individuals these assumptions do not apply. If even one of the assumptions does not apply, this can change the game dramatically. It will create tension and instability, make it impossible to resolve conflicts and sabotage any effort to implement the Promises.

Some partners do not value goodwill. They may be so full of anger, hurt and resentment that they will do what they can to frustrate their partner and cause them grief. *Some partners do not want their conflicts to be resolved.* They are comfortable arguing, sniping and undercutting their mate. For them to give up blame and resentment would be more difficult than to continue their harmful patterns of interaction. *Some partners are unable to comprehend the personal origins of their problems.* They cannot or will not look into themselves to search for the true sources of their relationship issues. They blindly insist that their partner is the cause of their pain. *Some partners lack the persistence and discipline that it takes to resolve conflicts and work with the Loving Promises.* Once they take on a difficult issue, when the initial excitement wears off and the difficult work begins, they will slack off and have difficulty carrying through to completion.

For these couples and individuals, the approach I have recommended in this book – which requires goodwill, genuine desire to resolve conflict, self-examination and prolonged effort – cannot apply. Probably one or both of the individuals in this relationship have strong unconscious motives that keep them bound. Most likely, they will require extensive self-inquiry and rehabilitation. Extricating themselves from their conflicting predicaments is probably not a "do-it-yourself" project. Professional help may be required if they are motivated enough to seek the advice of clergy or a mental health professional. After working with and through their personal issues, they may be able to mindfully work on their conflicts and take on the Loving Promises at a later time. There is no fault in this. I am an example. In the relationships before Alice I simply was not mature enough to be a good partner. I needed to do my "growing up" before I was ready for her.

Anger

Since anger is often a byproduct of conflict, it is helpful to make friends with it. There is nothing wrong with anger *per se*. Anger is a valuable resource in that it guards your boundaries and is an instrument of your healthy assertiveness. Angry confrontation, with loving intention, can shock you and your partner to "awakeness" and wash away bullshit. It can be like a fire that burns away impurities. It should not be wasted by being suppressed, diluted with mental analysis and rationalization or by incessantly imposing it on your partner.

In order for anger to be befriended, it must first be known. Anger is powerful energy, and if it is subconscious, it can be destructive. Unexpectedly, feelings of rage, a temper tantrum or an impulse to hurt may suddenly arise and surprise both partners. Acts of cruelty and vindictiveness may take place that are unwarranted and totally out of context. As long as you are unaware of your anger, it controls you. Once you are caught up in your anger, it is usually too late, and the fierce emotions will likely run their course. When angry feelings first arise, that is the time to be aware. The first stirrings of anger is the moment when you have a choice—allow it to spill out, or restrain it, examine it, learn from it.

Anger is not a dumb emotion. Almost always, there is truth in anger. Rarely will a person get angry without a reason. It may be an unreasonable reason, but somehow it makes sense to the one who is angry. If you can befriend anger, yours and your partner's, it can be a rich field for exploration that can bring in self-knowledge and mutual understanding. For that, anger needs to be honored.

Simply stated, anger is a response to an uncomfortable experience. You come up against frustrating circumstances or someone says or does something that touches off an anxious, resentful, threatened, vulnerable feeling in you. You react with clenched fists, tightened muscles, aggressive stance. Feelings of rage take over your mind. You get ready to do battle. Anger is powerful energy. The energy of anger doesn't just go away by itself. It finds outlets and can be channeled in several ways.

You could *discharge it*. It might feel good to "go off" on a person who upset you, but it can lead to mutual upset and outright war. While there is something to be said for the healthy release of the pent up energy of anger, it can become a habitual, knee-jerk response to frustration and conflict. And it's not exactly enlightened behavior to go around dumping on people. You could *suppress it*. Out of fear or intimidation, you could avoid a flare up by sitting on anger and holding it inside. There is evidence that suppressed anger is turned inside and can cause numerous health problems. Anger withheld is ineffective – it does not address the issues that provoked the anger and they remain as before. You could *rationalize it or spiritualize it*. This involves "rising above" anger by understanding anger as an ignoble response and meditating it away, or witnessing it dispassionately without expressing it. While this seems like an elevated response, it distances you from the fire and fails to address the source of the anger.

Working skillfully with anger varies with each person's "anger style." Those who are easily upset and quick to anger need to mindfully pause, moderate and sometimes withhold their anger. Those who tend to withhold anger need to feel it, and when appropriate, express it. While anger is a valid feeling, frequently and habitually indulging in expressing it is harmful, just as is habitually holding it in. Anger suppressed doesn't disappear but can take many indirect forms that aim to punish the partner, like emotional withdrawal, sexual withholding and such passive aggressive acts as "forgetting" important engagements, sulking, procrastination, sarcasm, nagging and chronic lateness. Anger passively expressed is still aggression, and like aggression, the aim is to hurt.

Each of these three ways of addressing anger have their positive and negative points and each might be appropriate in the right situation, at the right time, with the right person. Experience has shown me, no matter which way I deal with anger, I need to do my best to keep my heart open. *Anger with an open heart supports love.* Anger with a closed heart, devoid of love and compassion, can be mean and hurtful. I have found when I work at it, even in the midst of a fierce, passionate encounter with Alice, that it is possible for me to still feel great love for her. This is not the easy or natural thing to do. Our natural inclination when immersed in the heat of anger is to shut down our heart and be swept away by the emotion. Once swept away, anger is in charge. Or we can be overwhelmed by it and withdraw by stonewalling or going blank or numb. It takes energy and focus to keep coming back to love. When we combine our love with our anger, intimacy deepens.

It is beneficial to be able to incorporate "loving anger" not only when you are angry, but also when your partner is angry at you. It is difficult for me to hear Alice's anger. When she is mad at me, my tendency sometimes is to go numb and cut off feeling. I become deaf and dumb, erecting a brick wall to avoid the intensity of Alice's wrath. Alice senses this and my passivity adds another layer to her fury. My task is to keep opening to receive her anger without shutting down and trying to protect my ego.

It is difficult when you are on the receiving end of another's anger, because anger directed at you can easily upend you emotionally. Then you can react mindlessly by trying to deflect, blame, manipulate, minimize, shut down or retaliate – anything that will stem the flood of angry words directed at you. Another's anger signals rejection or put down. What is most needed, and most difficult to do when anger is directed at you, is drop the defensive stance, open to receive the anger your partner is expressing, and *listen*. If you listen carefully, you may be able to hear your partner's feelings behind the anger; the hurt, vulnerability and helplessness that their anger is covering up. For both expressing and receiving anger, it is beneficial to scan yourself and attempt to stay centered and steady in mind and body . . . and heart.

When listening to your anger, especially anger that seems unreasonable, erupts unexpectedly and with force that is out of proportion to what arouses it, you may discover that you are not responding to the present situation, but triggered by memories and events from the past. You may hold a reservoir of anger and resentment from as far back as early childhood. An event that happens in the present, perhaps a partner's disparaging look or harsh word, may spark a flood of feelings that have been penned up, waiting to explode. If both you and your partner are aware of the true source of the anger, that simple recognition can take blame and pressure off, and allow for space and perspective.

Like a cyclone, anger has a way of building in intensity. One partner expresses their anger and the other reciprocates with their angry response, and what began as a minor scuffle can quickly escalate to a major battle. What to do when you are seething in rage and want to tear into your partner? This might be a time to hold your tongue and wait until you are able to communicate without the intention to hurt. Breathe. Try to relax your body. Leave the scene if you are so worked up that you need a timeout. There is an appropriate time and way to strongly express your frustration and anger with your partner and there are circumstances where it is productive to do so. However, I believe conflicts can best be worked out if you first look inside, center yourself and share your feelings. With loving intention, and with a desire to resolve conflicts fairly and with a cool, composed mind, you have a much better chance of avoiding needless hurt and upset.

It may seem like I'm saying, "Don't rock the boat, carefully keep the situation at a reasonable level, and avoid emotional argument." However, playing it safe may not always be the best strategy. The worst kind of argument can be the one that never takes place.

Are you OK? What's the matter?
Nothing
You seem distant.
I'm fine.

Now what happens is *nothing*, except an air of heaviness all around, a feeling of incompleteness and a sense of foreboding. The argument that never took place dams feelings that can build and build.

Sometimes what is needed is a full – on, uncensored, top of lungs argument. While there is the risk of saying things you may regret later, an uncensored blow-up has the potential to reveal true feelings and clear the air. Anything less than that will rob anger of its truth and passion. It is difficult to be honest if your goal is to tamp down passionate feelings in order to avoid a flare up. Doing that will short circuit the truth.

I think the key to a positive outcome of an argument, even a forceful and impassioned one, is intention. If you maintain your goal as uncovering truth and deriving mutual benefit, and you wish to do so in a loving way, you and your partner could come away from a spat feeling like you've both gained.

Working with Conflict

Cultivating a mature, loving, adult approach with your partner won't eliminate conflict from your life because conflicts are an inevitable part of relationship. However, approaching disagreements with a loving heart will make combat less likely, reduce the amount of conflicts you have, decrease the intensity of your conflicts, shorten the time it takes to resolve your conflicts and improve your experience of your conflicts so that they actually become a positive encounter for you both.

When Alice and I have one of our rare disagreements, kindness and goodwill do not evaporate. In fact, we instinctively feel the urgent need to get more in touch with our loving-kindness. The sense of impending conflict awakens us and makes us hyper-vigilant. We seem to instinctively go through a process of conflict resolution that tends to contain the following elements, generally in this order:

- *We acknowledge there is a conflict.* This is the essential first step. We address the fact that a conflict exists. We don't ignore the problem, minimize it, sweep it under the rug or wish it away.

- *We try to understand the other's position.* This is a time for careful, focused listening, rather than asserting our position. We try to enter each other's experience and sense from the other's point of view. We ask ourselves questions like, "What does she really want? Why is this so important to him?"

- *We probe to discover the strength of the other's position.* We can simply ask "How important is this to you?" and govern our action by considering their response. Sometimes we test each other to see how strongly each of us is committed to hold on to our position. The way we do this is at first we maintain our position, or at times Alice or I will take an even more extreme stance in order to "negotiate back" later. This plays on the edge of manipulation, but it is what we do and part of the way we test. And it is part of the process of how we come to agreement.

- *We remain sensitive to the arousal of the "tendencies to combat."* We avoid accusations, blame, negative judgments ("you" language) and try to speak from our heart about what we are feeling ("I" language). There is no opening to argue against when a sentence begins with "I feel." At any point in our conflict, an ill-tempered word, a demeaning glance, the hint of the other taking a rigid position, can awaken our tendencies to combat. We are sensitive to timing and continually monitor the other to see if they are open to receive or are shut down. We keep close check on the temperature of our interaction to make sure it doesn't boil over and get out of hand.

- *We use humor when appropriate to lighten the situation.* At the right moment, humor can break the tension, or at the wrong moment, it could make it worse. In the midst of a dispute, there are times we have loudly exclaimed in jest, "I hate your guts. I want a divorce." That over-the-top declaration tends to give perspective and lighten things up.

- *We keep to the specific issue that is causing dissonance.* It becomes crazy and complicated if we lose track of our core conflict and begin to bring in irrelevant concerns, additional complaints and unresolved issues from the past.

- *We explore for areas of compromise.* We negotiate for some sort of agreement where we both get our needs met. It is almost invariably an amicable process of give-and-take in order to find a satisfying solution for both of us. Our intention is to be generous without "giving away the shop."

- *We delay making a decision.* If we are at an impasse and there is no time pressure, sometimes we can solve the conflict by simply doing nothing, putting off the decision. This cooling off period, where we forget about the problem, allows the subconscious mind to incubate. Just the passage of time can allow the situation to mature to the point where it can resolve itself or ripen so that a perfect solution can make its appearance.

- *We leave it to chance.* If each of us is willing to accept either outcome, and we can't decide which, we flip a coin. This works best if neither of us has taken an unyielding position. The coin makes the decision, and it clarifies our feeling. And, if we don't like the decision the coin makes, we go two out of three.

- *We examine our own willingness to surrender our positions.* This is not "giving up" in order to avoid conflict. Part of our spiritual practice is to turn our needs into wants, our wants into preferences, and our preferences into being OK with any outcome that occurs. We can say to each other, "Whatever makes you happy." But we still need to ask ourselves, "Will I have regrets, resentments? Will I feel it's unfair? Will I feel that I lost if I surrender? Will I be OK if I don't get my way?"

Overall, when we are in conflict we try to tune in to ourselves and into each other at all times. Conflicts are occasions that require heightened awareness. They are also opportunities to test our goodwill. When Alice and I have a disagreement, maintaining goodwill is uppermost in our minds. As unusual as it sounds, we want our conflict to be a positive experience. The following is our intention for the way we want to feel during and after we go through the process of resolving our conflicts.

- *We want each other to be pleased.* Alice genuinely wants me to be satisfied with the outcome and I want her to be satisfied too.
- *We want a fair outcome with each other.* We want the conclusion we arrive at to be balanced.
- *We don't want each other to lose.* We are unwilling to take advantage of each other.
- *We want the process of coming to resolution to be harmonious.* Neither of us wants angry arguments, hurtful words, manipulation or power struggles. Force begets force, kindness begets kindness.
- *We want there to be no lingering ill will.*
- *We want, as much as possible*, for there to be no unadressed issues, no leftover resentments, no unexpressed bad feelings and no unspoken expectations about the future.

While we have not met all these intentions in every disagreement we have ever had, these consequences are our goal. That goal is important to us. Because it is so important, we look deeply into our hearts for loving solutions. We work through the resolution process carefully, patiently, consciously, trying not to hurry through just to get it over with.

We recognize that conflicts are an important part of a healthy relationship. They allow us to feel our power by asserting our self, test our limits and gain trust of ourselves and the other. Through conflict and power struggle, couples learn who they really are as individuals and as a unit. Alice and I can honestly say that our conflicts have actually brought us closer together. The process of working through disagreement has been a healthy expression of our love.

ENCOUNTERING CONFLICT

Perpetual Conflict

The foregoing discussion concerns disagreement conflicts that can be worked with, conflicts where there is a solution and where partners are willing to work toward that solution. What about those disagreements that keep coming up again and again, ones that involve the same tired old arguments and end up in stalemate, each partner feeling exhausted and misunderstood? Then those same disagreements recur in the next week or two.

Couple's conflicts that are ongoing usually revolve around several common thorny issues – money, intimacy, parenting, in-laws, lifestyle, etc. With these issues there will always be fertile ground for ongoing disagreement. Tough, perpetual conflicts are often the result of a deep divide, a divide not easily bridged. They often entail the clash of differing values, differing ways we view the world and ways of behaving that we believe are proper and right. These ways of seeing and behaving are deeply embedded in our mind and in our body. They originate from diverse influences, such as from our innate temperament, our gender, our childhood upbringing and our life experiences. They are so much a part of us that they have become knee-jerk responses, unconscious and not amenable to reason. We firmly believe that our own ways of being are universally true and proper, and our partner's way is false and improper. Problems arise when we don't just believe our way is best, but we try to impose our way on our partner. When we continuously attempt to tenaciously impose our position against their will, we are in perpetual conflict.

Perpetual conflict results from the collision of the two partners' differing values, beliefs, goals and behavior. For example, one partner may have been brought up in an affluent household, where money was never an issue and they could obtain whatever they wanted simply by asking. They marry a person who was raised in an environment of poverty, where every penny was pinched. No matter what their present economic status, when the affluent-minded one purchases a nonessential item or pays without shopping around for the cheapest price, the thrift-minded one gets aggravated, judges and criticizes, causing an angry or defensive response, and another round of the same old argument begins. "You're wasteful and reckless and have no concept of the value of money. We have to plan and budget our purchases." "No" says the one with the loose purse strings, "You're cheap and controlling. Trust – the universe will provide for our needs." Another example: One partner's goal is to drink, carouse and have fun, while the other's is to seek salvation at the feet of Jesus. Just think of the host of perpetual conflicts that relationship will bring up.

There are many varieties of divergent values that can lead a couple into persistent, recurring conflicts. The following is a description of some of the more common ones. Each of these opposing values provides fodder for recurring arguments.

Cautious vs. Impulsive

Cautious – *The desire to be safe and protected, to know that there is enough for the future.*

Impulsive – *Willing to be spontaneous, take risks, trust that things will turn out well by themselves.*

"Slow down, you're driving too fast."

"Let's buy it now. We can borrow from your parents."

These are not simply the complaining person's problem. These are their compelling needs. The conflict is not only about driving speed or expenditure of money. It's about feeling safe and secure. For the partner who is not security minded, the other person can seem unduly fearful and overly cautious. For the one with strong security needs, the other one can seem reckless.

Gregarious vs. Isolative

Gregarious – *Desire for frequent social interaction.*

Isolative – *Desire for privacy and aloneness.*

"It was rude that you disappeared when we had company over."

"I don't want to go to the party tonight. We were out last night."

Some people are energized by social interaction and could easily fill their social calendar; others become drained and need time alone to find their center. Differing degrees of sociability can lead to a variety of conflicts, like disagreements over the frequency of attending social occasions, use of leisure time and time spent apart or together.

ENCOUNTERING CONFLICT

Dependable vs. Unreliable

Dependable – *Sense of duty and obligation, importance of completing tasks and doing things correctly.*

Unreliable – *Tendency to flaunt rules, desire for freedom from obligation.*

"Why didn't you get those bills paid when you said you would?"

"Nothing starts on time. They won't mind if we're late."

People have different ways of viewing the importance of rules and obligations. The partner who is more lax about responsibility will see the other as unbending and overly conscientious. The responsible partner will view the other as careless and untrustworthy.

Devoted vs. Indifferent

Devoted – *The need for the intimate partner and the primary relationship to have priority over other people and things.*

Indifferent-- *Energy and interests lie outside the relationship.*

"It seems more important for you to be with your friends than to be with me."

"I stared at the pretty woman who walked by because I appreciate feminine beauty."

One partner feels the relationship is of primary importance – more important than friends, family and work. The partner who is less invested in the relationship will think of their mate as "needy" and feel hemmed in by the other's demands. This will tend to create distance, causing their mate to feel threatened or abandoned.

LOVING PROMISES

Nurturing vs. Detached

Nurturing – *Taking personal interest, exhibiting concern, caring for and tending to your partner.*

Detached – *Passing concern for your partner's welfare, greater self-interest.*

"You say you love me but you didn't show up when I needed you."

"I was busy and assumed your friends would help you."

The partner who is the more nurturing of the couple will view the other as uncaring, disinterested and self-concerned. While the detached partner might welcome being cared for, nurturing others is not their natural inclination.

Meticulous vs. Disorganized

Meticulous – *Wanting things organized, planned in advance, under control.*

Disorganized – A *haphazard, unsystematic approach.*

"Your garage workshop is a disaster."

"Why do you have to have every minute of our vacation planned?"

The partner who is "looser" will see the other as too rigid, detail oriented and lacking spontaneity. The methodical one will see the other as inefficient, messy and chaotic.

Close vs Distant

Close--*Desiring physical presence and emotional intimacy.*

Distant--*Requiring physical and emotional space and clear boundaries.*

"Why don't you come and sit next to me?"

"I just need some time alone to get my head together"

ENCOUNTERING CONFLICT

The partner who needs closeness will experience the other as cold, rejecting and standoffish. The partner needing distance will pull away from the other from fear of being controlled and smothered.

Emotional vs Cerebral

Emotional – *Willingness to feel and express emotions.*

Cerebral – *Logical, intellectual, reluctant to feel or express emotions.*
"Tell me how you feel, not just what you think."

"You don't have to go ballistic over a minor thing."

The partner who is more emotional might put their mate down as cold, shallow and unfeeling, while the other may dismiss their partner as temperamental and overly emotional.

Gentle vs Assertive

Gentle – *Soft, patient, flexible approach.*

Assertive – *Brusque, overbearing, direct way of communicating.*

"Don't yell at me."

"You're wrong."

The placid partner is sensitive and flows with the moment. When faced with an assertive partner, they can feel overwhelmed, their thoughts and feelings not given due consideration. The assertive partner can feel impatient and frustrated and are inclined to enforce their will.

Despite the negative or positive connotation of some of the wording, there is no greater preference to be placed on one or the other divergent value. They are just different ways of being, part of an individual's natural inclination. There are times when it is ok to be impulsive, unreliable or detached, and times that it is undesirable to be devoted, nurturing and dependable. It is when a person is out of balance and consistently takes the extreme positions – like constantly being overly cautious or overly impulsive, overly meticulous or overly disorganized – that problems can arise. And when one partner continually judges and denigrates the other for their values, perpetual conflicts will keep recurring.

It is important to recognize that some of these divergent values that lead to perpetual conflicts have, as their origin, gender differences. In some ways, men and women are from different planets. Men are from Mars, women from Venus, as author John Gray reminds us. Of course, there are no ironclad differences between men and women in their orientation, but research has shown that women tend to have more concern than men about feeling and connection. You can see the differences for yourself at a social gathering. Men and women tend to clump together by gender. If you drift from group to group and listen to the conversations, the differences will be apparent. Men will tend to talk about objects, ideas, activities, and ways of solving problems. Women are more concerned with people and tend to value interaction, emotional expression and personal issues. These differences impinge on couple relationships and can be a source of friction and misunderstanding. Because the genders encompass such different ways of being, this can cause persistent, recurring conflicts. Understanding and allowing for the fact that your partner is from another planet can help soften the conflict. It's not that they are wrong or bad, they are just from Mars or Venus.

These divergent values are relatively unchangeable because they are so deeply ingrained in each person's personality. No amount of self-effort and no amount of pressure from others can force a transformation. Don't expect to change an introvert to an extrovert, or a disorganized partner to a meticulous one. Coercion, whether external or internal, may modify the surface a bit but, in most instances, can never radically alter a person's underlying personality. Hold transformation as a possibility, but don't expect or demand it.

Widening Perspective

Since you can't expect or demand your partner's transformation, are you perpetually stuck in the same issues for the remainder of your relationship? A way out of being trapped in the same worn out, deeply entrenched conflicts is to enlarge your perspective. I suggest you look at your partner's divergent way of being in a different, more accepting light. Rather than make them wrong, look for the validity in their values. Be open to learn from them. See their beliefs and behaviors as a message that will expand your own perspective and bring you more balance in your life. Maybe you are too rigid, maybe they are too lax. Maybe you are a recluse, maybe they are overly gregarious. Maybe you are a daredevil, maybe they are exceedingly cautious. A rigid person might benefit by loosening up. A recluse might benefit from more social interaction. A daredevil might benefit by being more cautious. If each of you could co-opt some of each other's attitude and integrate some of their behavior into your lives, it might help you both be more well-rounded and whole. At the very least, lightening up on judgments and understanding the validity of your partner's values and behavior will allow them space to be themselves and will help make persistent conflicts less frequent and less intense. It is not necessarily the divergent ways themselves that create conflict, but stubbornly maintaining the "rightness" of your way and the "wrongness" of their way hardens each person's position. When you are locked into your righteousness, perpetual conflicts remain perpetual.

My tendency is to be more gentle and cerebral while Alice tends to be more emotional and assertive. This has led to conflicts and misunderstandings, but I have come to admire and value the way Alice handles herself. By watching her, I see that sometimes my reluctance to assert myself hides a fear of confrontation and a tendency to manipulate. And I tend to escape uncomfortable feelings by "going cerebral." My openness to learn from Alice has helped me understand myself and change some of the unskillful, unproductive ways I have used when interacting with people.

The conflict that has the most relevance for working with the Loving Promise practice is one in which one partner is gung-ho for growth, change and progress in the relationship, while the other isn't. The reluctant partner refuses to participate and digs in his or her heels to avoid any change in the status quo. Yes, you don't absolutely require their participation. You can soldier on alone and take 100% responsibility. You can accept them as they are and try to see value in their differences. You can surrender and forgo trying to improve the relationship. You can demonstrate compassion and loving kindness and hope that they will be attracted by the love that you have cultivated through the Loving Promises. However, these strategies may not be effective. The reluctant partner's continued reluctance creates a persistent issue. When you are revved up and ready to grow, their foot on the brake is painful and frustrating for you. It might be of help to step back and gain some perspective about this common conflict.

An enlarged perspective can arise from understanding that relationships and individuals naturally go through periods of growth and periods of stability. Periods of expansion often tend to be followed by periods of quiet, where it seems that nothing is taking place. But actually, often the new experiences are in the process of being subconsciously digested, worked on and integrated. It is unreasonable to assume that these growth cycles will occur in an orderly fashion and in full view. And it is too much to expect that couples will always go through these cycles at the same time – thus the conflict endures.

Growth and expansion are destabilizing. New experiences and behavior can be challenging and stressful. The impetus for growth is often the result of uncomfortable circumstances that demand change (such as recurrent, festering problems coming to a head, intense protracted gridlock, confrontational therapeutic intervention or dawning awareness of long-term dissatisfaction.) These events create anxiety. Some people's natural response to the anxiety brought about by the need for change is to withdraw to the known, to retreat to the status quo of old, tried and true maladaptive patterns. This could possibly be a positive thing. It allows a person time to safely garner their energies and ready themselves to enter a new, challenging phase in their life and relationship. Sometimes, though, a partner's tendency when faced with stress in the relationship is to burrow in and to resist any change, now and forever. Insistent pressure by you to force them to take action to change will only make them burrow in more deeply.

I don't mean to make excuses for a recalcitrant partner, nor do I want to minimize the seriousness of this situation. Our cousin Pam has an analogy that illustrates this dilemma. She says that relationships are like a tennis game. You want to make sure that you play at a similar level of skill as your tennis partner. If not, you'll find yourself serving lots of balls that don't get returned. That's no fun. You might even find yourself running around the net to the other side in order to try to return your own serve. This gets old real fast.

What to do? Of course there is no one answer because people and circumstances differ. However, I think certain suggestions may apply when you are in a phase where you are raring to go, but your partner is resistant to making needed changes in themselves and in the relationship.

Work on the Loving Promises and on your own growth. That is the most productive thing you can do for yourself that will also have a positive impact on your partner and the relationship.

Keep the channels of communication open. Maintaining your connection allows for greater understanding.

Treat them with compassion and loving-kindness. That will allow them unpressured space to breathe, gestate and open to change.

ENCOUNTERING CONFLICT

Have patience. Let go of your need for them to be the way you want them to be–right now. Know that tomorrow may bring a change of heart, but don't expect or demand it.

Be gently persistent. Even in the face of your partner's resistance, recurrent non-demanding invitations and gentle loving will make it harder for them to resist.

Do not threaten unless you mean it. If the situation is intolerable for you and you cannot remain in the relationship as it is, separation or threat of separation or other drastic measure is a last-ditch effort. Separation is a powerful message that can motivate your partner, but it should be used judiciously and after much serious contemplation.

Trust in the process. Within each person is an innate tendency toward health and wholeness. It is a very powerful force. Your love, patience, communication and positive energy will facilitate that tendency in your partner and allow the events in their life to bring them the insight and motivation to grow.

The other evening, a large owl perched on the limb of the ancient oak in our front yard. A flock of crows was upset by the owl's presence. They sent up a racket and zoomed close in an effort to try to scare the owl away. The big bird remained unperturbed, maintained its calm center, and did not try to defend itself or chase the crows away. It seemed to be confident of its powers and willing to allow the noise and chaotic activity to just be as it was. After about twenty minutes, the owl decided it had business elsewhere and glided off.

This is actually quite an admirable approach to conflict. See yourself as bigger than the conflict. Feel your strength, maintain your center, don't rush to force or defend, espouse kindness, keep your integrity and don't attach too much importance to all the "sound and fury." Trust that what needs to happen will happen in its proper way and time.

The reality about conflict is that all relationships have them. Some can be resolved, some cannot. It is a fantasy to believe that all our relationship problems can and should be fixed. When we don't accept the reality that our irresolvable problems will persist, we constantly criticize, argue, cajole, blame and manipulate until we drive our partner and ourselves crazy. Or our partner will do the same to us and drive us crazy. If we can acknowledge that some of our problems will remain without a solution, we can let go of conflict and come to terms with our partner being who they are, as they are. This will set us free to move on and do what we need to do – appreciate them, love them, work for the common good and make our relationship into the magnificent edifice it can be.

As relationships evolve and more and more disputes are resolved through each person's increasing goodwill and graciousness, the rock tumbler of conflict will have done its work. The rough surfaces will have been worn away, revealing a smooth and beautifully polished loving partner, an exquisitely burnished loving self and a sparkling, lustrous relationship.

Chapter 7

Ways to Work with the Loving Promises

The Loving Promises are oriented toward behavior. They are about speaking and acting in loving ways with your partner. Rather than waiting for loving feelings to come to you before acting lovingly, the Promises ask you to act lovingly, with the understanding that your actions will bring on the feelings. As St. John of the Cross said, "Where there is no love, put love – and you will find love."

In taking on and working with the Loving Promises, the point is not simply to change your behavior, though acting in loving ways toward your partner is beneficial to both them and yourself. Your intention is far more ambitious. The primary reason you work with the Loving Promises is to transform your consciousness and change the underlying motivation behind your behavior. You wish to progress from being primarily self-centered, toward being other-centered, from demanding to receive, toward desiring to give, from concern predominantly for your own happiness, toward concern for the happiness of others. This is the way to a fulfilling life. True contentment lies through easy, open-handed generosity of spirit. A committed relationship is the perfect container for learning generosity of spirit and releasing the obsession with "me, me, me."

Self-centered motivation can usually take the form of greed – giving to others in order for you to receive back, or fear – giving in order to avoid losing what you have. On the surface, the behavior that originates from the motivation of greed or fear can look very much like giving from the heart. As with heartfelt giving, you follow the Loving Promises, you cooperate, you do and say things that make your partner feel happy and loved, but inside, your motives are quite different. With greed-based giving, there is the subtle or not-so-subtle expectation that your partner should reciprocate. And with fear-based giving, there is the underlying thought, "I must be on my best behavior or my partner will stop being generous to me or they will leave me or withdraw their love."

These are not attitudes that are conducive for true love. It is unlikely that you will be able to sustain the consistent practice of the Loving Promises for long if your behavior is motivated by fear and greed. It becomes so much hard work, and the reward – your partner's love and gratitude--is tainted by your deceit. However, when you devotedly practice the Loving Promises, over time, fear and greed-based giving will fade and be replaced by their opposite-- genuine courage and true generosity.

Resistance to Change

Much of the book applauds the beauty of the Loving Promises and their power for transforming your relationship and your life. Now for the bad news. *The cards are stacked against you.* Your mind and body have strong impulses to maintain the status quo and likely will stubbornly oppose any changes you try to make. They may even try to sabotage you. No matter how strongly you desire change and how much you recognize the need for the Loving Promises, you, (the part of yourself that wants the best and highest for yourself), are at a grave disadvantage. That healthy "you" is trapped in opposition to your mind and body's habitual patterns.

You may be like me. When the New Year rolls around, I start to dream up resolutions. These are good and noble vows, things that would be very beneficial if followed up . . . but I often don't. After a week or two, my resolve begins to weaken. I might begin to bend here and there, make excuses, backtrack and eventually give up and end where I began – eating more of the foods I had sworn not to and exercising less than I decided I would – except now I'm feeling guilty for being so weak and letting myself down. This is the classic conundrum we all face when we embark on a path of change. As soon as we commit, resistance to and rebellion against the change we wish to make begins to set in.

The most potent weapon you have in your arsenal for grappling with resistance and creating change is your willpower. The Promises are about summoning your will. ("I *will* stand steadfastly by you." "I *will* remain present with you.") However, as everyone knows who has tried to quit smoking or alter their diet, the will is notoriously weak when it comes up against a deeply-ingrained habit. Will resides in the domain of the mind. It concerns an intention for the future. The reward is in the future and it takes concerted effort over time to make real that intention and claim that reward. Instituting willpower in order to coerce yourself to do something to which you have resistance puts you in the world of reluctance, of forcing yourself, of "I should," "I must," and "I have to."

In contrast, an established habit is in the world of craving, immediate pleasure, comfort and ease, of "I enjoy," "I want," "I like." Pushing yourself to change by sheer force of will is usually not a very efficient, pleasant or long-lasting method.

If this sounds familiar to you, please don't blame yourself or put yourself down. You are in good company. Concerning the war within, even the Apostle Paul has written "I do not understand my own actions. For I do not do what I want, but I do the very thing I hate….For I have the desire to to do what is right, but not the ability to carry it out." (Romans 7)

With repetition, habitual patterns become deeply ingrained in the synapses of the brain and embedded in the muscles and in the gut. Habits form a groove. With each repetition, the groove becomes deeper and more difficult to escape. Old habits "feel right," while new patterns feel odd and uncomfortable. We naturally gravitate to our usual ways of doing things unless we receive a strong, immediate, pleasurable reward for novel behavior, which rarely happens. (Immediate reward trumps future reward.) So, for example, in my mind, I know that it is entirely right and beneficial for my relationship, my partner and myself for me to try to forgive them if they have hurt me (Promise #16). However, my emotions of anger and resentment say, "No way am I going to let that bastard off the hook." Even though I know that dishonesty is harmful to our relationship (Promise #18), my fear of the uncomfortable consequences of telling the truth to my partner prompts me to lie to them. It will take determined effort for me to undo those ingrained patterns.

The collision between behavior toward my partner that is beneficial in the future but uncomfortable now, and behavior that is detrimental in the future but convenient and comfortable now, sets up an inner conflict, in which one part of me is fighting against another. The classic picture comes to mind, of a person with a devil on one shoulder and an angel on the other. The devil is their sense cravings, supported by their devious mind. The angel is their benevolent intention, supported by their vacillating will. The devil keeps whispering in the person's ear, "Go ahead, have that delicious chocolate chip cookie," while the angel keeps saying "Be good. Think about your waist. Munch on a raw carrot instead." The devil has a much more compelling argument (immediate pleasure vs. future reward).

By deliberately trying to change a habit, you come to the realization of how powerful are the forces that impel you to maintain the habit. When you put an intention into practice, it often brings its opposite into being. A positive intention creates the conditions for negative intention to arise. For example, I want to avoid eating sweets, yet when I deny myself a chocolate chip cookie, I become hyper-aware of my desire for the sweet. I want to control my temper, yet

WAYS TO WORK WITH THE LOVING PROMISES

the more I try to dampen it, the more intensely my anger boils up. Denying yourself pleasure or forcing yourself to maintain an uncomfortable condition puts you in a quandary between the flesh and the spirit. What often happens is, if the angel prevails and you refrain from eating the cookie, the devil redoubles his efforts. Once you give in to the temptations of the devil, the angel shames you with blame and self-recrimination. Then you promise that you will restrain yourself, but here comes that ol' devil's temptation. This process can lead to endless cycles of restraint, giving in, self-blame, restraint, giving in, self-blame etc., and is the origin of the binge/purge cycle.

I offer the Loving Promises as a solution. Yet, the Promises are themselves based on willpower and therefore are subject to the same conflicts between the angel and devil. The Loving Promises treat love as a conscious decision, a deliberate choice to become a more loving person. Yet change is rarely the result of a simple deliberate choice. Change in thought and behavior may involve deliberate choice, but generally, the motivation for change is far more complex. Change, when it occurs, will most likely evolve from the confluence of a variety of mental, emotional and situational factors that lead a person to the condition of being "ripe." To ripen is to be ready. A ripe fruit is one that has matured to the point where the flavors are at their peak and it is ready to drop from the branch of its own accord.

To be ripe for change means that you have gone through some sort of an awakening process. Perhaps you hit bottom, had a painful breakup, awoke due to a realization brought on by illness, or came to a deep insight through longstanding contemplation. The difficulty and pain of your situation has finally broken through to your awareness, sounded an alarm and woke you up. Something has changed inside and you now view the world with different eyes. This awakening has made you hungry for change and given you resolve to follow through with actions that will facilitate that change. When you ripen, you eagerly embrace change and engage easily in activities, like the Loving Promises, that will bring change about. When you are not ripe, you are faced with an uphill struggle. Your devil is invigorated.

Being ripe is a good beginning. Becoming ripe can be the impetus to initiate change and can possibly make it easier to maintain change. But becoming a magnificent lover is a long-term project for most people, and staying with that level of loving partnership is the work of a lifetime. The devil can be expected to repeatedly make his appearance, sometimes often. His arguments are persuasive and his temptations enticing.

Let us not be so quick to demonize our devil and so anxious to banish him and pursue our angel. The Prince of Darkness can actually be a source of light.

He gives voice to a real part of us, a voice that we should listen to and not ignore. His words illuminate the conflict that is going on within us. When we become aware of that conflict, attend to it, work with it, dig in and get our hands dirty, we can move through it. If we are unconscious, we can be blindsided.

The Loving Promises call up the devil. Every one of the Promises is an invitation for our devil and angel to get into the boxing ring and duke it out. To have to be dependable when you don't feel like it, to be generous when you don't feel like it, to be forgiving when you don't feel like it, brings your internal conflicts right into the bright lights of the arena. It is important to pay attention to the conflicts and resistance you have about entering more deeply into love with your partner. Embracing and exploring the resistance is a legitimate path to loving. The resistance consists of the barriers you have erected to love.

Working with the Promises

With such a devious opponent as your personal devil on your shoulder and your own stubborn mind and body, and with so unreliable a weapon as your willpower, you will need as much support as you can get. This chapter is meant to offer some help, in the form of ways you could approach working with the Loving Promises.

The ideas put forward are meant as suggestions. It is beyond the scope of the book to go into detail about ways an individual can initiate a personal action plan. Some of the suggestions have already been covered in other parts of the book and so will just be touched upon here. See the following ideas as seeds. Each of them holds powerful truths. If you contemplate them, consider how they apply to your life, you will encourage the seeds to germinate, sprout and grow.

-Do whatever works for you to fortify body, mind and spirit. Use everything you can to make your practice of the Loving Promises easier and more effective.

Before entering battle, the samurai warrior is fully prepared. He checks his armor and makes sure his sword is sharp. He readies his mind through focus and meditation. He beseeches his ancestors to protect him and give him strength. He makes sure there is nothing left undone. His life depends on it.

Engaging with old destructive habits and tackling new, productive ones is like entering into battle. When you are fully prepared, you have the best chance of victory. Make use of everything at your disposal. The ensuing suggestions can be

WAYS TO WORK WITH THE LOVING PROMISES

of help to make your work with the Loving Promises more effective. Your success depends on it.

-Motivate yourself by understanding and valuing the Loving Promises. Your knowledge of and respect for the Promises will serve to empower you.

Like many people, I find it helpful to have a conceptual understanding of things I am involved with. Knowing how the Loving Promises work and why they work is motivating. Understanding the Loving Promises will also serve to bolster your confidence in them. That understanding will carry you through when you hit a bumpy road. The Loving Promises make sense. The concepts behind them are logical and internally consistent. When you appreciate the rationale behind them, you strengthen your incentive.

Don't just read the Loving Promises. Deeply contemplate them. Consider how they apply to your life. They contain deep truths and are powerful and potentially life-changing. Understand them as a gift that can change your relationship and your life.

-Don't judge yourself harshly or compare yourself to others. Accept the totally unique individual that you are.

Two days a week Alice attends a yoga class. She has been taking yoga since before we met and has derived great benefit from it, and finally convinced me to go. The first few times I went to class I injured myself – hurt my neck, strained my back, pulled my shoulder. What happened was that I would see others stretching into poses and compare myself to them. I would attempt to force myself into positions my body was not ready for. Judging is comparing, and comparing can be harmful because every person is different from all others. Each has individual strengths and weaknesses. Each person moves in their unique direction at their own pace. Respect your uniqueness. Accept your differences and **start from where you are**. Admit who you are and stand in the center of your truth. If you start with wanting to be different, you are coming from an idea in your mind. If you try to start from where you want to be, or expect to be, or think others want you to be, you are in fantasy. Seek to move forward from your own center rather than trying to conform to some image of perfection.

LOVING PROMISES

-Don't demand change from your partner. Embarking on the Loving Promises is your adventure.

Practically speaking, Loving Promises work best when both partners are on the same page, when there is a sense of teamwork, where both are moving toward creating a more perfect union. Without that unity of purpose and concerted effort, it is more difficult to sustain the Loving Promises. By all means try to enlist your partner to work together with you. If they are amenable to taking on the Promises, great! If not, no amount of discussion or cajoling will get him or her on board. Your time and energy is better spent working the Loving Promises on your own. Do a good job and your partner may get sucked into your energy and the powerful energy of the Loving Promises. Be the change you want to see in your beloved.

-Practice. Repetition is the way you learn.

Old habits are deeply ingrained. Through repetitive practice, old behaviors become extinguished, and new ones are reinforced. Love is a set of learnable skills that can be acquired, refined and integrated through practice. Choose the generous response over the selfish one. Choose to calm yourself rather than emotionally react. Choose to apply the brakes when you see yourself becoming defensive. Make these choices over and over again. With each repetition, you are increasing the probability that the desired behavior will occur. A well-practiced behavior will recur automatically. When you practice loving behaviors they will become your natural response.

-Keep a journal. Writing down your thoughts and experiences makes them more solid.

Thoughts, experiences, dreams and inspirations are ephemeral. They can float around in your head like butterflies and then take off, never to be seen again. Any of those inspirations could be life-changing. Using a journal to write down those thoughts and experiences makes them more solid. Once you have put them down in black and white, you can revisit them, think about them, allow them percolate. You will also be able to chart your progress over time if you maintain a record. When you track your progress, positive results from practicing the Promises will energize you; negative results will inform you.

WAYS TO WORK WITH THE LOVING PROMISES

-Cultivate endurance. Understand that fulfilling the Loving Promises is a lifetime project and takes prolonged effort.

If you expect instant results, what you will get is frustration. Change happens slowly. If there is a rapid change, it is usually the result of the gradual summation of a number of proceeding changes. My aunt called the ability to follow through with a difficult task "stick-to-it-ness." There are a number of aspects of stick-to-it-ness. Determination is the motivation to put out continuous persistent effort. Patience is the ability to wait and let go of having to have things happen when and how you want. Endurance is the ability to keep going over the long haul. Working with the Loving Promises is not a short sprint; it is a marathon, a lifetime project. It is important to understand this from the beginning. Keep reasonable expectations. If you don't, you'll give up when you are faced with your first major challenge.

-Aim to be consistent. Consistency generates trust.

Consistency is required in two ways. The first is *consistency within each Promise*—working each Promise at all times, not letting up from time to time because you don't feel like it or it's too difficult. The second is *consistency between Promises*—working all the Promises, not ignoring some because you are having a hard time or you don't consider one to be as necessary as the others. When your partner senses your inconsistency, they cannot help but question your willingness or ability to comply with the Promises. They will lose trust.

-Take on the small things. Big love is expressed in a multitude of small ways.

Mother Teresa said it beautifully, *"We can do no great things – only small things with great love."* The Loving Promises sound sweeping in nature – "I will stand steadfastly by you," "I will serve your best interest," "I will participate in your life." These grandiose pronouncements are actually abstract. In real life, love is expressed in small, concrete ways – making coffee for your beloved, showing up on time, rubbing their aching shoulders, listening patiently to their complaints. Love is compounded action by action. If you could concentrate on doing the small things with great love, you will be giving "great love" to your partner.

LOVING PROMISES

-Don't overwhelm yourself. Be considerate of your needs and limitations.

In any undertaking, there are moments when "the force is with you" and you can make tremendous progress with little effort. And there are times when the force is absent, and any amount of "forcing" gets you nowhere. It is important to keep aware of what your energies are telling you. The Loving Promises require a dynamic balance. If you push too hard and take on too much, too soon, you can go beyond your present limitations and throw yourself into overwhelm. On the other hand, if you lie back and fail to apply yourself, you can easily go nowhere and stagnate.

-Acknowledge your partner as your teacher. They know you better than anyone else.

Your partner is perfectly positioned to provide you feedback about yourself and your behavior. They live with you, interact with you intimately and know you far better than others do. Every day they hold up a mirror that allows you to see yourself. Of course, you want to see how grand and smart and beautiful you are, but sometimes the image that is reflected back to you is of one who is greedy and insecure. Your ego may be bruised at times, but if you can acknowledge and be thankful for the feedback you receive from your partner, it will provide valuable insights that are available to you no other way.

-Accept slip-ups and setbacks when they occur. Reverses are an important part of the learning process.

You are not perfect. If you were, you wouldn't need the Loving Promises. There will be times when you are not kind and compassionate, but would rather fight, times when you are not supportive, but are absent, times when you are not truthful, but choose to lie rather than face your partner's ire. There will be times when you are manipulative, selfish, judgmental, non-communicative. When these times occur, don't wallow in self-blame. Pick yourself up, dust yourself off (and dust your partner off) and use the incident as a learning experience. Determine what it was that you said or did that created distance, hurt or upset them. Your understanding of your part and commitment not to repeat the offense will make it less likely to happen in the future. There are two ways to learn your lesson. You get it right, or you get it wrong. Though getting it right may be more comfortable, the learning may be less effective than getting it wrong. Understand that your failings are just part of the process of learning to love and can provide you with valuable insights if you are willing to listen.

-Seek support when you need it. Don't be a solitary hero.

Problems that exist in the relationship can hang on for years – or forever. Rather than trying to be a hero and tough it out alone, consider seeking professional support from like-minded mental health professionals or clergy. Sometimes the intervention of a disinterested and knowledgeable third-party can help an individual or couple find clarity and inspiration. It is also possible to obtain guidance from books, classes, recordings and workshops. For those who have a religious bent, appealing for blessing or intervention from a higher power through prayer is an important and valuable way of obtaining support. To be able to admit to yourself and to others, that you cannot handle your problems alone and seek help is a sign of maturity and strength rather than weakness. Arriving at the point where you acknowledge your need for help is the greatest difficulty.

-Lighten up and maintain a sense of perspective. A broader view will keep things in perspective if you become too serious.

When you are feeling down and things are not going the way you want, it's easy to fall into a dark funk. Everything wrong dominates your mind. This is "catastrophizing," where the negative is blown way out of proportion. It's not life or death. Everything changes. Pleasant follows unpleasant; unpleasant follows pleasant. When you understand this, you'll feel more at ease when you see pleasure leaving and pain coming. Turn it around by widening your view and remember, "This too shall pass." Find the humor, count blessings, and place your attention on the positive. You are on a journey and are bound to take wrong turns and find yourself in dead ends before you reach your destination. Blow your perspective wide open by reminding yourself of your mortality. Even your worst problem will not matter when you are gone. Go outside on a clear night and look up at the stars. Your problems will pale when compared with the grand scale of the universe.

LOVING PROMISES

-Keep the company of like-minded couples. Being with happy, healthy couples will inspire you.

Alice and I are energized by being in the presence of couples who have a magnificent relationship. There are so many miserable couples whose conflict, anger and competition can drag you down if you spend a lot of time with them. The atmosphere around loving partners will raise your spirits. Being in their presence is an education in love. It is truly a pleasure knowing couples who love each other and are putting their love into action. Their happiness serves as a confirmation that magnificent relationship is possible and their presence in your life will reinforce your love for each other.

-Focus on the positive parts of your relationship. The affirmative will propel you forward; the negative will bog you down.

With relationship everything is flux. The easy times are not the real relationship. The difficult times are not the real relationship. The good, the bad, the happy, the sad – all are part of the flow that is the stream of relationship. If you define your relationship as "troubled," you solidify that which is fluid. By focusing on problems, you give energy to problems. Attend disproportionately to what is dissatisfying in your relationship and that aspect will be blown out of proportion. You will be bathed in negativity, obstacles and discouragement.

Rather than attempting to just reduce your unhappiness in your relationship, try increasing happiness. Focus on what's working, on the good parts. Put your energy into creating fun, closeness and good feelings. Attend to the positive things about your partner. Contemplate those things. Write them down. This positive focus will create an atmosphere where, when problems arise, they can be solved more easily. Positive focus is an affirmation that opens your life to positive experience.

-Address problems immediately. Don't wait until bad situations get worse.

Problems don't normally go away by themselves. If you ignore them, they usually get worse. Do not tolerate the persistence of bad feelings between you. Sometimes just a willingness to make things better and a heartfelt conversation will do the trick. "I've been sensing a distance between us. Are you feeling that too? I don't want things to stay this way. How about you? Let's explore what it is that is causing this distance and see what we can do to get back in connection." It would be hard for anyone to reject such an open hearted offering. It's so much easier dealing with hurt feelings, discontent and anger right off the bat, rather than trying to clean up the mess after an explosion.

-Assess your behavior. Determine if your actions are in line with the Loving Promises.

The Loving Promises do not happen without your volition. You must apply your energy and attention. Attend to yourself. Are you slacking off or ignoring one or more Promises? Attend to the interactions with your partner. Are you speaking and acting with loving-kindness? Observe yourself without judgment or blame, but correct your course if you are off base with the Promises.

-Re-envision issues that arise in your relationship as opportunities to practice loving more. Problems are occasions to further your practice.

Everything is fuel for the fire of love. When times are good and there are no problems, the joy you both feel cements your love. When times are bad and you experience painful challenges, that pain deepens you and opens you to greater compassion and wisdom – if you are able to envision problems in a productive way. When your partner is acting unloving, that is the best time to for you to practice love. The question to ask yourself is, "What is there for me to learn in this situation and how can I best learn it?" Looked at in this way, problems are portals to self-discovery. Their purpose is to help you awaken.

-Allow the practice of surrender. Letting go when appropriate is powerful medicine.

Surrender is not giving up. It is not giving in. It is not being defeated. Surrender is a choice. It is choosing to let go of a behavior, feeling or idea that you tightly held onto in the past, but now is not appropriate and no longer serves you. So, you release it, and in that release is a relaxation and a sigh of relief. An example of surrender is letting go of insisting your partner go on a healthier diet when they are not ready, or giving up a day of golf in order to stay home and help take care of the kids. The Serenity Prayer of Alcoholics Anonymous is a statement of surrender. "God grant me the Serenity to accept the things I cannot change, Courage to change the things I can, and Wisdom to know the difference."

Surrender is not always a choice you make. rather, it may be a choice made for you by the overwhelming intensity of the circumstances you find yourself in. Everything you do seems to have no effect or only makes things worse. You feel helpless, hopeless. You are frozen and depressed. You have reached "the dark night of the soul." All you can do is give up trying to control. . . and surrender.

-Be willing to delay gratification. Putting off your own immediate pleasure in favor of future benefit will pay dividends later on.

Magnificent relationship involves giving, and giving often involves putting off or foregoing your own gratification in order to meet your partner's needs. Delaying gratification includes a whole basket of related skills – tolerance, restraint, abstinence, patience, sacrifice, persistence, surrender, endurance, self-discipline. These are all qualities that help you become comfortable with hard work and repetitive practice.

I work out in the gym five days a week. Most days, I don't like it. The other days, I hate it. Sometimes, if it's hot or I stayed up late the night before or I'm just not in the mood, I'm inclined to skip the workout or abbreviate it. I know myself, though. Barring a major calamity, if I fail to show up on the gym floor because of some rinky-dink excuse I give myself, I will have just lowered the bar and, next time, it will be easier to make excuses.

The secret behind every creative endeavor of lasting value, be it sports, arts, business, or relationships, is the ability to postpone immediate pleasure in order take the sometimes laborious actions that will help us accomplish our desired goal. If we lack discipline, we will be a helpless slave to passing whims and momentary desires and cravings. Many of the Loving Promises require us to practice this skill in some form or another. Discipline is a necessity when working with the Promises.

-Maintain an awareness practice. Clarity of inner perception is an essential tool for the Loving Promises.

An awareness practice – meditation, yogic postures and breathing, quiet contemplation, focuses your consciousness. It cultivates "choice-less awareness" –

WAYS TO WORK WITH THE LOVING PROMISES

a seeing without preferences. These kinds of practices are tools, like a magnifying glass, that will help you explore with precision what's going on inside your mind and heart. Clarity, insight and inspiration spring from the quiet of an inner-focused mind. That quiet mind, in addition to giving you self-awareness, will enable you to more clearly see and understand your partner. You bring the serenity you obtain from awareness practices to your partner, and, as a result, your relationship becomes more peaceful. As a bonus, these are excellent techniques for reducing stress. The Appendix at the end of the book provides instruction in various forms of meditation.

-Understand the Loving Promises as part of your spiritual practice. The root causes of most problems in relationships and in life are spiritual in nature.

When Alice is shopping and I am waiting for her, tolerating my restlessness becomes a spiritual practice of patience. When Alice and I are in a conflict that cannot be resolved, my spiritual practice is to let go and accept. I sometimes find myself trying to prove I am right with Alice. If I realize that this is pride and ego speaking and I am able to hold my tongue, I'm engaging in the spiritual practice of humility. When I reach for the perfect peach for myself, I pause, reflect and then offer it to Alice – this is my spiritual practice of generosity. These are all part of my intention to become a more spiritual person by making patience, acceptance, humility and generosity more prominent parts of my character. When I am impatient, judgmental, prideful and greedy, I cause pain to myself and Alice and cause problems in our relationship.

-Treat your work with the Loving Promises as a practice of loving-kindness toward yourself. Become your own best friend.

Befriending yourself, accepting yourself just as you are, is the foundation of the Loving Promises. Trying to improve your relationship with your partner while despising yourself, hiding from others and being unkind to yourself is an empty exercise. It cannot be done. Your self-love enlivens the Promises and gives them power to transform. And, at the same time, working with the Promises energizes your self-love.

LOVING PROMISES

-Apply the Loving Promises to the one you're with. They have shown up for you to love.

It is an extremely rare thing to have found your soul mate. Few are fortunate to be with their perfect partner. You ask for love, yet, when love knocks on your door, you don't open because the visitor standing before you is not the image of perfection you have in your mind. If you won't accept anyone less than the perfect mate of your dreams, you're in for a long wait. There's always something wrong, something that doesn't fit. And who's to say that once you choose that perfect person, they will choose you.

When you are in a relationship with a partner who is less than perfect, should you withhold committing, keep shopping around until you find that perfect mate? I say "No." Unless there is a "deal killer," some quality your partner has that you simply cannot live with, or some internal voice warning you not to commit, I say give the best of your love. (This doesn't mean you should choose someone just because they have shown up at your doorstep. You should use discrimination when offering your gift of love.) The person you are with may or may not be "the one," may or may not be "forever," but it doesn't matter. If you love half-assed you are cheating yourself and your partner. However, if you apply the Loving Promises, serve up your heart and love with integrity and kindness and generosity, you cannot lose.

-Honor the spirit of the Loving Promises. Don't just follow the word.

The spirit of the Loving Promises is different than the words. You can impress your partner by talking a good game and you can sleepwalk through the Loving Promises by rote. If you are inclined, you can probably even manipulate your partner for sex and induce other goodies by simulating compliance with the Promises. You can fake forgiveness by mouthing the words while seething in anger inside. You can fake transparency by sharing some genuine-sounding revelation, but withholding the real you. You can fake being present with your mate at the same time you are roaming about in your mind. These pretenses are empty and ultimately will end up harming you, your partner and the relationship. To really follow the Loving Promises you must surrender to them – put your heart and soul behind them, embrace them as your own. Only then will they transform you and your relationship.

WAYS TO WORK WITH THE LOVING PROMISES

The Loving Promises read as if they are strict commandments. They are not. They are pliable guidelines, not rigid regulations. They are directions in which to go rather than unequivocal destinations where you must end up. They aren't meant to be meticulously followed, at all times, in every circumstance. There are times when the raw truth is hurtful to others and should be modulated when dealing with a sensitive person, times when a little manipulation gets the job done more efficiently, times when it is not necessary to be fully transparent, times when it is OK to raise your voice in anger.

When is it alright to bend the Promises? What is the criterion to use? For Alice and me, some Promises are not meant to be broken or even altered. I consider committing to the permanence of our relationship (Promise #1) to be inviolable, as is accepting Alice as equal (Promise #9), and sexual fidelity (Promise #26). Vows like these, if broken, would cripple our relationship. I don't take lightly deviating from the words of the Promises. And I rarely deviate from the intent. If I do waffle, I do not do so solely for my own comfort or convenience. The overriding principles for applying the Loving Promises are kindness and compassion--kindness and compassion toward Alice, and kindness and compassion toward myself. Loving Promises are love. If you work with the Promises in an unloving way, you are violating them.

Michelangelo was asked about the process he used to create such beautiful sculptures. He replied that in his mind he first envisioned the image of the sculpture within the stone. Then he would chip away anything that was not the image. To become more loving, keep chipping away and remove thoughts, feelings and behaviors that are not loving.

The process is so simple – simple but not always easy. Pay close attention – to yourself and your partner. If you see a way in which you can act more lovingly or if you sense that you are behaving in a way that is harmful or is creating pain for your partner, change your behavior and act in a more loving manner.

The way to practice love was shown long ago and stated much more eloquently than I, in a prayer attributed to St Francis:

> Lord, make me an instrument of Your peace. Where there is hatred, let me sow love; where there is injury, pardon; where there is doubt, faith; where there is despair hope; where there is darkness, light; where there is sadness, joy. O Divine Master, grant that I

may not so much seek to be consoled as to console; to be understood as to understand; to be loved as to love; For it is in giving that we receive; it is in pardoning that we are pardoned; it is in dying that we are born to eternal life.

Self-Awareness

Each of us have a vast store of material—thoughts, emotions, bodily sensations—which are unavailable to our conscious mind. Even though we are unaware of these unfounded fears, obsolete childish beliefs and expectations, unjustified guilt and confused thought patterns, they still have a tremendous influence on our behavior and our life.

Subconscious ideas like "I don't deserve to be loved," "I will be rejected if I show my feelings," "If I love I will be hurt," can prevent us from fully loving and being loved.

An essential key to becoming a more loving person is to cultivate greater self-awareness—become conscious of these subconscious internal processes. Obviously, when you are more closely in touch with the contents of your mind, you are more closely in touch with the world, because your mind and senses are the way you have connection with the world. By developing greater focus and acuity on the contents of your mind, your picture of yourself, your partner and your world becomes more accurate. Therefore, grounded in reality, your decisions and actions can be more effective and your relationships more fulfilling.

Self-awareness is a precursor to an invaluable skill, which will serve you in your life and relationships, as well as in working with the Loving Promises. This skill consists of the ability to separate yourself from your perceptions and to be a witness to them.

Normally, we are totally absorbed in what we are experiencing, so much so that we are not even aware that we exist. For example, you are sitting on your comfortable couch, watching a TV program. You are fully engaged in the plot, seeing the actors moving across the screen, hearing their voices, experiencing your own emotions in response to the action you are viewing. There is no "you." Your consciousness resides only with the sights, sounds and feelings. You, the "experiencer," have merged with the objects you are experiencing. This is a wonderful state, to be able to fully lose yourself – that is, until the drama turns disturbing and you begin to identify and suffer along with the actors.

WAYS TO WORK WITH THE LOVING PROMISES

At those times it is beneficial to be able to consciously pull back and watch yourself watching the show – to be aware that you are aware. Your awareness allows you to know the thought you are thinking the moment you are thinking it, the feeling you are having the moment you are feeling it. Awareness brings you awake.

In your daily life, when you are going about your business, if you watch the passing show of your senses and your mind, but are not identified with the show, you are in *witness consciousness*. Whether you are aware of it or not, the *witness* exists within you and everyone in potential form. It is a place of clear, undisturbed awareness. It is simple awareness that takes in whatever comes in front of it. It doesn't become involved in emotions, it doesn't get lost in thought. It watches emotions as they arise and fall away. It watches the passing parade of thoughts as the mind thinks.

You can obviously see how potentially useful this mind state can be. If you have even a modicum of witness consciousness, and someone were to insult you or put you down, you wouldn't have to lose it and go off like a bomb. From a clear space, you could observe the emotions arising, the heart racing, the fists tensing, the jaw clenching. You watch from the perspective of an uninvolved third party. "How interesting, the body is tensing and the mind is racing." From this neutral vantage point it is possible for you to be able to objectively survey the situation and act from perspective and wisdom.

The job of the witness is to simply observe, not to try to change anything. By seeing, and in turn, understanding, the impetus to change and recognition of the appropriate solution can, without effort, naturally arise. Your clear minded observations will show you the path and lead you to where you need to go.

Another invaluable skill that utilizes self-awareness is the ability to allow your psyche to remain open when feeling anxious and unsafe. Remember from Chapter 1, the first Necessary Condition for Love to Survive is *safety*. On the physical level, if your body integrity is threatened, you feel fear and cover up to protect yourself. It is the same on the psychological level. If you feel your ego or self-concept is threatened, possibly when a person who is important to you judges you or withdraws from you, you might shut down and go into protective mode. You might close off your heart and either attack or withdraw from them. Shutting down is aimed at damage control, but it is an attempt to hide from problems rather than repair them, defend rather than resolve. Doing this prolongs problems and prevents growth because as long as the perceived threat remains, your closed off, protective stance must be maintained. Fear takes up so much space that there is no room for love to dwell.

LOVING PROMISES

Fear is not the only thing that compels you to shut off feeling. Anything that draws you away from your heart draws you away from feeling. If you cannot feel, you cannot love. Dwelling in your mind is the primary way you keep yourself from feeling. Your mental apparatus predominates and your heart closes down when you engage in mental activities like judging others, working yourself into an angry snit, devising ways to manipulate someone and when your mind is confused or in a very active state.

The opposite of closing down is remaining open – allowing whatever thoughts and feelings that are arising to bubble up, and when they surface, accept them or release them. If you are sensitive to yourself, you can be aware of the actual experience of when you close down and open up. A subtle tightening in the belly, a faint change in train of thought, the tiniest upwelling of emotion are the early signs to look for. This is where self-awareness is so valuable. It alerts you just as you begin to close down. At this early point, it is not too late – you have the ability to choose to remain open without a struggle. The moment you feel yourself closing down you can make the decision to relax and let go of resistance before you are drawn in by fear or judgment and locked down or are whisked away in a wash of emotion. With an open heart, you more fully open to the moment. And you won't make the mistake of doing damage by reacting to others from a place of fear or defensiveness. When you keep attending to when you are closing down and keep releasing fear and defensiveness, you will feel light and free and your lightness and freedom will help your partner remain open.

Self-awareness is essential because so much of what motivates us is below our conscious mind. The things we don't know about ourselves *can* hurt us. There are many unconscious hidden land mines we are unable to see that can explode and cause problems for us. The classic psychological defense mechanisms – repression, denial, projection and all the others that prevent us from living in the aliveness of the moment – operate on the subconscious level. The things we reject in ourselves – our own shortcomings and unacceptable impulses that we can see and harshly judge in others, but are blind to in ourselves – are all relegated to the subconscious. Aptly called the "shadow," this Dr. Jekyll/Mr. Hyde mechanism allows an angry, impulsive sub–personality to live within a mild, compliant person, a sexual predator to coexist within a solid, church-going citizen, and allows a severely depressed, suicidal introvert to be hidden within a person who plays the happy social butterfly.

These shadow parts of ourselves can sabotage us if they remain in the dark corners of our psyche. Think of the problems that could be caused by unconsciously seeing and responding to your girlfriend as if she was your mother or by passive-aggressively attacking your boyfriend from a well of anger you are not even aware you have. In order to avoid these kinds of problems and for us to be fully ourselves, the shadow must be brought to the light of awareness, named, acknowledged and accepted as part of us. One instrument that can bring the light of self-awareness is the practice of mindfulness.

Mindfulness is a conscious state of attention on the present moment. It involves active observation of the arising and passing away of thoughts, feelings and sensations. Without judging good or bad, right or wrong; without "efforting" at holding on or letting go; mindfulness allows everything to be as it is, simply watching. The self-awareness that results from the focus on the present moment maintains presence in the here and now. Mindfulness has ancient roots in Buddhism but is now being touted by physicians and psychologists as an effective, evidence-based practice for stress reduction and treating a variety of ills from heart problems to mental illness. Mindfulness strengthens with practice. Instructions for mindfulness practice can be found in the appendix.

With intention, attention and practice, self-awareness will increase over time. As awareness increases, you gain greater control over your behavior. You become able to intervene sooner in the cycle of impulse-intention-action, and actually choose to inhibit unloving actions at their source. Lacking self-awareness, you are blind to when you are speaking and acting in an unloving manner. Your behavior is kind of a habitual, unconscious response. Since you are unaware of the workings of your mind, the hurt or angry reactions of your partner are the only signals available to you alerting you that your behavior is causing upset. After numerous times of being alerted by your partner, you become more conscious of the effects of your behavior and begin to catch yourself after you have spoken and acted without love. Too late. . . but progress. Then, as you become clearer about your upsetting behaviors, you begin noticing in advance when you are about to speak and act in ways that might cause your partner pain. You start seeing and feeling subtle urgings as they just begin to arise. Now, once you are aware of the initial impetus before you have acted, maybe even before you have formed a conscious intention, you have gained the ability to effectively choose to refrain from unloving actions. Finally, with loving intention and self-awareness firmly established in your psyche, the impulse to speak and act without love does not arise.

Self-awareness tends to retreat when we are distressed. Our natural human tendency is to avoid that which makes us uncomfortable. Yet, becoming a more loving person entails the opposite – turning towards your discomfort, exploring it, becoming friendly with it. If you try to create a safe, predictable world around you and keep avoiding the things that make you feel unsafe and uncomfortable, you will be giving in to laziness and fear. And by letting laziness and fear run you, you will likely never grow beyond the restricting bounds of the familiar and unchallenging.

It helps to play at the boundaries between where you feel safe, and where you feel challenged. Uncomfortable being generous? Experiment with how it feels by attempting to give more to others. Uncomfortable with aspects of your partner's personality? Explore by trying to understand and accept those parts. Uncomfortable feeling someone may have taken advantage of you? Probe what it feels like to take a stand and demand to be treated fairly. Uncomfortable with the level of vulnerability in your relationship? Investigate by opening yourself up and expressing your inner feelings more. Enter into your discomfort. Feel it. Welcome it. The fear you experience means you are approaching your edge, the place where growth takes place. The Promises demand it. Every one of the Loving Promises presents challenges that can take you out of your comfort zone and into a place you find difficult and disturbing. When you move beyond your comfort zone, every Promise has the potential to propel you to greater heights and depths of love.

Consciously engaging with that which disturbs you is not easy. It takes courage and dedication to move beyond what feels safe and enter into the fearful unknown. Taking on the Loving Promises is akin to embarking on a Hero's Journey, the mythic archetypical tale about an ordinary person called to adventure in a quest to solve some problem that has disrupted the peaceful safety of the community. The hero must overcome his or her personal fear and reluctance, cross the boundary of the comfortable known, and enter into unknown, uncharted territory. There they are tested, and must face their fear, call up their courage and struggle with and vanquish a formidable monster or villain. After winning their battle, they are able to cross the barrier, return to safety and home, having obtained a boon or precious gift. They will never be the same. Facing their fear and triumphing over their demons has transformed them and the gift they received has enriched and empowered them.

You take a similar heroic journey with the Loving Promises – experiencing dissatisfaction in your relationship, overcoming internal resistance, committing to engage with your self-defeating thoughts and behaviors that have been holding your relationship back. You confront those issues and with courage and determination, work through them. In the process of engaging in this heroic work, you become a hero. The windfall you receive from your successful battle with your demons is a more loving heart, a magnificent relationship and a glowing sense that you have become a hero in your life, a power with which to be reckoned.

WAYS TO WORK WITH THE LOVING PROMISES

The image of the lone hero is very seductive. How gutsy and brave, calling upon our own power and overcoming all obstacles by ourselves. We may feel that needing the help of others somehow indicates a weakness on our part and an affront to our pride. We may also feel that the Loving Promises are such powerful medicine that they alone are all we should need to become a magnificent lover. This is not the case. Sometimes we have such stubborn habits, deep wounds and profound misperceptions that we cannot find our own way unaided. Our blindness in certain critical areas may be so complete and our defenses so strong that we may be faced with the impossible task of trying to lift ourselves up by our bootstraps. In these kinds of circumstances, we can benefit from another set of eyes that can help us see what we ourselves cannot. Most times, it is best if those eyes belong to someone who is independent and not entangled in the relationship. The intervention of a skilled psychotherapist or other competent mental health professional or spiritual advisor could be very healing. The open, nonjudgmental space and wise counsel they offer can provide needed insight and guidance.

Practice makes perfect. As you work with the Loving Promises, you will get better at it. Engaging the Promises will become easier for you. They will seem normal and become part of you. You will not consider any other way of being. As your relationship becomes more magnificent and you become more sensitive, even the slightest deviation from the standard set by the Loving Promises sets off alarm bells. That is the way it is with Alice and me. When we are out of alignment with each other, even a little bit, it feels so bad that we immediately reconnect and do what is necessary to get the love flowing again. Our love is so sweet; we do not do anything that will jeopardize it in any way.

Gentleness and Power

When you boil down the Loving Promises to their condensed essence, you must make two choices about how you will live your life. The first is "Will you maintain integrity within *yourself*?" The second is "Will you extend generosity to *others*?" Integrity is steadfastly choosing to adopt and uphold your moral, ethical, psychological and spiritual ideals. By maintaining integrity within yourself, your speech and actions with your partner and with others will reflect that integrity. Generosity in relationship is choosing to consistently take into consideration the needs, desires and well-being of your partner. By extending generosity to your partner, you grow generosity within yourself. So, in general, if you behave honorably toward righteous ends, and if you give open-handedly what you are able when needed, you will be well on your way to adhering to the Loving Promises.

Bringing integrity and generosity into your relationship is tantamount to bringing the best and highest aspects of you to your partner. When the best of you speaks and listens to the best of your beloved, nothing but good can result.

Integrity and generosity require of us different personal qualities. Maintaining integrity requires toughness, discipline and perseverance, the ability to take a stand and follow through. Extending generosity requires empathy, tenderness, patience and sensitivity. These energies, in their most basic manifestation, are the qualities of power and gentleness. These seemingly polar opposites, through the Loving Promises, synthesize and make us whole and complete. Together, the power of integrity and the gentleness of generosity are two wings. Both are required in order that we may soar.

Integrity and generosity are one-way paths. You must progress forward. You cannot go back. When you have attained a certain level of integrity and generosity, that becomes your new starting point. Your pain threshold is lowered. If you have a lapse of integrity and act in a dishonorable way, you will feel it acutely and suffer for it. If you have a lapse of generosity and retreat into selfishness and hungrily grasp only for your own satisfaction, you will feel the pain of your greed acutely. This sensitivity to backsliding provides an impetus to keep growing and progressing on the path. Your happiness threshold is also lowered. Acting with integrity and generosity brings on more joy, more harmony and more intimacy into your relationship, and this too multiplies the impetus for you to continue growing on the path. The same mechanism is at work with your engagement with the Loving Promises, the same mechanism is involved with love itself. Over time, as you grow in love, it becomes easier and easier for your love to expand and advance, and more difficult for your love to contract and retreat.

In working with the Loving Promises and learning to be a more loving person, there will be many times when you fall short. You'll lose your temper, shade the truth and place your own interests before your partner. You are allowed to make mistakes. Mistakes are part of the process. It might seem at first that there are more failures than successes. That's OK. Nobody learns to be a magnificent lover all at once. You just show up every day and love to the best of your capacity. If you fall, pick yourself up and keep on loving. There is really only one mistake you can make. That is to be content with living with a closed heart.

It's like in the yoga class I'm taking. Everyone gets into the yoga postures as best they can, and there is a lot of variation. Some lithe beauties can easily do a

WAYS TO WORK WITH THE LOVING PROMISES

forward fold and touch their palms to the floor, and some old fogies like me have trouble reaching their ankles. But when I extend myself to my limit, I am maximizing the benefit to my body, just as the young person is maximizing hers. It's all relative. Do the best you can.

Comparing yourself and your relationship to others can be deadly. The Loving Promises are a beautiful path and a magnificent relationship a wonderful destination. This book is meant to be a inspiration on the path. However, some readers, rather than be inspired, might become dispirited. When they read how wonderful a loving relationship can be and compare it to the one that they have, they become depressed. They think that they can never attain such love, put themselves down and feel hopeless. Comparing takes you away from the task at hand, which is being the best, most loving and lovable partner you can be in this moment. As the sages say "The journey of a thousand miles begins with one step." They neglect to tell that you must take the next step, and the next, and the next. Everyone is on their own journey, and everyone has progressed, so far, to the place they need to be.

The Loving Promises are not merely ideals for you to admire; they are actions for you to take. They are not a collection of dry abstract formulas. Each Promise is alive. They are brought to life in our day-to-day interactions, with every problem encountered, every decision made. They are embedded in our thoughts, our speech, our actions. They guide us, inspire us, embolden us. And when we imbibe the Loving Promises, they become us.

If the Loving Promises and this book have touched a chord in you, where can you go from here? Since everyone has different needs and desires, this is a decision that is up to each individual to make. A firm understanding of the principles of the Loving Promises is essential. You might start by re-reading the book. I have often found that a second reading can clarify and can often reveal new insights that I missed in a first reading. If your mate is also interested in the Promises, you might try reading together out loud, chapter-by-chapter, and discussing in detail the points you find relevant, interesting or confusing.

There is an abundance of material that goes into greater detail than I have here. A cursory search will reveal a wealth of information about meditation, family dynamics, spirituality, etc. Retreats and workshops can provide extended, experiential programs. Try to avoid the pitfall of spending all your effort accumulating more and more information. The Loving Promises are about action.

Ongoing support and discussion groups working with the Promises would be valuable. An online telecourse is in the planning stages as of this printing. A website is provided at the end of the book with news and updates for those interested in keeping abreast of latest developments. What remains is to practice the Loving Promises day-by-day and enjoy the results.

Years ago, Alice and I were vacationing in Hawaii. Someone told us to take the road to Hana, at the time, a quaint town on the edge of the island of Maui. We set out and soon encountered fabulous vistas overlooking the ocean, secluded beaches, lush tropical forests, streams, pools, waterfalls. We were stunned by the beauty. We arrived in Hana, a relatively nondescript little village. It turns out that the reason for the trip was the road, not the town. The beauty was in getting there. It's like that with life and relationships, and with working the Loving Promises. There's great meaning in the way you get to where you want to go. If you focus only on your destination, you can miss the joy of the journey. Your work with the Loving Promises is your journey, your life. Enjoy the scenery as you navigate your path.

The great German philosopher, Goethe, wrote beautifully about the power of taking on difficult projects, and this has relevance for the Loving Promises. "Concerning all acts of initiative and creation, there is one elementary truth: that the moment one definitely commits oneself, then providence moves too. All sorts of things occur to help one that would never otherwise have occurred. A whole stream of events issues from the decision, raising in one's favor all manner of unforeseen incidents, meetings and material assistance which no man would have dreamed would have come his way. Whatever you can do or dream you can, begin it. Boldness has genius, power and magic in it. Begin it now."

Chapter 8

THE PROMISE OF LOVING

The book began with the question "What is your life's purpose? Why were you born?" This final Promise is an attempt at an answer.

The human mind is ingenious. We can to fly through the air like a bird, swim under the ocean like a fish, travel to distant planets. We are able to instantaneously see and speak to another person on the other side of the Earth. Through nanotechnology, we can build objects molecule by molecule. Our brain, using the Internet, has become centralized outside our skull and has instant access to the contents of a thousand libraries.

We now have in hand capacities that previous generations ascribed to Gods. Yet these powers can be and are being used for evil purposes – for destruction, for greed, for mayhem, for enriching the few at the expense of the many. If guided by love, these powers could create a beautiful world. Guided by hate, greed, fear, delusion and separation, these powers can create a hell.

The promise that loving makes to humankind is to bring heaven to earth, to make our relationships, our friends, our abode, our life, into a paradise. Not at a future time or in another place, but right here, right now. Every moment spent in heart open loving is a joyous moment. When we are loving, our consciousness is flooded with feelings of peace, unity, openness, acceptance and goodwill. So every moment spent loving is a heavenly moment, every moment spent hating is a moment in hell. Thus, the final Promise.

39. I WILL EMBRACE LOVE AS THE GUIDING LIGHT OF MY LIFE.

My ultimate goal is to think more loving thoughts, feel more loving feelings, speak more loving words, act in more loving ways – at all times, in any situation, with every person – including myself. I will monitor my journey by taking a loving inventory. My intention is to bring more goodness into my life, into your life, into our relationship and into the world.

THE PROMISE OF LOVING

If you think about what is important and meaningful in your life, many things lose their luster. How important is the label on the clothes you wear, the model of car you drive, who you're seen with, how your favorite sports team is doing? What really matters, what gives your life meaning, is giving yourself in love and receiving love from others. Giving and receiving love is your ultimate reason for being.

This Promise invites you to not limit love with the people in your life, but to expand love to include "all times" and "any situation." Love doesn't happen only when you are with your sweetheart. Loving feelings can well up when you are taking out the garbage. It is entirely possible to imbue the little things in life with the same heartfelt care and affection as if you were cavorting with your beloved. Is it possible to love the commute to work? To feel love as we are waiting in line purchasing groceries? As we are cleaning out the cat box? Why not? We spend much more time in everyday activities than we do with our lover. Why shouldn't we aspire to experience everyday life as an opportunity to imbibe and express love.

Just today, in the space of one single day, my heart burst open and I fell in love with a white egret as it glided over the tree tops in the morning, the open, smiling face of the young waitress as she guided us to our table for lunch, the changing reds and yellows of the setting sun and the sound of the pianist playing classical music on the upright piano in a basement bar. These "little loves" arise and pass away, arise and pass away, but are as essential to our love life as the "big love" of our one and only. By themselves, the egret, the waitress, the sunset and the pianist I experienced today are mere sensory phenomena. As I am able to pour caring, attention and appreciation into these passing events, my life becomes filled up with love and I become more loving and lovable. By appreciating these ephemeral moments, the love I am able to bring to my partner is enhanced.

We must not wait until we encounter someone or something we consider "worthy" before we are able to experience love. Love is not an automatic response to that which is lovable. We don't become a more loving person by looking around for and discovering objects we consider more worthy of our love. *Love is a conscious decision we make.* We decide, by focusing our attention and intention, to consciously imbue the objects and people that come before us with more love. We commit to make the effort to see them with more loving eyes. Love is a choice to bring care and show up with a loving heart.

When you adopt this final Loving Promise, you are committing to make love the central purpose in your life. More accurately, you adopt the Promise because you have come to the realization that love **is** the central purpose of your life. And because love is your central purpose, you give your life over to love, and love becomes the organizing principle around which you build your life.

Your commitment to love provides a framework to which you can return again and again. When in a quandary, you don't rely on your feelings of the moment, which can change with the wind. With this Promise, and with the other Loving Promises, you have an anchor, a stable value and a set of practices you can hold onto that you trust and know is true and effective.

This final Loving Promise has its own chapter because it is different from the others. It is not a vow that you make. Rather, it is a realization that comes upon you. It is the fruit of all the other Loving Promises. It dawns upon you and beckons after you have worked the Promises for a while and have grown within them. Because it requires a certain degree of ripeness, it is necessary to refrain from taking on this Promise unless you feel strongly moved to do so and until you have matured in love. You cannot rush this Promise, it happens of its own accord, in its own way and in its own time.

Over time, as you worked with the Promises, your goals have evolved. At first it was all important for you to overcome some of the problems and frustrations you were having in your relationship. You initially began working with the Promises with that goal in mind. But as you worked with them and integrated them into your life, you changed, you evolved, and you deepened. By bringing loving awareness to your heart, loving feelings started to take over your consciousness. Gradually, all that was loving began to increase; all that was unloving weakened and began to dissolve. Acceptance increased, judgment weakened. Sharing increased, selfishness weakened. Compassion increased, uncaring weakened.

Your goal expanded to more than just resolving relationship issues. Your goal now became to have a great relationship, a magnificent relationship. You saw that in order to have a magnificent relationship, you needed to turn within, live with integrity and generosity, transform yourself into a magnificent person and evoke magnificence in the people in your life. You set your intention on accomplishing that purpose. Your work has borne fruit. Now it is time to move on to a higher level, time to live love, be love and make love your goal and your ultimate purpose.

What will this look like? How will this Promise be expressed in action?

Throughout your day you will maintain a heightened awareness of loving/non-loving thoughts and actions. You will take a gentle, non-judgmental inventory, being attuned to when your love flows, when it stops, when anger or blame arises, when it subsides. At the times when non-loving thoughts make

THE PROMISE OF LOVING

their way into your consciousness, you release them, and avoid empowering them by giving them the energy of your attention. And if you cannot or will not release them, you hold yourself in loving awareness, without blame or self-accusation. All the while, you keep the intention to bring in more love, more love.

> *You are driving your car and another driver blindly swerves into your lane and forces you off the road and almost into a ditch. You pull to a screeching stop in a cloud of dust. Your heart is racing and you feel the hot sting of anger rising, but make the choice to not give the anger free reign. Instead, you keep awareness that the driver's action was probably not on purpose and you are awash in a sense of gratefulness that you are safe and there was no damage.*

> The same situation occurs. *Your heart races, anger rises, builds and overcomes you. You speed and catch up to the offending driver, scream at them, threaten, and make obscene gestures. . . Then you realize what you are doing. You cease, let go of your anger, let go of blame, forgive yourself and are awash in a sense of gratefulness that you are safe and there was no damage.*

Working with this Promise, as with all the others, is an ongoing process. In the examples above, both were opportunities for you to learn love and forgiveness. In the first example you learned more quickly. The second example illustrates the truth that you can learn as much or more from your mistakes and failures as you can from your progress and successes. When growing in love, the way you handle your lapse of loving action is as significant as the lapse itself.

The way you work with this final Promise is simple, but not easy – discern what is the more loving action, continually choose it, despite your resistance, despite your lethargy, despite what wrongs *they* have done or are doing to you. Choose love especially when stressed and frustrated and pissed off. Choose love, kindness and courtesy anyway. Choose it every day, in every situation, with every person – no exceptions. Choose it because you know in your heart that pain in relationship and in life comes from withholding love. Joy comes from extending love.

At times you will be faced with a fork in the road, one of two alternative actions you must take. A question you can ask yourself when deciding on a course of action is this, "Which action will bring more love?" This powerful question, carefully considered, can be your reference point, your yardstick to help discover the highest and best action for any situation. To follow the Loving Promises, this one question is a basic one you need to ask yourself. You know how to do this. Instinctively, you know what actions bring more love, more peace . . . and which don't. You know what will make another person feel happy and loved. You know what will make you feel more empowered. You have an unerring inner voice that speaks with love and integrity. It's a matter of listening for that voice, and following it.

As you go through your day and interact with friends, lovers and strangers, reflect on the ebb and flow of the energy of love. Observe yourself. Are you being a messenger of love and acceptance? Are you being a messenger of dissatisfaction and frustration? Are you looking to find goodness, or looking to find fault? Wanting to be special and superior, or harboring feelings of inferiority? Seeking gain for yourself, or opening your hands in generosity? This is "loving inventory." It is "loving" because you are not looking to find fault or criticize yourself. You are observing yourself and your behavior with loving eyes. Your intention is only to learn to be more skillful so you can improve your ability to love.

Let your mantra be, "I intend love." Send your loving intentions into the world wherever you are and whenever you think of it. Respond with lightness and graciousness. Do it especially when you are feeling frustrated. When the cashier is slow at the grocery store, *intend love*. When your child is having a screaming tantrum in a crowded restaurant, *intend love*. When a salesman calls during dinnertime asking you to take a "quick survey," *intend love*. When your beloved partner is ignoring your wishes and insisting on having their way, *intend love*. By intending love, you bring the Loving Promises to bear in whatever situation. Follow up your loving intention with loving action.

Toward this end, your intention to feel and express love can be made manifest with a simple but powerful exercise, similar to the ones described in more detail earlier in Promises #3 and #14. That process involved experiencing love for your partner through your heart (Promise #3), and radiating love out to your partner from your heart (Promise #14). To use this process, feel love entering your heart and visualize love radiating out but, in this case, don't include only your partner. Receive and radiate love to all beings as they come into your life – your waiter in the restaurant, your boss at work, the old lady hobbling down the street. Keep it up. This is a potent practice, especially when done for prolonged periods of time. The longer you do it, the more potent it becomes. The more often you do it, the more deeply ingrained it becomes. The more you do it, the more natural it becomes. I have worked with this practice for

THE PROMISE OF LOVING

full days at a time and the effect has been transformative. It fills your heart and mind to overflowing with loving thoughts and feelings.

This final Loving Promise speaks of "goodness." Bringing goodness into your world means spreading the experience of joy, peace, truth, harmony, and goodwill to all persons, known and unknown. This seems like a tall order, but it is not impossible. What makes it possible, in fact, what makes it easy, is to aspire to be a joyful, peaceful, honest, harmonious person of goodwill. When these attributes characterize your personality, you cannot help but bring the blessing of goodness into every interaction. Goodness is the only thing you know. You see, hear and speak only goodness. Goodness is the only thing you have to give.

As we saw in Promise #38, about expanding your love into the world, love will wither if reserved for those select few to whom you are related and with whom you find it easy to get along. But what about those who are not so easy? Will your love be diminished if you leave them out? This can be a difficult challenge, but are you willing to send goodness even to those who you judge harshly, maybe even find disgusting? How about sending love to the drunken bum who accosts you on the street corner, stinking of booze and soaked in his own urine? That's a tough one.

As difficult as it is to extend love to those you judge, it is an even more difficult challenge, because it affects you personally, to send good wishes to your enemies, those infuriating people who frustrate you and purposely do what they can to cause you pain. Use the final *metta* affirmation to wish goodness for these trying people in your life.

> May . . . be happy.
> May . . . be peaceful.
> May . . . be free of suffering.
> May . . . love and be loved.

When you take on the challenge to offer good wishes to the difficult people in your life, you will be accruing great personal benefit. It is easy to offer good wishes to the ones you love and those who are nice to you with whom you get along. It is even easy to send out impersonal love to all of mankind. But to desire goodness for those who wish you harm is a real stretch. The benefit from stretching your love this way is that your ability to love will grow bigger, stronger and more inclusive.

Years ago there was an angry, vindictive man in our life who purposely created problems for us that cost us a lot of money. We never knew what evil surprise the next day would bring. Alice and I were stewing in anger and plotting ways to get back at him when we realized that by giving vent to those feelings, we had "become him." We felt bad being him. So together we worked on our anger using affirmations, wishing him well. After a surprisingly short time, our fury subsided and we were able to reclaim our loving selves again. What a relief! The affirmations were a great help.

This incident is infinitesimal compared to the burden some people must endure. In some countries, innocent citizens are stripped of their wealth, murdered in cold blood, women raped, families separated, cultures destroyed, people treated as 3rd class citizens in their own country or sent to live as exiles in horrible conditions in refugee camps. How is it possible to deal with the searing anger from this excruciating suffering? The Dalai Lama, leader in exile of the Tibetan people is an example of a way to transmute suffering. His country was taken over by the Chinese. Every day, he spends hours in prayer, seeking to purify himself, cultivate compassion and asking that the Chinese be forgiven and that they be free from suffering. His religion, he says, is kindness.

In the corner of the altar in our meditation room is a photo of a terrorist a moment before he is about to behead an innocent victim. When I feel up to it, I try to work through my outrage and hate by looking at the photo and wishing goodness, through *metta,* to the perpetrator of that heinous act. It is not easy, but occasionally I can do this.

A reasonable question that could be asked is, "Why should I even try? It is probable that this hate filled person cannot be touched by human mercy, but to hate him and wish him pain is to wall off my heart, (just as he has done). I truly believe this-- *there is never any justification for closing down my heart.* Never, not in any way, not for any reason, not towards any person, no matter how vile their behavior. To hate, to carry resentment, to want to retaliate, to wish to cause suffering, is to bring the venom of hate and suffering into my own consciousness. I don't want it there to poison me.

This is not to say that I never feel rage and never experience the desire to hurt or retaliate. Even with Alice I have had flashes of pure hostility and impulse for revenge in response to something she has said or done. But my greater intention is that these feelings not take up residence in my mind and heart. When they arise, I do whatever I can to best allow them to quickly pass through me.

It should have been obvious from the beginning that the Loving Promises are not just about your relationship, but about your life. The skills needed to have a magnificent relationship – integrity, generosity, patience, etc., are the very same skills needed to have a magnificent life. Therefore, as you grow in magnificence as a couple, you will grow as an individual. As you grow in magnificence as an individual, you will grow as a couple. It works both ways.

THE PROMISE OF LOVING

The promise of loving and the pledge that the Loving Promises aim to fulfill for your magnificent relationship is a lifetime of sweet harmony together. Being in harmony is wanting a good life for each other and working together with kindness and goodwill to create that good life. Harmony is the reward for treating each other kindly and graciously. There is no guarantee that your life together will be easy – every life will have its portion of suffering and pain. There is no escaping that. But to have a companion and helpmate to share in life's ups and downs is a blessing and takes some of the sting out of the "downs" and amplifies the joy of the "ups."

When you practice the Loving Promises in your relationship and develop them in yourself, you cultivate the most precious quality a relationship could have – trust. Trust is the fabric that holds your relationship together, the foundation upon which it is built. Trust is the unquestioned conviction that you and your partner will protect each other's vulnerable heart and honor each other's sovereign soul. All the Loving Promises are designed to do this.

Trust does not happen automatically, and it doesn't appear full-blown. Trust develops day by day, tested and proven again and again through your words and actions. You demonstrate your trustworthiness by standing steadfast by your partner, serving their best interests, being unselfish with them, participating in their life, etc. – all vows of the Loving Promises.

The Loving Promises develop your partner's ability to trust you. Through the Promises, you also gain trust in your own self. By working with the Promises, your integrity, inner strength and autonomy grow. Cultivating these potent inner forces makes you steadfast in your trust for your own self and confident in your power. Seeing your strength, your partner will recognize your trustworthiness and relax, knowing they are safe in your presence. Thus their trust of you will grow ever deeper.

A yardstick for measuring your progress with the Loving Promises and the depth of your magnificent relationship is contentment. You feel fulfilled in your relationship. There is nothing more you need in your partner; nothing more you want. Of course, no relationship is perfect, but there is nothing that need change with this one. You are satisfied.

In addition to harmony, trust and contentment, magnificent relationship promises an ever-growing love. This was a surprise to me. I could never have imagined that the love Alice and I have for each other would keep on deepening and maturing as it has over the years. It is the nature of true love to not just remain static, but to gather momentum and strengthen with the passage of time. With every kindness extended, with every emergency weathered together, with every conflict resolved fairly, the bond of love and genuine friendship becomes closer. The couple's appreciation of each other, the preciousness of that love and the preciousness of every moment they are privileged to have together becomes stronger.

The sense of appreciation brought about by magnificent love is not limited only to your partner or your relationship. Appreciation saturates everything. Everything becomes more precious to you because of the preciousness of the love you share with your partner. That love brings you more into the present. Because of the depth of your love is deeper, and width of your love is wider, you have greater capacity to feel more. The emotions that arise are more consciously available to you. You feel more joy and pleasure, but you also more grief and pain. The feelings you experience generate aliveness. The aliveness you experience generates feelings. Embracing all feeling, you become more vital and alive.

Love from a relationship that is magnificent cannot remain within the confines of the relationship. The love for one another is a sanctuary of peace. It is the nature of true love to expand outward from that sanctuary to include others and touch them with that peace. The light from a magnificent relationship shines on everyone. Family, friends, coworkers, acquaintances – all are recipients of the luminous glow that emanates from a loving couple. All are loved more deeply because the love within the primary relationship has grown in magnificence.

The reflected glow of that love is inspiring for everyone. In essence, simply by having a magnificent relationship you are serving others. The beauty of your relationship reassures others of the truth of love. It displays the power of love. It demonstrates the delicious fruits of love. And it confirms that such love is attainable. Your love can inspire others to know that they too can aspire to magnificent love.

When you exercise the Loving Promises and your love flourishes, you tap into power. Love is a power, a power that you can actually feel. You sense it radiating towards you when in the presence of a person who loves you. You feel it radiating from yourself toward the person you love. Your love feeds off the love of your partner and vice versa. Together, your loves merge to create a dynamo. Other people around you pick up the "vibration" that emanates from you both and can easily sense your love for each other.

What if you were in the presence of a person who had developed the power of love, unconditional love, to the nth degree – a person who exists in a continuous vibration of love? That person would be a love generator whose energy of kindness, acceptance and goodwill would be broadcast out and attract people just as the fragrance of blossoms drifts and attracts bees to a flower. Christ was one such love generator, as was the Buddha, Krishna, and other great beings whose hearts opened completely and embraced all who were moved to enter. Their love was so powerful that even after more than two millennia, people's lives are still being touched and transformed by that love.

The mesmerizing power of pure love isn't only relegated to ancient history. Years ago, I attended a large event in India where Mother Teresa was a keynote speaker. She was a humble nun, but a towering presence of love. When she entered the giant, packed auditorium from the rear, the whole energy of the place instantly changed. All conversation stopped. All eyes followed this tiny, bent figure as she slowly walked down the aisle. With reverence, people struggled to reach out to touch her, many with tears in their eyes, as she made her way to the podium. Simply to brush her garment put them in contact with love inside themselves. Such was the power of the love she generated. I felt it. I was one of those who touched her cloak.

My personal experience of that powerful love occurred in the presence of an Indian guru. He passed his love down to me, as the love of his guru had been passed down to him. I have been with other evolved persons and the experience was the same. Their years of spiritual practice in pursuit of enlightenment brought them the fruit of that practice – a love so deep and so wide that it left no one out. The all-encompassing love they embodied awakened a place in me and others that was available to open to love.

I had a life-changing awakening with an Indian holy man. That was the way it occurred in my life. Awakenings don't always have to be so exotic. They can occur, as it did with my stepson, after a life-threatening illness. They can occur when you become new parents and gaze at the face of your newborn baby. They can occur when you feel the touch of Spirit during the Sunday service at your neighborhood church. And they can occur when you fall in love, as it did with Alice and me. The awakening to love has less to do with the situation that causes it, and more to do with your readiness to open to awaken. Alice and I were ready. When you are ready for love, it is as if you are dry kindling. Even the slightest spark will light a flame in you. That's what happened to us.

Here lies the simple secret of the power of the Loving Promises--*the flame of your love will kindle love in your partner's heart.* The greater the intensity of your flame, the more quickly and easily will love be ignited in your partner. When you and your partner are open to be touched by love, love will burst forth in your hearts. The purpose of the Loving Promises is to intensify your flame. And their goal is to make it more easy for your own heart to be set afire. Your flame can cause a conflagration. It is contagious. That is its nature.

LOVING PROMISES

Laying in bed this morning, musing about how I could end the book, I asked myself, "What is the message of this book? What one idea is behind all the Loving Promises? What would encompass everything I'd written?" The answer came to me immediately, but it seemed so hackneyed and simple and cliched that I felt hesitant to share it. But I will. *"It is better to give than to receive."* So plain, yet so powerful and so, so true. If you could incorporate this simple understanding into your life and relationships, you wouldn't even need the Loving Promises. You would simply enjoy giving to your partner, and enjoy their enjoyment from receiving your gift. You would both swim in this warm ocean of openhearted generosity.

The ocean is there, waiting for you to dive in. I can declare now without a shadow of a doubt or hint of false pride, that my relationship with Alice is magnificent. The fact that it is magnificent doesn't mean that it should be held in awe, or seen as something only a few special couples could achieve. If I felt a magnificent relationship like ours was unattainable by others, I never would have written this book. I take comfort in the knowledge that Alice and I are not alone. Many other couples we know and know of, have embarked on this incredible journey and are living immersed in harmony and love. We all stand as examples and inspirations. Know without a doubt that loving communion is real and is possible. Let that knowledge be an affirmation for you. Alice and I are not some special form of humans. We are as you are. If a magnificent relationship is possible for us, it is possible for you.

May *you* hold the promise of loving. May that promise be fulfilled in you. And may your love be magnificent.

Epilogue

OUR STORY by Alice

Who would have thought I would meet the love of my life by chance at my girlfriend Roni's house. I was introduced to Richard in the kitchen just as I was leaving. He was standing on the right side of the room - a cute, tall, thin, silent person. I was standing by the door, alive with energy, decked out in my dancing skirt with scarves tied around my waist - excited to be on my way to Dance Home, a freestyle dance studio in Santa Monica where I would religiously go three times a week. Richard was 39 and had just returned from living in an ashram in India. I was forty-three. There are some events in life that stand out in minute detail. Those first few seconds of our meeting are one of those poignant moments.

I had been single mother and sole supporter of my children for ten years after the divorce from my first husband. My thirteen-year marriage produced a son, Jason, and a daughter, Angela. We were young when we married, and although he was a nice guy, our core values were too different and I did not feel happy. It became apparent to me that I could not spend the rest of my life with him. I was a stay-at-home mom, my kids were seven and eight years old, and I had no job, but that didn't stop me from divorcing. A lot of people wait until the kids are grown, but I felt it was better to be apart than to have them be witness to an unhappy relationship.

Fortunately, a perfect job showed up almost simultaneously with my decision to separate. I became a teacher's assistant in a private school. The hours were perfect as I could be home when my kids got out of school, and we shared the same school vacations. I supplemented the low pay and the lack of child support with food stamps, and it all worked out. A couple of years later, I became the school's art teacher, and remained in that job for eight years.

EPILOGUE

During my ten years as a single mother I also had several other unfulfilling relationships. Through those unsatisfying experiences I learned what I didn't want in a partnership. I saw that I lost myself trying to seek approval, and vowed never to do that again. I knew that if I ever had another relationship, it would be one of fidelity, equality, trust and joy - one where my partner and I could grow together and expand.

That decade was spent soul searching – looking inside myself for ways to be happy, contented and open-hearted. I attended various personal growth workshops during this period, which helped me to open my mind and heart and come to terms with the things that were holding me back from living to my full potential.

Fortunately, I had lots of good friends and was enjoying my single life and my family. I was not actively looking for a partner, but was open to the possibility.

A few days after my first meeting with Richard in the kitchen, I was invited to the celebration of Roni's birthday at a local restaurant. Thanks to the sweet hand of fate, Richard and I ended up seated next to each other at the end of the large booth. It is amazing to think that if he didn't sit next to me, we might have never connected with each other. Although there were ten other people present at the table, we "only had eyes for each other." It was as if no one else existed. We were engaged in a silly conversation about nothing, but we were so familiar and at ease - like we were old friends. At the end of the evening, I invited him to come and dance with me the following Friday. He accepted.

We fell in love on that day, September 20, 1982 at 7:30 P.M. while driving together in my VW Rabbit on the Santa Monica Freeway between the Lincoln and 5th Street off ramp on our way to Dance Home. Richard took my hand in his, gazed at me and began telling me that I was so beautiful - that I was ageless and deep - that I could be a young girl or an old lady. He was seeing me in different lights. I looked at him and thought to myself, "This really is one adorable person." We recognized each other at the deepest level. This recognition didn't happen in our minds. It happened in our hearts.

Pianist George Winston's beautiful album, *Autumn*, was playing in the background on the car stereo. I parked the car in the lot, and we immediately began kissing each other. I wasn't "the kind of girl" who made out with "boys" in the parking lot, but here I was, and enjoying every minute. Dance was very important to me and I wanted to dance with Richard to see if we were really in rhythm with each other on a more subtle level. Our first dance told the whole story. We were whirling around the floor like we were an old married couple

LOVING PROMISES

who had been dancing together forever. We went back to Richard's home and made love. That was our first date, and we have never been apart since that time.

We were exhilarated by the overwhelming feelings of love we felt for each other, and within days of that memorable evening, began announcing to everyone we encountered that we were in love. Immediately we introduced each other to my children, our parents, siblings and friends who were all delighted about our meeting. Our family and circle of friendships instantly grew larger.

On November 1, 1982, about six weeks after Richard and I met and fell in love, he officially moved into my home. The fact that I had two teenage children didn't faze him. He said he never had a thought about it. The kids loved him, and were happy that I had fallen in love with such a wonderful person after ten years of being single. One day he thoroughly surprised me by paying my dentist bill for over a thousand dollars saying that he loved me and, "What's yours is mine." I added his name to the deed of my home saying, "What's mine is yours"! Richard merged naturally into our household as a loving father figure and a darling, affectionate, trusted and supportive partner.

1982 – First photo together 3 days after we met (early digital photo)

A couple of weeks after we began to live together, we took a trip to Big Sur for my birthday. I admired a gold and sapphire ring he was wearing and he, without thought, removed his treasured ring from his finger saying, "It's yours," and offered it to me. I put out both of my hands, unsure of which finger it

EPILOGUE

should be slipped on. Of course, he put it on my left ring finger where it has remained since that day. Only later did we realize that this was our engagement.

In January, 1983 we decided to go to India and visit the ashram that Richard had lived in. That experience had been life changing for him and he wanted to share it with me. When we stepped off the plane at the Bombay airport, it was like nothing I had ever seen or smelled!!! We entered into a shore-to-shore sea of women clad in colorful saris, men with dark faces, white teeth and deep, soulful eyes, carrying everything imaginable on their heads, in their arms and on their backs. Families were spread about on the floor with piles of odd suitcases, pillows, blankets, food, etc. The smell was a sickening combination of incense, spices, diesel fuel, cow dung fires, humanity. (After a short while in India, that nauseating smell became like perfume to me because it was a reminder of what a beautiful and amazing adventure we were experiencing.)

From the airport, we then embarked on a third-class train on our way to the ashram, completing the last part of the trip in a three-wheeled motorcycle with a top and a seat for the driver in the front, and 2 seats behind him. We sat crammed in with our two suitcases and a rather large man with a huge suitcase of his own. We were laughing as we bounced down the main "highway" to the ashram on a narrow two-lane dirt road, sharing it with a sea of people walking, cows, cars, buses, water buffalos, people in horse drawn carriages, three-wheeled, two-seater cars loaded with six or eight people, women in bright colored saris walking with baskets on their heads, cars, dogs, bicycles with cages of chickens and furniture strapped on the back, and wrecked vehicles lying by the side of the road. It was like Mr.Toad's Wild Ride.

Finally, we arrived at the ashram - an oasis of serenity. Colorful doors shaped like lotuses greeted us. We entered the cool marble courtyard to total silence and the smell of incense. Here the life is very scheduled. We would arise at 3AM and spend the day chanting, meditating, listening to inspirational talks with the guru, and performing seva (selfless service). Everyone had some kind of job so that the ashram could run smoothly.

After about a week, I was sitting with a group of people shelling peas for one of the meals. Richard came to me and said, "I was talking to a friend and he said that Indian weddings are beautiful. Do you want to get married?" Of course, my response was, "Why not?" Within days we were in Bombay (Mumbai) having a ring made for Richard that matched the one he had given me, and buying my red silk wedding sari trimmed with real gold thread and his white silk shirt and *lungi* (an Indian sarong).

Upon returning to the ashram, we were informed that our wedding had been arranged to happen in a few days – January 23, 1983 - four months and three days after we met. It was to be held in the home of the ashram's head Brahmin priest. With a few friends in tow, we boarded the crowded local bus enroute to our wedding. We were dropped off at the tiny village of Yeola, where some of the dirt streets were so narrow that no car could drive on them, and you could stretch out your arms and almost touch buildings on both sides of the street.

The home of the Brahmin priest was small and simple. The cooking was done on the floor on burners. The water came from a faucet in the courtyard. Within minutes of our arrival, I was whisked into the bedroom by the daughters of the priest. They proceeded to wrap my sari around me, fix my hair, polish my nails and put a jewel on my forehead.

Upon entering the main room, we sat on the floor with the priest, and a beautiful hour and a half traditional Indian ceremony began, complete with chants, prayers to the gods, spices, incense and small ritual fires. We even went outside to get the blessings from the sun. There was a part in the ceremony when Richard held my hand as I put my big toe in seven piles of rice that were on the floor. In this ritual he was promising to be there for me through all the stages of my life. I was adorned with a *mangala sutra* – a traditional necklace that is worn as symbol of devotion and protection for Richard. I never take it off.

There was a moment in the ceremony when priest's daughters held a sheet between us, supposedly hiding us from each other. This was our opportunity to escape with no questions asked if one or the other decides not to marry. Once the sheet is removed, it is too late—it's a done deal. In our case, the sheet was held too low, so we were able to see each other's faces. Our eyes locked and filled with tears of love.

After the ceremony we were taken by *tonga*, (colorful, horse drawn carriage) through the narrow streets of the village. It was like a parade. Everyone from the village was outside on the road and on their rooftops waving and cheering and children were chasing after our carriage. We felt like the king and queen on parade. When we returned to the priest's home, we were amazed to find that his wife and daughters had prepared a magnificent feast served on leaves, which we ate with our fingers while sitting on the floor. At the end of the day, we were taken through the beautiful countryside back to the bus station where we returned to our hotel in a nearby village. Our wedding day was truly a magical experience—beautiful beyond words.

EPILOGUE

January 1983 – Indian Wedding – Receiving Blessings from the Sun

LOVING PROMISES

January, 1983 Indian wedding ceremony

Our trip to India then became our honeymoon. We travelled to many parts for about a month, totally awed by our sweet and easy connection, and by the unusual sights of India. Spirituality runs deep in that country, and the experience of being in that amazing place, especially with my loving husband, inspired me to open up more to the spiritual life. I soon began devouring books by the great masters, listening to talks, being in their presence whenever possible. The teachings have informed my life and opened my heart.

When we returned home in March, we had an afternoon potluck wedding in the backyard of our home so we could share our marriage vows with our family and friends, and make our union legal. (It was too confusing in India to do that). My brother, Robbie, had become a minister with the Universal Life Church and performed the ceremony. It was a casual, laughter-filled event with friends and family offering sweet and funny statements. Our German

EPILOGUE

Shepard/Husky dog, Goalie, was even a part of it. She was the "Best Dog." The potluck feast was spectacular as everyone prepared their favorite dishes, and the celebration continued well into the night.

1983 – Backyard Potluck Wedding. Ruth and Jack Matzkin, Angela, Us, Robbie, Jason, Beulah & Sumner Long

We settled into our married life with the usual ease of our relationship. Richard was working at a private psychiatric hospital as a therapist. I would come to work with him from time to time and volunteer with the patients, teaching yoga and creating art. Eventually seeing what a great team we were, the owner of the hospital offered us a job as Program Directors. We were thrilled to be able to spend all day together and get paid for it. We accepted the job with the idea that we would work for a while, save our money and then leave for a year-long, round-the-world trip.

When the time came, to our co-workers' shock and awe, we gave our notice and booked the flight for our trip. It was perfect timing as both of the kids were working and becoming independent and our parents were all healthy. We were free as birds to explore the world. We travelled for thirteen-and-a-half months with no reservations anywhere except our first night in Hong Kong. We took planes, ships, trains, buses, sailboats, taxis, donkeys, rickshaws, camels, and wore out the soles of several pairs of shoes. The adventure took us to mainland China, Pakistan, India, Egypt, Israel, Greece, Turkey, Yugoslavia, Czechoslovakia, Hungary, Austria, England, Spain, Portugal, Morocco, France, and New York. For all that time we were with each other 24/7. As usual, we were in the same rhythm and totally enjoyed our togetherness. We had only one argument, which lasted about an hour. It was about what time the ferry left from the Greek mainland to the island of Santorini.

1985 World Trip – Egypt, Great Pyramid of Giza, After Riding Camels Through Desert

Once home from our adventure, we saw that our love we shared rekindled a rebirth in our artistic gifts that we had left behind. I had stopped painting for twenty-two years while I was raising my kids. Richard had left his jazz band and stopped playing drums for about the same amount of time in order to get his master's degree and pursue a career in psychology. My son expressed an interest in learning to play the drums. Richard bought a drum set in a thrift shop for Jason who banged on it a few times before giving up. Richard sat down and began playing and hasn't stopped since. My paints and brushes were in storage in the garage, and with intense excitement I began painting again. I signed up for an art class and enrolled Richard in a sculpture class. He is a natural artist, so sculpting was easy for him and he began producing beautiful pieces in clay. Our daughter's bedroom in our home was immediately turned into an art studio the very day she moved into her own place.

Eleven blissful years later we moved into a sweet home in Ojai at the end of a country road where we share a beautiful art studio and love it when we are working at the same time. We are not in competition, and totally support, encourage and enjoy each other's artistic successes and endeavors. We value and trust one another's opinions and perceptions of our work, and from time to time

EPILOGUE

Richard has even put a brush to my paintings, and I have dug my fingers into the wet clay of his sculptures.

Richard and I have renewed our wedding vows three additional times since our wedding in India, and our potluck wedding in our back yard. The third wedding was a traditional Native American wedding in the field behind of our Ojai house, the fourth, a Las Vegas Wedding in Cupid's Chapel, and the fifth, a wedding in the Jewish tradition, where we made the final vow to always remember that each day we have together may be our last.

February 1995 - Native American Wedding with Grandfather Semu, Chumash Medicine Man

February, 2005 Las Vegas Wedding – Cupid's Wedding Chapel

EPILOGUE

June, 2006 Jewish Wedding

LOVING PROMISES

It is difficult to condense these precious thirty-three years (at this writing) into a few pages. There are so many experiences – both joyful and sad – that we have shared. The sweetness, affection and devotion we have for one another still flourishes. We have always totally supported each other in all our endeavors. His family and my family have become OUR family. We are truly best friends, equal partners, lovers, mother, father, sister, brother to each other. We always love being together. I have learned so much from Richard, and he has learned a lot from me - we are each other's teacher and student at the same time.

So much of our life is ordinary, but made special because it is infused with love. Laying in bed together reading, cleaning up the kitchen, walking hand in hand down the road, making the bed together – these little things are the brick and mortar of our love. We can be alone in each other's presence. We have absolutely no backlog of hurts or anger. Each morning upon awakening we are always happy to see each other and start the day with sweet hugs and kisses. We express our love to one another many times every day and have so much gratitude for the life we have been given. Generosity, peace, respect, humor, trust and unconditional love have always been the main focus of our relationship, and we do anything from the bottom of our hearts to enhance those qualities and make each other happy. Being loved by Richard is feeling safe, protected, accepted and worshipped totally for who I am. When I reach for his hand, it is always there. Loving Richard is easy because he is so lovable in every way.

As we grow old together, our love becomes deeper. It took on even greater depth when Richard had a sudden heart attack on a family trip to Sicily a few years ago. This was a poignant reminder of the fleeting moments of time, and the preciousness of our life together. During his six-day stay in the hospital he was in a state of bliss and overcome with thankfulness for his life, and remains so until this day. He even enjoyed the horrible hospital food! We were all blessed by his quick recovery with no damage to his heart as we continued our trip as if his heart attack was a minor blip. There are no words to describe the profound gratitude we feel.

EPILOGUE

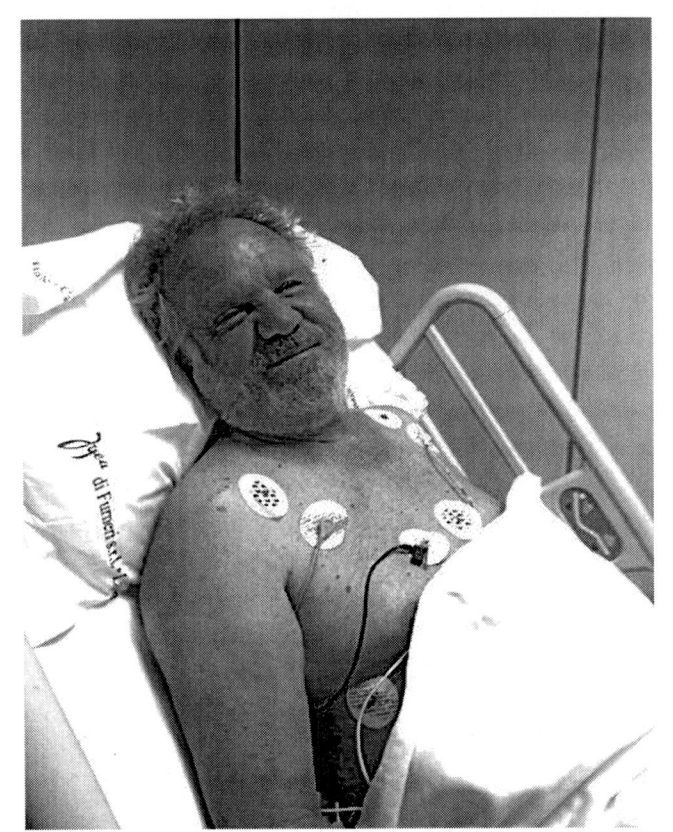

2013 – Richard in hospital in Sicily after his heart attack

2013 Jason, Alice, Angela and Richard in Agrigento, Sicily the day after Richard's release from hospital

LOVING PROMISES

Living the Loving Promises has been our way of life since the day we met and fell in love. It just came naturally to us. It is the product of all of our life's experiences. Personally, I took so much pleasure watching Richard write this book. He would work every spare moment writing each word by hand. Often, in a half sleep during the wee small hours of the night, I would hear the scratching of his pencil on paper. It was like music to my ears knowing that completing this book was fulfilling his dream. Putting our thirty-three years of loving marriage into words is a gift and a contribution to the world. It is a love poem dedicated to our love, and truly a recipe for happiness. Richard and I are living proof that it is possible.

"Richard Writing His Book On Love" painting by Alice Matzkin

Afterword

WORLD PEACE

Meher Baba, an Eastern mystic has said; *"True love is unconquerable and irresistible, and goes on gathering power and spreading itself, until eventually it transforms everyone whom it touches. Humanity will attain to a new mode of being through the free and unhampered interplay of pure love from heart to heart."*

Heart to heart. This is how love expands. And the touch of love from one heart to another is the way towards world peace and understanding. In this time of so much darkness, where millions are suffering from poverty, war, prejudice, hunger and alienation, humankind is in dire need of the light of love. Only light dissipates darkness. Only love dissipates hate. The real task of bringing in light and transforming the planet will not happen by force or decree. It will happen one person at a time. That one person is *you*. Want to stop war? Stop the war within your own mind. Incensed by abuse? Stop mistreating yourself with abusive, self-depreciating thoughts. Disgusted by prejudice? Observe the harsh way you judge yourself. Peace in your relationship, your family and the world can only begin within you.

The causes of suffering in our planet are simple, but are deeply rooted in the collective psyche – greed, hatred, fear and ignorance. These are the same things that cause suffering in your own life. You cannot expect to diminish the suffering of even one other person if you have not addressed the greed, hatred, fear and ignorance in yourself. In order to make a difference, you must be the difference you wish to make.

So what can you, as only one person among billions inhabiting the earth, do to contribute to make the world a more hospitable place for peace to dwell? Love. Love. Open your heart to more love. Know the Other not as separate, not as a stranger, not as *"us"* or *"them,"* but as *you*. The child starving on the street in Somalia, the terrorist in Syria, the rich Wall Street trader, the homeless person holding a handwritten sign you just passed on the street corner, the beloved one

AFTERWORD

you are cradling in your arms; these are not strangers. You know them. They are you. They have needs and fears, hopes and dreams, pain and joy. . .as do you. They have taken birth, and they will die. . .as will you. No matter who they are or what they do, as souls, they deserve happiness, peace, freedom from suffering and to love and be loved. They are deserving of your lovingkindness. Cultivate your love.

The light of your love is a powerful energy. And it can spread. A candle is lit in a darkened room and the flame is passed on to light another candle. Though the flame is shared and shared again, it is never diminished. Each person receives the flame and lights another person's candle, and they in turn light another, and then another. Soon the room is bathed in light.

May the flame of love in your heart blaze ever more brightly and may you ignite the world. The world needs your love. Start with yourself. Start with your beloved. Start now.

Appendix

MEDITATION

Mindfulness and meditation have become a topic in the popular media, with researchers claiming its usefulness for relaxation, stress reduction, physical and mental health. It is all that, and more. The end goal of meditation can be for whatever purpose you intend. If you want relaxation and stress reduction, meditation can help provide that. If you want to free yourself from suffering and attain enlightenment, meditation can help do that too.

Meditation is a turning of your attention inside. Think of your consciousness as a camera. Normally your camera is focused outside yourself, on the sights, sounds and occurrences that make up the drama of your life. Meditation reverses the camera and turns your consciousness to the events that make up the landscape of your inner world. When you turn your awareness within, you normally experience a raucous mix of voices, feelings, images and thoughts. This cacophony is the contents of your mind.

Meditation is not a method of escaping reality. It actually brings reality it to sharper focus. Through meditation you can see with greater clarity. If you take a glass jar, fill it with muddy water and then shake it, the fluid in the jar will be dark and opaque. Let it stand undisturbed for a while, and the dirt particles will drift to the bottom, leaving clear water in the remainder of the jar. This is an analogy for the way meditation works. When you sit quietly and empty your mind, the body calms, the mind calms and sensations and thoughts become clear. Without the disturbing chatter of the mind, you sink into presence, and the serene experience of the true Self can shine forth.

Well. that's the way it's supposed to work. What often happens though, especially for beginning meditators, the minute you get quiet and comfortable, the mind really kicks up and jumps around like a mad monkey. You flit from one thought to another, one fantasy to another, one sensation to another. Your legs hurt, your back aches, and you wonder how much more time before this session will end. (It's amazing what crazy stuff can come up. In this morning's

APPENDIX

meditation, the word, "wingymanone" was repeatedly coursing through my brain. I looked it up. Wingy Manone is an obscure jazz musician from the 30s.)

This ceaseless mental activity is the reason why the ancients have invented techniques to tame the mind and senses during meditation. Many of these techniques involve tethering awareness to a simple, non-changing stimulus. The procedures of focusing your attention on the tip of a candle flame, following of the subtle sensations of the breath or repeating a simple phrase over and over, are all devices to occupy the mind and allow the detritus of thoughts to settle.

Practical Matters

The process of meditation is simple and the instructions are not that difficult to follow. Very little is needed. All you have to bring, as one meditation teacher has said, are three things; a restless body, a wandering mind, and out of control emotions. Here is how to do it.

Create a meditative space. If a separate area is not available, even the corner of your room will do nicely. You can burn incense, place flowers, create altars, hang pictures, include statues if you wish. Try to keep the space for the exclusive use of meditation. It is said the spiritual "vibes" from meditation will permeate the area.

Schedule meditation sessions. Time for meditation must be scheduled. If you only wait till you feel like it, you will keep putting it off. Schedule certain days of the week and certain hours of the day that will work best for you. Sticking with a schedule creates a physical and mental readiness.

Best time. Early mornings are traditionally considered a good time to meditate, while you are still peaceful from the night's sleep. The activity, disturbance and noise of the day has not yet begun. Many people feel that evening is best, after the activity of the day is done. However, any time that works for you is the best time. Avoid eating immediately before meditation and for sure, do not drink coffee or consume caffeine.

Duration. Don't overdo. Start with the length of the session and number of days of the week that are comfortable for you. Ten or twenty minutes is a good beginning. You can increase minutes and add days as you become more experienced.

Time each session. Decide in advance how long you will be meditating and set an audible alarm so that you won't be sneaking glances at the clock.

Alone or together? Some people find meditating with others helpful. The shared energy can make your meditation easier and deeper. There are meditation communities throughout the globe that hold group meditations. Even though meditation is a solo activity, somehow, a meditation session with your partner can enhance your sense of connection. We definitely feel more present and in tune with each other after we have meditated together.

Posture. Wear loose clothing and loosen any constricting belts. There are cushions and chairs made specifically for meditation use, however, a firm pillow or comfortable chair will also work. It is not advisable to lie down as it will be easier to fall asleep. Sit relaxed with back straight, supported or unsupported, arms and hands resting easily. If you keep your hands on your knees, palms up, this will help maintain an erect posture. Get comfortable. Take a few deep breaths, then breathe normally. Keep eyes softly closed. More advanced, keep eyes half closed, unfocused on the ground around three feet in front of you. You don't need to remain rigid. If your body hurts, you can move and refresh your posture to make yourself more comfortable.

Ending. Be gentle with your mind and body when you hear the alarm ending the session. Don't immediately jump up. Slowly bring your awareness into your waking world. Feel your butt on the seat. Take a deep breath. Wiggle your fingers and toes. You're here.

Techniques

Awareness of breath. A common technique is to bring your attention to the sensations of breathing. Breathe naturally. Focus on the subtle sensations of the breath as it enters and leaves the nostrils or on the rising and falling of the belly.

Awareness of space between breaths. Breathe normally and focus your awareness on the point in time where the in-breath ends and the out-breath begins, and the point where out-breath ends and the in-breath begins. You will notice that these are moments where the mind is still.

Mantra. Repeat a word or phrase over and over. It could be any words, however, if the words you use have special meaning for you, that meaning can permeate your mind. Words that have positive connotations, such as "love," "I am peace," God loves me," are good. I was taught a Sanskrit phrase, *Om Namah Shivaya*, which has been used for centuries and translated means, "I bow to God." A traditional mantra is said to be powerful because it carries all the meditative energy of those who have repeated it.

Staring. Keeping your eyes focused on an object such as the tip of a candle flame, complicated design, (mandala), picture, statue or other stationary form is a traditional meditation technique called *tratak*.

Naming. When a thought, sensation, vision or emotion arises in your consciousness, sub-vocally label it with a single word or two that describes the experience, such as "thinking," "hearing," "itching," "angry." Continue with the name until another experience arises, or until you find yourself in a clear, mindless meditative state.

Walking. Select a quiet indoor or outdoor spot that is level and unobstructed for 30 or 40 feet. (9 to 12 meters.) With eyes half closed, walk slowly, with a steady gait. Remain conscious of each step; the sensations of muscles of the leg, the pressure of the foot on the ground, the lifting and placing of the next step. When you reach the end, center yourself, turn around, and continue.

Awareness of the contents of the mind. This method is different from the other techniques in that it doesn't restrict the mind, but follows whatever thoughts, feelings, visions and sensations are arising. Make these the object of your meditation. As these experiences come into your consciousness, allow them to be, without trying to force them away, judge or follow them. Just observe. New experiences that will attract your mind will always come. The point is not to get caught up in them.

There is great value in this kind of meditation practice. By allowing the mind its freedom, we are able to more clearly see and understand the way the mind functions. We actually experience it as a machine that continuously manufactures thoughts, images and emotions. With this understanding, it is easier to allow the mind go about its ceaseless chatter and avoid getting caught up in its convoluted machinations.

This form of meditation can also make it easier to accept ourselves as we are. Normally, we blind ourselves to the negative aspects of our personality. We don't want to see our weakness, fear, greed and stupidity. Even though we push these negative views of ourselves out of consciousness, they still remain active within us. This makes it difficult to see our positive qualities and know the lovely human that lies behind our self-judgments. Meditation allows it all to bubble to awareness, the good, the bad, the ugly, where we are able to note it, accept it, let it go, and move on.

There are other meditative techniques such as visualization and contemplation, but these can be complicated and are better left for more advanced meditators.

Everyone has their favorite meditative technique that works best for them. Once you find one that works well for you, it's better to stick with it and not continuously switch around.

The Process

Each of the above techniques will help to stabilize and harmonize the body, breath, mind and heart. As the breath calms, the body relaxes and the mind opens. An open mind is able to see more clearly and develop a tolerance and

LOVING PROMISES

acceptance for whatever enters. That openness makes room for more love and compassion.

Meditation is a practice for training the mind. An untrained mind is like an untrained dog that will run around sniffing where it wants, peeing on the carpet, and not come when called. Training requires discipline. Meditation techniques provide a container wherein discipline can develop. When the mind wanders, as it will, the task is to bring your attention back to your selected technique--back to your breath, back to your mantra. If you don't discipline your mind, it will simply wander here and there, and your meditation session will consist of twenty minutes or an hour of sitting and thinking. Even if your entire session consists of bringing your mind back, losing your focus, bringing it back, losing it again, and bringing it back, you will have gained discipline and concentration. And you will reinforce your inner power as you resolve to forgive yourself for not being perfect and begin again, begin again.

Meditation is not all hard work. It can bring on ecstatic states of peace, joy, clarity and insight. It can put us in touch with our higher Self. Attaining those elevated states is a major purpose of meditation. However, we don't meditate in order to experience bliss for the half hour duration of our session. We want to bring the peace, joy, clarity and insight we attain in our session into the other twenty-three and a half hours of our day. And we want to be able to share those attainments with our partner and with all who we meet.

About the author

Richard Matzkin has a magnificent relationship with his wife Alice. Retired now, he has been a men's therapy group leader, director of a domestic violence program, program director of a psychiatric hospital and meditation teacher. He is an accomplished sculptor, jazz drummer and author, with Alice, of the award winning book, THE ART OF AGING: Celebrating the Authentic Aging Self. The Matzkin's live on an acre at the end of a country road, outside the village of Ojai, California. Their website for the book is www.lovingpromisesbook.com.